John

A n d r e w   M i s e n h e i m e r

ISBN: 979-8-9913127-0-7

Front cover image purchased from iStock Images

Published by 4Gospel Publishing
607 S Main St
King, NC 27021
Printed by IngramSpark, in the United States of America

First printing edition 2024

For additional copies of this book, please contact Andrew Misenheimer
Email: drewmize@gmail.com
Mobile: 1-704-223-2215
www.TheUnsearchableRiches.podbean.com

PREFACE

A warm greeting to every one of you in the name above every name, the name of our Lord and savior Jesus Christ. I find it a sheer joy and privilege that you have decided to read a copy of this book. It is my hope and prayer that the information you read will be a help and blessing to your heart, and that it will edify, exhort, and comfort you as a saved child of God.

WHAT TO EXPECT IN THIS BOOK

The intent of writing this book is twofold. First, we will read each verse within the Gospel according to John so that we can examine those verses in their context. I am convinced the number one reason for false doctrine being taught in churches today is a direct result of individuals taking verses out of their context, thereby making the verse's statements stand alone, for the purpose of supporting that person's thoughts and/or opinions. I do not want their opinions. I do not want your opinions. I do not want their thoughts. I do not want your thoughts. I, and hopefully like you, want to know what God's word says ... period. Therefore, I would ask that you read each chapter of John at least twice before reading the commentaries found in this book. That way you can personally familiarize yourself with the Bible's context before you consider this book's commentaries.

Secondly, while we are examining every verse in John, we will also look at hundreds of other verses in God's word to see how this Gospel fits within the context of the entire Bible. The truth of the Bible is simple. Each verse has a context based on the verses that precede and follow after it. Those verses collectively have a context based on the chapter of the book, and the book has a context based on the Bible as a whole. 2 Peter 1:20 states **that no prophecy of the scripture is of any private interpretation**. Verses cannot stand alone. Chapters cannot stand alone. Books cannot stand alone. We must search the scriptures (John 5:39) and rightly divide them through study (2 Timothy 2:15) to correctly understand it. Isaiah 28:13 states this concept perfectly. **But the word of the LORD was unto them precept upon precept, precept upon precept; line upon line, line upon line; here a little, and there a little**.

Furthermore, in our study together we will come across pieces of information in John that pertain to doctrinal or factual truths of the word of God. Some of these truths will be fully discussed within the commentary of the chapters, while others will be set aside to the Appendix to be discussed once the chapter's commentary is complete. Please read the book in that fashion. In other words, when you come across a footnote reference directing you to the Appendix, please wait to read that material until you have finished reading the chapter at hand. The reason for this is to help us stay focused on the context of the verses.

I hope you are as anxious to get started as I am, but there is one more thing to mention before you begin reading. You should expect to see additional footnotes pointing you to other commentaries or literary works that I plan to write or am in the process of writing. I have organized my writing in this way simply because there are certain topics, doctrines, or truths we will come across in John that are discussed in more detail in another book of the Bible. Thus, the discussion of those ideas is set aside to the book containing the greater details.

In summary, my desire for each of you is that our study together would give you a greater understanding of John, and all the word of God, along with answering many of the questions you might have. Nehemiah 8:8 sums this up perfectly. **So they read in the book in the law of God distinctly, and gave the sense, and caused them to understand the reading**. Simply put – I want to help you understand the word of God.

May this book be a blessing to your hearts and an encouragement for you to have a closer walk with Jesus Christ. May your desire to spend time with His word increase, and may God bless you and your time spent in this study.

If you would like to contact me for any reason, I would be glad to hear from you. My information is provided below. Also, please consider listening to *The Unsearchable Riches of Christ: Commentary Series* podcast for additional Bible teaching.

Andrew Misenheimer
Email: drewmize@gmail.com
Mobile: 704.223.2215
www.TheUnsearchableRiches.podbean.com

Table of Contents

Overview

John contains 19,097 words, 21 chapters, and 879 verses. The red-letter editions of the Bible present 8,160 words to be spoken by Christ – that is 42.73% of the book.

Each of the four Gospels in the Bible are unique. Many stories and truths overlap, but close examination reveals them all written with a specific theme. Matthew presents Jesus as the King of the Jews. Mark presents Him as the servant. Luke presents Him as the Son of Man, and John reveals Jesus Christ as God.

As God, Jesus has no beginning (John 1:1 with 1:14, 17:5, 1 John 1:1, Ephesians 1:4, Proverbs 8:23, Psalm 90:2, Revelation 1:8-11, 3:14), which is why this Gospel begins at the beginning where we read that Jesus *was* – meaning He had to exist prior to creation (see also John 17:5). Furthermore, no genealogy is given as is found in Matthew and Luke.

In John, Jesus will not be referred to as the Son of David, as He is often called in Matthew. That is an earthly title specifically for an earthly throne. A throne that Jesus, as both God and man, will not possess until His second coming (Revelation 20:1-6).

John does not mention the word repent, for in John individuals are dead needing life. Nor does John mention the word forgive. Only the Son of man on earth can forgive (Matthew 9:6), but the Son of God gives eternal life (John 10:10).

Only this Gospel states that Jesus has power to lay down his own life and take it up again (John 10:17-18). A power only God Himself possesses.

All these truths support John's theme to present Jesus as God. In fact, every chapter declares Jesus to be God. While progressing through this book you should expect to see each chapter's heading provided with that chapter's specific verse illustrating this truth. Often, more than one verse in each chapter could be selected, but only one will be provided.

The most oft recurring number in the book is seven – the number of completion or perfection. A few examples are listed below …
- 7 times the penman of John refers to himself, but not by name.
  - 13:23, 18:16, 19:26, 20:2-8, 20:25, 21:7, 21:20
- 7 sermons by Jesus using the words: I am – showing He is the God of Exodus 3:14: **I am that I am**.
  - 6:35, 8:12 & 9:5, 10:7, 10:11, 11:25, 14:6, 15:1

- 7 miracles recorded before Jesus' crucifixion.
    - 2:1-11, 4:46-54, 5:1-9, 6:1-14, 6:15-21, 9:1-7, 11:38-45
- 7 times Jesus mentions the **hour** of His death.
    - 2:4, 7:30, 8:20, 12:23, 12:27, 13:1, 17:1
- 7 statements by John the Baptist in Chapter one
- Jesus speaks to the woman at the well 7 times in chapter four
- Jesus refers to Himself as the bread of life 7 times in chapter six
- In chapter ten, Jesus mentions 7 things the good shepherd (Jesus) does for His sheep, and 7 descriptions of the sheep are given

More examples will be given throughout this commentary, and a detailed list of each occurrence is provided in the appendix.

Below are a few things NOT found in John that the other Gospels include. They are excluded by the Holy Spirit because to include them would counteract John's purpose to present Jesus as God.

- The temptation of Jesus by Satan (Matthew 4:1-11, Mark 1:12-13, Luke 4:1-13) – excluded because God cannot be tempted with evil (James 1:13).
- The agony Jesus experienced in the garden – an experience for the man Christ Jesus (not fitting for John's theme to present Jesus as God).
- The transfiguration account on the mountain – in John, Jesus is already viewed as God.
- The manger scene – as God Jesus has no beginning.
- Only one parable is found in John – chapter 10. However, the interpretation is immediately given for all to hear (unlike the parables in the other Gospels). God conceals nothing and wants all to be revealed to man.

The Gospel's summary verses are found in John 20:30-31: **And many other signs truly did Jesus in the presence of his disciples, which are not written in this book: But these are written, that ye might believe that Jesus is the Christ, the Son of God; and that believing ye might have life through his name**. Everything written in John, and the entire Bible, is exactly what we need to believe Jesus is the Christ, the Son of God. Have you believed in Him? Do you have life through His name?

Without dispute, this Gospel sets forth our Lord and savior Jesus Christ as God manifest in a body of human flesh.

John 1

Nathanael answered and saith unto him, Rabbi, <u>thou art the Son of God</u>; thou art the King of Israel – John 1:49: *Jesus is declared to be the Son of God*

¹In the beginning <u>was</u> the Word, and the Word <u>was</u> with God, and the Word <u>was</u> God. ²The same <u>was</u> in the beginning with God.

Notice the past tense use of the word was. At the start of this book, God takes us back to the beginning, and we see that He "was," and the Word "was" – implying God existed before the beginning.

These verses also prove God's existence is plural. We do not have specific evidence to the trinity here, but in the beginning, God existed with the Word, and the two are equal. Therefore, we know that God exists as more than a singular entity.

Even in the creation account according to Genesis the same truth prevails: **And God said, Let <u>us</u> make man in our image, after our likeness: and let them have dominion over the fish of the sea, and over the fowl of the air, and over the cattle, and over all the earth, and over every creeping thing that creepeth upon the earth** (Genesis 1:26).

To locate a single verse supporting a trinity, see 1 John 5:7: **For there are <u>three</u> that bear record in heaven, the Father, the Word, and the Holy Ghost: and these <u>three</u> are one.** Who or what is the Word? If you jump ahead to John 1:14 you see **the Word was made flesh, and dwelt among us...as of the only begotten of the Father**. The Word is Jesus Christ our Lord **who took upon him the form of a servant** and was **found in fashion as a man** (Philippians 2:5-8), and whose **name is called The Word of God** (Revelation 19:13).

So, the start of John declares this book will be all about our Lord and savior Jesus Christ: God manifest in the flesh (1 Timothy 3:16).

³All things were made by him; and without him was not any thing made that was made.

Fact #1: Keeping this verse in its context, ALL THINGS were made by the Word, and the Word is Jesus Christ. Therefore, if the word of God is true (and it is), the theory of evolution should be abandoned for the truth of creation. The earth did not appear by chance, an explosion, a big bang, coincidence, or any other ill-conceived scientific theory. God created it – specifically Jesus Christ.

An argument has existed since at least 325 A.D. where some members of the Council of Nicea[1] claimed that Jesus Christ was created by God the Father. The words "only begotten Son" in John 1:14 and 3:16-18, Acts, Hebrews, and 1 John apparently caused controversy among the council members. The argument that was presented: *If Jesus was begotten then He must have been created.* However, John 1:3 completely refutes this logic because it was Jesus who created ALL THINGS.

Furthermore, consider the prophesy from Micah regarding Jesus as the ruler in Israel. **"But thou, Bethlehem Ephratah, though thou be little among the thousands of Judah, yet out of thee shall <u>he</u> come forth unto me that is to be ruler in Israel; whose <u>goings forth have been of old, from everlasting</u>** (Micah 5:2). Jesus has no beginning because He is the beginning (Revelation 1:8). His goings forth have been FROM everlasting so you cannot put a start date to His existence. If the statement "He created all things" means He created Himself, how is that possible if He did not exist when He was created? If you need more proof, read Colossians 1:9-17.

We will deal with the statement "only begotten Son" when we come to it in John 1:14.

Also, keeping this verse in its context while looking elsewhere in the Bible for verses about creation, we will see that Jesus, GOD, and LORD are used interchangeably.

- Exodus 4:11: **And <u>the LORD</u> said unto him, Who <u>hath made</u> man's mouth? or who <u>maketh</u> the dumb, or deaf, or the seeing, or the blind? have not I <u>the LORD</u>?**
- Psalm 89:8a and 11: **O <u>LORD</u> God of hosts, The heavens are thine, the earth also is thine: as for the world and the fullness thereof, <u>thou</u> hast founded them.**
- Jeremiah 32:17: **Ah <u>LORD</u> GOD! behold, thou hast made the heaven and the earth by thy great power and stretched out arm, and there is nothing too hard for thee**

Considering John 1:3 states that Jesus created all things. The cross-reference verses above stated the Lord God made man and founded the

---

[1] Please see the Appendix: *The Trinity*

This council is historically stated to be the first ecumenical council of Catholic bishops orchestrated by Constantine to settle the observance of Easter, establish the nature and relationship of the Son of God with God the Father, and to write the canon law.

heavens and the earth. Therefore, only one conclusion is acceptable: Jesus is God.

It is also necessary we note that even though Jesus, God the Father, and the Holy Spirit are equal, they are not always in the same place at the same time. **And Jesus, when he was baptized, went up straightway out of the water: and, lo, the heavens were opened unto him, and he saw the Spirit of God descending like a dove, and lighting upon him: And lo a voice from heaven, saying, This is my beloved Son, in whom I am well pleased** (Matthew 3:16-17).

Fact #2: Our God created all the other gods that different religions choose to worship: the sun, moon, waters, and even the gold, silver, and bronze these religions use to create their idols. So, why would anyone continue to worship such things if they have the truth that Jesus Christ created all things?

He is the ultimate God, the only true God (1 Timothy 2:5), and all these gods throughout the world will one day be destroyed. **But the LORD is the true God, he is the living God, and an everlasting king: at his wrath the earth shall tremble, and the nations shall not be able to abide his indignation. Thus shall ye say unto them, The gods that have not made the heavens and the earth, even they shall perish from the earth, and from under these heavens** (Jeremiah 10:10-11).

[4]In him was life; and the life was the light of men. [5]And the light shineth in darkness; and the darkness comprehended it not.

Jesus Christ is the origin of life for life is in Him. This living, breathing life that makes every individual person in the world alive is the light of men. This simple understanding of being alive is the initial bit of truth you and I have that God exists, He created us, and we are accountable to Him.

The Athenians in Acts 17 are proof of this truth. **Then Paul stood in the midst of Mars' hill, and said, Ye men of Athens, I perceive that in all things ye are too superstitious. For as I passed by, and beheld your devotions, I found an altar with this inscription, TO THE UNKNOWN GOD. Whom therefore ye ignorantly worship, him declare I unto you. God that made the world and all things therein, seeing that he is Lord of heaven and earth, dwelleth not in temples made with hands; Neither is worshipped with men's hands, as though he needed any thing, seeing he giveth to all life, and breath, and all things; And hath made of one blood all nations of men for to dwell on all the face of the earth, and hath**

13

determined the times before appointed, and the bounds of their habitation; That they should seek the Lord, if haply they might feel after him, and find him, though he be not far from every one of us: <u>For in him we live, and move, and have our being</u>; as certain also of your poets have said, For we are also his offspring (Acts 17:22-28). These Athenians worshipped an "unknown god" but the one thing they knew and understood, for even their poets wrote of it, was it was Him who created them and gave them life. They just needed someone to tell them God's name – Jesus!

However, this light shines in darkness and the darkness does not comprehend it. John 3:19 proclaims **that light is come into the world, and men loved darkness rather than light, because their deeds were evil**. Those that do not comprehend the truth about God, though the evidence exists in the very life that they live, is because they do not want to comprehend it. They love the darkness they are living in and do not want the light of the truth to expose their evil ways.

Concluding the events with the Athenians in Acts 17 shows that some mocked Paul (vs. 32) while certain others believed (vs. 34). Some of them wanted light while others wanted to remain in darkness. As we progress through this Gospel, we will see Jesus (the Light) often ignore questions asked of Him. This is because those questions are stated as argumentative rebuttals against Him and His words rather than heart felt inquisitions desiring truth. Simply put: if you want truth, God will provide it; but if not, He will allow you to remain in the darkness that you so desire.

⁶There was <u>a man</u> sent from God, whose name was John. ⁷The same came for a witness, to bear witness of the Light, that all men through him might believe. ⁸He was not that Light, but was sent to bear witness of that Light.

John was indeed a great man sent from God for even Jesus said, **Among those that are born of women there is not a greater prophet than John the Baptist** (Luke 7:28). Nonetheless, he is just a man[2] sent to bear witness of Jesus.

⁹That was the true Light, which lighteth every man that cometh into the world. ¹⁰He was in the world, and the world was made by him, and the world knew him not.

Here again is the same truth from verses four and five. EVERY MAN that comes into the world is given light by the Light (Jesus) and they know

---

[2] See the author's work: <u>Matthew</u> for a more thorough commentary regarding John the Baptist.

God exists simply because of creation that surrounds them. They may not know God's name, but they know He exists, and they are accountable to Him. We believers have the great responsibility to present every man with the gospel truth, and then every man has a decision to make - believe or believe not.

Here is what the Bible says regarding this truth in Romans 1:16-32. **For I am not ashamed of the gospel of Christ: for it is the power of God unto salvation to every one that believeth; to the Jew first and also to the Greek. For therein is the righteousness of God revealed from faith to faith: as it is written, The just shall live by faith. For <u>the wrath of God is revealed from heaven</u> against all ungodliness and unrighteousness of men, <u>who hold the truth</u> in unrighteousness; <u>Because that which may be known of God is manifest in them</u>; <u>for God hath shewed it unto them</u>.**

How was it shown unto them? **For the invisible things of him from the creation of the world are clearly seen, being understood by the things that are made, even his eternal power and Godhead; so that they are without excuse:**

Do you see? Everyone knows of God's eternal power and Godhead because the visible things of creation bear witness of Him who is invisible. **Because that, <u>when they knew God</u>, they glorified him not as God, neither were thankful; but became vain in their imaginations, and their foolish heart was darkened. Professing themselves to be wise, they became fools, And changed the glory of the uncorruptible God into an image made like to corruptible man, and to birds, and fourfooted beasts, and creeping things.** This is where men ignored what they knew to be true based on the evidence in and around them and decided to create images as their gods to worship.

How does God respond? **Wherefore God also gave them up to uncleanness through the lusts of their own hearts, <u>to dishonor their own bodies between themselves</u>: Who changed the truth of God into a lie, and worshipped and served the creature more than the Creator, who is blessed for ever, Amen.**

Before we read the next verses, please understand something ... there is a movement in our society today in support of homosexual behavior. It is being glorified on every news channel, newspaper, television sitcom, and movie production across our country. Even some so-called preachers proclaim such abominable lifestyles to be acceptable (Leviticus 18:22). Upon reading the next few verses you will see how this behavior is one direct result of people disregarding the truth they hold within themselves. **For this cause**

God gave them up unto vile affections: for even their women did change the natural use into that which is against nature: And likewise also the men, leaving the natural use of the woman, <u>burned in their lust one toward another; men with men working that which is unseemly, and receiving in themselves that recompence of their error which was meet</u>. God just told us that there is a recompense of their error that is received in these people who partake in such a lifestyle. One such recompense is AIDS, or as it was first known: GRIDs – Gay Related Immune Deficiencies.

And even as they did not like to retain God in their knowledge, God gave them over to a reprobate mind, to do those things which are not convenient; Being filled with all unrighteousness, fornication, wickedness, covetousness, maliciousness; full of envy, murder, debate, deceit, malignity; whisperers, Backbiters, haters of God, despiteful, proud, boasters, inventors of evil things, disobedient to parents, Without understanding, covenantbreakers, without natural affection, implacable, unmerciful: <u>Who knowing the judgment of God, that they which commit such things are worthy of death</u>, not only do the same, but have pleasure in them that do them. There are pleasures to be had in sin, but only for a season (Hebrews 11:25) because **when lust hath conceived, it bringeth forth sin: and sin, when it is finished, bringeth forth death** (James 1:15), and then **after this the judgment** (Hebrews 9:27).

I do not know very many people who enjoy hearing this for the first time, but it is simply the truth of God's word.

[11]He came unto his own, and his own received him not.

Jesus was born, according to the flesh, an Israelite whose lineage could be traced back to David and Abraham (Matthew 1:1). As we progress, you will see the Israelites reject Him.

[12]But as many as received him, to them gave he power to become the sons of God, even to them that believe on his name: [13]Which were <u>born</u>, not of blood, nor of the will of the flesh, nor of the will of man, but of God.

Those that did receive Him by believing on His name were given power to become the sons of God. What does it mean to believe on His name? His name is Lord Jesus Christ (Romans 10:4-9).

He is Lord because He is deity – equal with God.

His name Jesus was the name given Him at birth, which is the name regarding His humanity. He is just as much man as He is God.

16

He is Christ because He is the prophesied Messiah come to save the nation Israel. You must believe this, and that God raised Him from the dead (Romans 10:9) to be saved. Romans 10:10 and 13 states: **For with the heart man believeth unto righteousness; and with the mouth confession is made unto salvation. For whosoever shall call upon the <u>name of the Lord</u> shall be saved**.

Then, according to John 1:12-13, once you believe on His name you experience a new birth. This birth has nothing to do with you: blood, will of the flesh, or the will of man. God gives you this new birth! This will be further discussed once we reach chapter 3 and deal with Jesus' conversation with Nicodemus.

[14]**And <u>the Word</u> was made flesh, and dwelt among us, (and we beheld <u>his</u> glory, the glory as of the <u>only begotten of the Father</u>,) full of grace and truth.**

As we have already discussed, the Word is Jesus Christ – the only begotten of the Father. When He became flesh and dwelt among us, those around Him beheld His glory and that glory was full of grace and truth. How marvelous it must have been to be around the Son of God **who did no sin, neither was guile found in his mouth** (1 Peter 2:22) **for in him dwelleth all the fullness of the Godhead bodily** (Colossians 2:9). Everything He did or said was FULL of grace and truth!

Now, let us continue the discussion we began in verse three. The word begotten has a three-fold purpose in scripture: First, it refers to one's physical birth. Second, it refers to one's spiritual birth. Third, in reference to Jesus Christ, the term is used to give Him an honored and exalted position. The third point is set aside for a later discussion – see the Appendix: *The Trinity.*

The word begotten is commonly found in the Bible's genealogies. **And the days of Adam after he had <u>begotten</u> Seth were eight hundred years: and he begat sons and daughters** (Genesis 5:4). Two things to note in genealogies are the males are primarily used, and every person that has lived on this earth, besides Adam and Eve, were born from the womb of a woman.[3] The reason the males are primarily mentioned is because God set up the family to take the father's name (Genesis 5:1-2), and also because

---

[3] An exception to this statement is Melchisedec. He is **without Father, without mother, without descent, having neither beginning of days, nor end of life; but made like unto the Son of God; abideth a priest continually** (Hebrews 7:3).

children are begotten by the man's seed through the man and woman's acts of procreation. However, for Jesus Christ there were no such acts between Joseph and Mary because the Bible declares in Luke 1:18 that **before they [Mary and Joseph] came together, she was found with child of the Holy Ghost**. His birth was by "her seed" and not man's (Genesis 3:15).

Again, every person that has been born, whether physically or spiritually, is said to have been begotten. Since Jesus came into the world (John 11:27), the word begotten must apply to Him as well. He entered this world as a man (1 Timothy 2:5) through Mary's womb, but not through the aid of man's seed: making Jesus **the only begotten of the Father** (John 1:14). He is the only one physically begotten of the Father according to scripture.

Begotten is also found in scripture referring to one's spiritual birth. Notice an interesting truth found in James 1:17-18: **Every good gift and every perfect gift is from above, and cometh down from the Father of lights, with whom is no variableness, neither shadow of turning. Of his own will begat he us with the word of truth, that we should be a kind of firstfruits of his creatures**.

If God the Father begat us with the word of truth, how can He say in His holy word that Jesus is the only begotten of the Father? ... Well, as we have just discussed: one statement refers to the physical while the other refers to the spiritual. Nonetheless, this is NOT a contradiction. The same statement is used by God in Genesis chapter 22, verses 2, 12, and 16 speaking of Abraham regarding his son Isaac. Isaac is described as Abraham's only son, when Isaac is not his only son because we know from Genesis 16 that he had a son named Ishmael by his Egyptian concubine Hagar.

Why call Isaac his only son? ... The definition[4] of only is *this above all others*. As for Christ, He is above all others because without Him humbling Himself, taking the form of a servant and being found in fashion as a man, and being obedient unto the death of the cross (Philippians 2:7-8), we would have no chance of being begotten spiritually. As for Isaac, he is above all others simply because he was the son of promise by God to Abraham, not Ishmael (Galatians 4:21-28). Please reference in the Appendix: *The Trinity* for further details on this topic.

---

[4] All definitions, where provided, are derived from an 1828 Noah Webster Dictionary.

15John bare witness of him, and cried, saying, This was he of whom I spake, He that cometh after me is preferred before me: for he was before me.

John puts Jesus in His rightful place: preferred before me. The interesting statement is the last one in the verse: **for he was before me.** If you reference Luke, chapters 1 and 2 that detail the births of both Jesus and John, you will notice that John was born before Jesus. So, how was Jesus before John? ... Jesus is eternal. He is God manifest in the flesh, with no beginning or ending because He is the beginning and the ending (Revelation 1:8).

16And of his fulness have all we received, and grace for grace. 17For the law was given by Moses, but grace and truth came by Jesus Christ.

His fullness is grace and truth (v.14), and all have received it. In the context, all have light that God exists, and everyone was created by Him. Also, God has been gracious to us all even though we do not deserve it. Please don't miss this wonderful truth! Whether you realize it or not, God has been extremely gracious toward you.

The example given for His grace being dispensed is the law given to Israel. One might conclude that the law came first and then grace. Even the majority of biblical dispensational charts list law before the age of grace because chronologically Moses was here on earth before Christ. However, Christ predates Moses (as has been thoroughly discussed) and truthfully, grace was given first. Noah will suffice as a perfect example for he was before Moses and the law. **But Noah found grace in the eyes of the LORD** (Genesis 6:8).

18No man hath seen God at any time; the only begotten Son, which is in the bosom of the Father, he hath declared him.

Many would argue, and have argued, that this is a Bible contradiction for there were men in the Old Testament who saw God. **Then went up Moses, and Aaron, Nadab, and Abihu, and seventy of the elders of Israel: And they saw the God of Israel: and there was under his feet as it were a paved work of a sapphire stone, and as it were the body of heaven in his clearness. And upon the nobles of the children of Israel he laid not his hand: also they saw God, and did eat and drink** (Exodus 24:9-11).

How does one explain this seemingly contradiction? ... Thankfully, the Bible explains itself. Verse 18 continues to say that the only begotten Son hath declared Him. When men saw God in the Old Testament, they were seeing the Son of God (John 14:9). Since Moses was mentioned, see Exodus 33:19-23 for an explanation that fits the context of John perfectly involving grace and seeing God in His glory. **And he [Moses] said, I beseech thee, shew me thy glory. And he [the LORD] said, I will make all my goodness pass before thee and I will proclaim the name of the LORD before thee; and will be gracious to whom I will be gracious, and will shew mercy on whom I will shew mercy. And he said, Thou canst not see my face: for there shall no man see me, and live. And the LORD said, Behold, there is a place by me, and thou shalt stand upon a rock: And it shall come to pass, while my glory passeth by, that I will put thee in a clift of the rock, and will cover thee with my hand while I pass by: And I will take away mine hand, and thou shalt see my back parts: but my face shall not be seen.** Moses beheld the back side of God's glory which is full of grace and truth: precisely what was recorded of Jesus Christ in John 1:14-17. Those in the Old Testament saw the Son when beholding God.

[19]And this is the record of John, when the Jews sent priests and Levites from Jerusalem to ask him, Who art thou? [20]And he confessed, and denied not; but confessed, I am not the Christ. [21]And they asked him, What then? Art thou Elias? And he saith I am not. Art thou that prophet? And he answered, No.

These verses prove how these priests and Levites (also "of the group of the Pharisees" – v. 24) knew the scriptures. Three people were prophesied to come according to the Old Testament, and they address all three:

1. Christ from Daniel 9:24-27
2. Elias (Elijah) from Malachi 4:5-6
3. That prophet from Deuteronomy 18:15

John confessed he was not any of these men.

[22]Then said they unto him, Who art thou? That we may give an answer to them that sent us. What sayest thou of thyself? [23]He said, I am the voice of one crying in the wilderness, Make straight the way of the Lord, as said the prophet Esaias.

John may not be one of those men mentioned above, but he is the voice of one crying in the wilderness preparing the way of the Lord (Isaiah 40:3-10), bearing witness of Jesus Christ.

When people claim there is no biblical evidence to support Jesus Christ being equal with God, they either have not read the Bible or they are simply repeating something they heard. Jesus is God and we have 23 verses thus far to support that fact.

[24]And they which were sent were of the Pharisees. [25]And they asked him, and said unto him, Why baptizest thou then, if thou be not that Christ, nor Elias, neither that prophet? [26]John answered them, saying, I baptize with water: but there standeth one among you, whom ye know not; [27]He it is, who coming after me is preferred before me, whose shoe's latchet I am not worthy to unloose. [28]These things were done in Bethabara beyond Jordan, where John was baptizing.

John simply answers that he is only baptizing with water. We will see a perfect definition of baptism in the next few verses, but please notice that Jesus is apparently there in the crowd based on John's response.

I also appreciate John's humility. He could easily boast about all he is doing for God and all that he has been able to accomplish. He comes in 400 years after Malachi preaching basically the same message as Malachi. His words turn the hearts of the people toward God while preparing the way of the Lord, but he acknowledges his unworthy place before an almighty God. Indeed, **among those that are born of women there is not a greater prophet than John the Baptist** (Luke 7:28).

[29]The next day John seeth Jesus coming unto him, and saith, Behold the Lamb of God, which taketh away the sin of the world.

Here is the greatest announcement the world has ever known. Abraham prophesied in the Old Testament, while preparing to sacrifice his son Isaac as commanded by God, that **God will provide himself a lamb for a burnt offering** (Genesis 22:8). This is He that was prophesied to come in Isaiah 9:6: **For unto us a child is born, unto us a son is given: and the government shall be upon his shoulder: and his name shall be called wonderful, Counsellor, <u>The mighty God</u>, The everlasting Father, The Prince of Peace**. Jesus, the mighty God, is the Lamb of God come to take away the sin of the world. Hallelujah!

Also, please take note of the progression involving sacrifices throughout scripture. In Genesis 4 one lamb was sacrificed for an individual. In Exodus 12 one lamb was sacrificed for an entire family. In Leviticus 16 we read of an annual sacrifice where one lamb was sacrificed for the sins of the entire nation of Israel. Now here in John 1 we have the last sacrificial lamb that will ever be needed, for His sacrifice will take away every sin of every person in the entire world. Thank you, Jesus!

³⁰**This is he of whom I said, After me cometh a man which is preferred before me: for he was before me.** ³¹**And I knew him not: but that he should be made manifest to Israel, therefore am I come baptizing with water.**

There is your definition for baptism. Jesus was baptized to be made manifest to Israel. In like manner, we are baptized to be made manifest to others that we have believed on the name of Jesus Christ.

A more thorough summary on baptisms will follow in John 4.

Why did he baptize? ... The simple answer is that he was told to (v. 33), and we are to continue the trend (Matthew 28:19, Acts 2:41 and 10:48). However, Matthew 3 can shed some additional light on this question.

In those days came John the Baptist, preaching in the wilderness of Judaea, And saying, Repent ye: for the kingdom of heaven is at hand. Bring forth therefore fruits meet for repentance: and think not to say within yourselves, We have Abraham to our father: for I say unto you, that God is able of these stones to raise up children unto Abraham. I indeed baptize you with water unto repentance (Matthew 3:1-2, 8-9, and 11a). John preached that all should repent from their wicked ways and turn back to the God they had long forgotten and ignored. When people heard this preaching and claimed to have repented, John responded by saying: **Bring forth therefore fruits meet for repentance**, i.e. You claim to have repented so prove it. Get down in this water and be baptized.

Please understand that there are many baptisms in scripture. Hebrews 6:1-2: **Therefore leaving the principles of the doctrine of Christ, let us go on unto perfection; not laying again the foundation of repentance from dead works, and of faith toward God, of the doctrine of baptisms, and of laying on of hands, and of resurrection of the dead, and of eternal judgment.** John is preparing the way of the Lord, and his baptism is not the same baptism as when someone is baptized after believing on the Lord Jesus Christ. **John verily baptized with the baptism of repentance, saying unto the people, that they should believe on him which should come after him, that is, on Christ Jesus** (Acts 19:4).

John simply preached that all should repent. When people claimed to have repented, he told them to prove it by submitting to baptism. During his preaching of repentance, he also proclaimed that someone was coming after him that they should believe on. He was preparing the people to believe on Jesus Christ.

32And John bare record, saying I saw the Spirit descending from heaven like a dove, and it abode upon him. 33And I knew him not: but he that sent me to baptize with water, the same said unto me, Upon whom thou shalt see the Spirit descending, and remaining on him, the same is he which baptizeth with the Holy Ghost. 34And I saw, and bare record that this is the Son of God.

It was God who sent John to bear witness of Jesus (v.6-7), and when John saw the Spirit descend like a dove to abide upon Jesus, he knew this was the Son of God.

Also, you and I might have been given power to become the sons of God (v.12) by believing on Jesus' name, but we are in no way equal to the Son of God. He is "before us" just as John rightfully placed Him (v.15).

35Again the next day after John stood, and two of his disciples; 36And looking upon Jesus as he walked, he saith, Behold the Lamb of God! 37And the two disciples heard him speak, and they followed Jesus.

Well, how about that! John is walking with two of his disciples and upon introducing them to the Lamb of God, they began following Jesus instead of John, and John did not have anything to say regarding the matter. That is how it's supposed to be. Jesus is the head, not any other man (Ephesians 1:22, 4:15, Colossians 1:18). If only the preachers filling the pulpits of America today would realize this truth. The members of the congregations can be followers of them as they follow Christ (1 Corinthians 11:1) but their role that God desires for them to fulfill is **being ensamples to the flock** and NOT **lords over God's heritage** (1 Peter 5:3).

38Then Jesus turned, and saw them following, and saith unto them, What seek ye? They said unto him, Rabbi, (which is to say, being interpreted, Master,) where dwellest thou? 39He saith unto them, Come and see. They came and saw where he dwelt, and abode with him that day: for it was about the tenth hour.

Of all the questions someone could ask the Lamb of God, these two disciples were only interested in where Jesus lived. Nonetheless, Jesus answered their question because they genuinely wanted additional light that the Light had to offer. As we previously discussed in verse 5, Jesus will provide light only to those that desire it. Keep this in mind because it will be a prevailing theme throughout John.

[40]One of the two which heard John speak, and followed him, was Andrew, Simon Peter's brother. [41]He first findeth his own brother Simon, and saith unto him, We have found the Messias, which is being interpreted, the Christ.

Apparently, these men knew at least this much truth from the scriptures: The Messiah is the Christ, a person promised to come, and they have officially found Him.

I think every Bible student should take a closer look at these disciples for many think them to be ignorant and unlearned men based on Acts 4:13: **Now when they saw the boldness of Peter and John, and <u>perceived</u> that they were unlearned and ignorant men, they marveled; and they took knowledge of them, that they had been with Jesus.** The word perceived means to know according to the senses. I would say this is a natural perception for these people to have because those that saw the boldness of Peter and John were Annas (the high priest), Caiaphas, and those related to Annas: people of elevated status in society. Therefore, when they heard and saw Peter speak, they instinctively drew a conclusion that Peter and John were ignorant and unlearned. What they perceived may or may not have been fact.

A similar example might be an educated Southerner talking to someone born and raised in the North. Usually with a southerner's accent, he or she might be taken as a simpleton despite having received a formal education. The point is you cannot accurately judge someone solely on looks or speech. Even in Acts 2 everyone thought that Peter and the other disciples were full of new wine based only on what they heard and saw. Yet this proved to be false.

Here are 2 facts we can gain from scripture about the disciples:

1. Peter and John were able to get into the palace of the High Priest in John 18 because John knew the High Priest. I would imagine you would have to have quite the status in town to have such an opportunity.
2. These fishermen brought fish to a town that lived on consuming fish. We have no idea if they owned one boat or many, or if they had a big or small business, nonetheless their occupation was an important one. It is quite possible they were important people.

I am simply saying that we must fully examine the scriptures before drawing any type of conclusion.

⁴²**And he brought him to Jesus. And when Jesus beheld him, he said, Thou art Simon the son of Jona: thou shalt be called Cephas, which is by interpretation, A stone.**

This verse along with Matthew 16:18 are used by the Catholic Church to support their belief that Peter was the first Pope and the foundation of the church (refuted by 1 Corinthians 3:11: **For other foundation can no man lay than that is laid, <u>which is Jesus Christ</u>**). However, the only fact we can gather from John 1:42 is that Cephas means a stone. We will have to proceed to 1 Peter to gather a little more information, but first we will deal with Matthew 16.

Matthew 16:13-18: **When Jesus came into the coasts of Caesarea Philippi, he asked his disciples, saying, Whom do men say that I the Son of man am? And they said, Some say that thou art John the Baptist: some, Elias; and other, Jeremias, or one of the prophets. He saith unto them, but whom say ye that I am? And Simon Peter answered and said, <u>Thou art the Christ, the Son of the living God</u>. And Jesus answered and said unto him, Blessed art thou, Simon Barjona: for flesh and blood hath not revealed <u>it</u> unto thee, but my Father which is in heaven. And I say also unto thee, That thou art Peter, and upon <u>this rock</u> I will build my church; and the gates of hell shall not prevail against it**. Many people read this and think the church will be built upon Peter, but that is NOT what Jesus said. Jesus declared the rock upon which the church would be built is what the Father in heaven revealed to Simon Peter: Jesus is the Christ, the Son of the living God. This fact is supported completely by the context of John 1 declaring Jesus to be the Christ, the Messiah, the Light, and that through Him you receive the power to become the sons of God by believing upon His name. He is the rock!

Now let's visit 1 Peter 2:4-8: **To whom [the Lord] coming, as unto a living stone, disallowed indeed of men, but chosen of God, and precious, Ye also, as lively stones, are built up a spiritual house, an holy priesthood, to offer up spiritual sacrifices, acceptable to God by Jesus Christ. Wherefore also it is contained in the scripture, Behold, I lay in Sion <u>a</u> <u>chief corner stone</u>, elect, precious: and he that believeth on <u>him</u> shall not be confounded. Unto you therefore which believe he is precious: but unto them which be disobedient, <u>the stone</u> which the builders disallowed, the same is made <u>the head of the corner</u>, And a stone of stumbling, and <u>a</u> <u>rock</u> of offence, even to them which stumble at the word, being disobedient: whereunto also they were appointed.** While it is true that

25

Peter, including those that believe, are lively stones, it is Jesus Christ who is the chief corner stone and a rock upon which the believers are built.

See Psalm 18:2, 31, 46; Psalm 27:5; Psalm 28:1; Psalm 31:2-3; Psalm 42:9; Psalm 62:2, 6-7; Psalm 71:3; Psalm 78:35; Psalm 89:26; Psalm 92:15; Psalm 94:22; Psalm 95:1; Romans 9:33; 1 Corinthians 10:4 for more biblical support on the topic.

[43]**The day following Jesus would go forth into Galilee, and findeth Philip, and saith unto him, Follow me.** [44]**Now Philip was of Bethsaida, the city of Andrew and Peter.** [45]**Philip findeth Nathanael, and saith unto him, We have found him, of whom Moses in the law, and the prophets, did write, Jesus of Nazareth, the son of Joseph.** [46]**And Nathanael said unto him, Can there any good thing come out of Nazareth? Philip saith unto him, Come and see.**

A great question. When people lean to their own understanding (as instructed not to do – Proverbs 3:5), similar questions often get asked. What good comes out of going to church? What good comes from witnessing to the lost? What good comes from reading the Bible? The answer to such questions is the same as v. 46: **Come and see**. Give it a try and find out.

I have no idea why Nazareth would be negatively looked upon. What I do know is that Isaiah 53:2 says **Who hath believed our report? and to whom is the arm of the LORD revealed? For he shall grow up before him as a tender plant, and as a root out of a dry ground: he hath no form nor comeliness; and when we shall see him, there is no beauty that we should desire him.** Jesus came as a root out of a dry ground – not a place you would expect a healthy root to flourish. He even was not much to look at physically. But what a savior He is! He is full of grace and truth. His mercy is everlasting, the very expression of love and compassion. On and on we could go describing how wonderful and marvelous Jesus Christ is. You've got to experience Him personally though. Come and see for yourself how wonderful Jesus is.

[47]**Jesus saw Nathanael coming to him, and saith of him, Behold an Israelite indeed, in whom is no guile!**

Oh, if people would desire to live such a life where they say what they mean and mean what they say. Nathanael is such a person - a man described as having no guile in him.

What is an Israelite indeed? My best answer comes from Romans 9:6: **For they are not all Israel, which are of Israel**. In the book of Leviticus, strangers and sojourners could choose to take part in the Israelite's way of life and thereby become an Israelite. Nathanael must have been born an Israelite making him an Israelite indeed and not a stranger who converted.

⁴⁸Nathanael saith unto him, Whence knowest thou me? Jesus answered and said unto him, Before that Philip called thee, when thou wast under the fig tree, I saw thee. ⁴⁹Nathanael answered and saith unto him, Rabbi, thou art the Son of God; thou art the King of Israel.

Before Philip even went to Nathanael to call on him, Jesus knew where Philip was and what he was doing. No doubt, this is God in the flesh.

Notice the order: Son of God first, then King of Israel. The order is vitally important because it summarizes His two advents. He came to this earth the first time to establish Himself as God and die on the cross for the sins of all the world. When He comes again it will be to establish His rule and reign over the kingdom of heaven as the King of Israel.

⁵⁰Jesus answered and said unto him, Because I said unto thee, I saw thee under the fig tree, believest thou? thou shalt see greater things than these.

Indeed we will see greater things, for Christ will heal a Roman official's son (John 4:43-54), heal a lame man (John 5:1-9), feed multitudes with a little boy's lunch (John 6:1-5), walk on water (John 6:16-25), give sight to a blind man (John 9), and raise Lazarus from the dead (John 11:1-44).

⁵¹And he saith unto him, Verily, verily, I say unto you, Hereafter ye shall see heaven open, and the angels of God ascending and descending <u>upon</u> the Son of man.

There is one other place in scripture where someone saw angels ascending and descending. It was Jacob in Genesis 28:12: **And he dreamed, and behold <u>a ladder</u> set up on the earth, and the top of it reached to heaven: and behold the angels of God ascending and descending <u>on it</u>.** This ladder directly represents Jesus, because the only way you are going to get from this earth and into heaven is through the Lord Jesus Christ. He said **I am <u>the way</u>, the truth, and the life: no man cometh unto the Father, but by me** (John 14:6). Praise the Lord!

John 2

This beginning of miracles did Jesus in Cana of Galilee, and manifested forth his glory; and his disciples believe on him – John 2:11: the glory of God is manifested

¹And the <u>third day</u> there was a marriage in Cana of Galilee; and the mother of Jesus was there: ²And both Jesus was called, and his disciples, to the marriage.

The overview of this book noted the number 7 as the oft recurring number throughout John. Here is another example. So far in this gospel, God has impressed upon John to mention a total of seven days (John 1:29, 35, 43, and 2:1). It is on this seventh day that we read of a wedding. If we compare this fact with Genesis 1, we read there about the seven days it took God to speak creation into existence and at the beginning of the next chapter we find ourselves dealing with the marriage of Adam and Eve. In John, we have dealt with creation (John 1:1), it is the seventh day, and now at the beginning of the next chapter we are reading about a marriage. One might claim this to be an interesting coincidence, but there is a greater truth afoot.

The more I study the Bible, with God shedding forth His light, the more I realize one infallible fact: these are God's words! I do not find it possible, nor do I consider it a coincidence that dozens of men, who lived centuries apart, could write sixty-six books and all the finer details of their writings line up without error. The only explanation is one person authored the Bible by instructing men to write His words. That author is the Word - Jesus Christ (John 1:1, 14; 1 John 1:1 & 5:7).

³And when they wanted wine, the mother of Jesus saith unto him, They have no wine. ⁴Jesus saith unto her. Woman, what have I to do with thee? mine hour is not yet come.

First to note is how Jesus does not over exalt Mary. The Catholic Church might give her a place equal to that of deity, but He simply addresses her as a woman for that is all she is.[5]

Even in Matthew 2, you read the following words describing Jesus and Mary: **the young lad and his mother** (2:13-14, 20-21). Isn't it curious that Jesus is mentioned first? I do not know of anyone that refers to a mother

---

[5] See the author's work: <u>Luke</u> for an explanation on why Mary was chosen by God, and for scripture references refuting Catholicism's view of Mariolatry.

and her child by speaking of the child first, but the Bible places them in their proper order.

Secondly, Jesus states His hour is not yet come. These words are used again in John 7:30, 8:20, 12:23, 12:27, 13:1, and 17:1, and they refer to His crucifixion. He came for one purpose, and that was to die on a cross at Calvary at an extremely specific time to pay the sin debt for the entire world (Romans 6:23). He will not submit Himself to death until this hour has come.

[5]His mother saith unto the servants, Whatsoever he saith unto you, do it.

When reading the New Testament from beginning to end, these are the last recorded words of Mary, and what powerful words they are: **Whatsoever he saith unto you, do it**. May God help us to live up to these words.

[6]And there were set there six waterpots of stone, after the manner of the purifying of the Jews, containing two or three firkins apiece. [7]Jesus saith unto them, Fill the waterpots with water. And they filled them up to the brim.

A firkin is a measure of capacity equal to a fourth of the overall volume of the container; therefore, these water pots were half to three-quarters full. Their purpose served guests arriving at the wedding an opportunity to wash their hands and quite possibly their feet, considering the dusty and sandy terrain they lived in, before entering the dwelling. Jesus simply had the servants to completely fill the pots. He did not have them washed out, nor did He tell them to dispose of the filthy water inside. He just told them to fill the pots with water.

[8]And he saith unto them. Draw out now, and bear unto the governor of the feast. And they bare it. [9]When the ruler of the feast had tasted the water that was made <u>wine</u>, and knew not whence it was: (but the servants which drew the water knew;) the governor of the feast called the bridegroom, [10]And saith unto him, Every man at the beginning doth set forth good wine; and when men have well <u>drunk</u>, then that which is worse: but thou hast kept the good <u>wine</u> until now. [11]This beginning of miracles did Jesus in Cana of Galilee, and manifested forth his glory; and his disciples believed on him.

This is the first of many miracles Jesus performs, and the first miracle biblically since Daniel 6. I would dare say that upon first reading this passage many people carelessly draw the following conclusion: Jesus made wine and people got drunk. Then, depending on their beliefs, morals, or code of conduct they will either doubt the fallibility of such a conclusion or accept it as fact.

My desire is to keep this simple. Alcohol is a sin. I refuse to beat around the bush or even be subtle with my remarks concerning the topic. Consuming alcohol is a sin.

With that being said, I do understand that confusion exists concerning the topic of wine in the Bible. Genesis 9:20-24 states that Noah, after the ark events, **planted a vineyard: And he drank of the wine, and was drunken**. Later we read of Lot's two daughters, in Genesis 19, plotting to make their father drink wine so that he would lie with them and preserve their seed. The Moabite and Ammonite nations came to exist because of this wicked sinful act. Thus far, it seems like wine is not a good thing.

Even most preaching against wine/alcohol references verses like the following…

- Proverbs 20:1: **Wine is a mocker, strong drink is raging: and whosoever is deceived thereby is not wise.**
- Proverbs 23:21: **Look not thou upon the wine when it is red, when it giveth his colour in the cup, when it moveth itself aright.**
- Proverbs 31:4-5: **It is not for kings, O Lamuel, it is not for kings to drink wine; nor for princes strong drink: Lest they drink, and forget the law, and pervert the judgment of any of the afflicted.** According to Revelation 1:6, He has made us kings and priests. Strong drink is not for us!
- Galatians 5:19-21: **Now the works of the flesh are manifest, which are these; Adultery, fornication, uncleanness, lasciviousness, Idolatry, witchcraft, hatred, variance, emulations, wrath, strife, seditions, heresies, Envyings, murders, <u>drunkenness</u>, revellings, and such like: of the which I tell you before, as I have also told you in time past, that they wich do such things shall not inherit the kingdom of God.**
- Habakkuk 2:15: **Woe unto him that giveth his neighbor drink, that puttest thy bottle to him, and makest him drunken also, that thou mayest look on their nakedness!**

Again, I must reiterate – drinking alcohol and drunkenness should be preached against! Even if God's word said nothing about the dangers of alcohol, I must ask why do men and women, who call themselves Christians, indulge in something that destroys families, leads to unwanted sexual relations, diseases, pregnancies, decreased internal organ function including liver failure, impaired mental and motor function, and even death? Common sense should tell you to abstain from the sin of alcohol.

The main point I want to make is that all the above information seems to be confusing when thinking about the fact that Jesus turned water into wine at this marriage supper. Even Paul told Timothy in 1 Timothy 5:23 to **drink no longer water, but use a little wine for thy stomach's sake and thine often infirmities**. So, again I must say that I understand people find this all to be confusing. The Bible seems to teach that wine is a terrible thing in some places, but then teach it as a good thing in other places. In truth, this is easily rectified if you are willing to examine the entire Bible as a whole and keep every verse in its context.

Wine in the Bible can be either grape juice or alcohol. Grape juice will eventually ferment and become alcohol if given enough time to spoil. The type of wine you are reading about, in any given passage of the Bible (whether pure grape juice or fermented alcohol) is all dictated by the context of each passage. For example: the passage from 1 Timothy above must be pure grape juice. The antioxidants found in freshly squeezed grapes are extremely beneficial for one's health, especially for Timothy being in a foreign country. Think about the rule for traveling abroad – everybody gets told not to drink the water because your body is not accustomed to the foreign contaminants found in that local water source.

The main reason confusion exists is because people lean to their own understanding concerning the words wine, and drunk. Wine is universally understood to be an alcoholic beverage, along with drunk being universally understood to be the result of consuming alcohol. However, the LORD uses these words in a different manner throughout scripture.

Drunk has two meanings: the first, being the world's application to one who is intoxicated, and the second meaning the past tense of drink. In the modern vernacular we say drank as the past tense of drink, but God often uses drunk to imply that someone has consumed a liquid. When someone has consumed alcohol and is intoxicated, God often uses the word drunken.

Now there was a certain man of Ramathaimzophim, of mount Ephraim, and his name was Elkanah, the son of Jeroham, the son of Elihu, the son of Tohu, the son of Zeph, an Ephrathite: And he had two wives; the name of the one was Hannah, and the name of the other Peninnah: and Peninnah had children, but Hannah had no children. And this man went up out of his city yearly to worship and to sacrifice unto the LORD of hosts in Shiloh. And the two sons of Eli, Hophni and

Phinehas, the priests of the LORD, were there. And when the time was that Elkanah offered, he gave to Peninnah his wife, and to all her sons and her daughters, portions: But unto Hannah he gave a worthy portion; for he loved Hannah: but the LORD had shut up her womb. And her adversary also provoked her sore, for to make her fret, because the LORD had shut up her womb. And as he did so year by year, when she went up to the house of the LORD, so she provoked her; therefore she wept, and did not eat. Then said Elkanah her husband to her, Hannah, why weepest thou? and why eatest thou not? and why is thy heart grieved? am not I better to thee than ten sons? So Hannah rose up after they had eaten in Shiloh, and after they had <u>drunk</u>. Now Eli the priest sat upon a seat by a post of the temple of the LORD. And she was in bitterness of soul, and prayed unto the LORD, and wept sore. And she vowed a vow, and said, O LORD of hosts, if thou wilt indeed look on the affliction of thine handmaid, and remember me, and not forget thine handmaid, but wilt give unto thine handmaid a man child, then I will give him unto the LORD all the days of his life, and there shall no razor come upon his head. And it came to pass, as she continued praying before the LORD, that Eli marked her mouth. Now Hannah, she spake in her heart; only her lips moved, but her voice was not heard: therefore Eli thought she had been <u>drunken</u>. And Eli said unto her, How long wilt thou be <u>drunken</u>? put away thy wine from thee. And Hannah answered and said, No, my lord, I am a woman of a sorrowful spirit: <u>I have drunk neither wine nor strong drink</u>, but have poured out my soul before the LORD. (1 Samuel 1:1-15)

Hannah obviously had drunk because the passage told us she did. However, she was not drunken. The liquid she consumed was neither wine nor strong drink so she could not have been intoxicated. This sheds great light on the John 2 passage revealing that the men were not drunken but had only drunk wine. Now we need to examine what God has to say about wine and we will see that the people at the wedding were not drinking alcohol.

Notice what the Bible says in Isaiah 65:8a: **Thus saith the LORD, As the <u>new wine</u> is found in the <u>cluster</u>**. God specifically said that wine is the juice found inside the grapes growing on the vine in a cluster. We call fermented grapes wine, but God defines wine as the juice inside a grape.

If another example is needed to satisfy your curiosity, see Deuteronomy 32:14b: **and thou didst drink the <u>pure blood of the grape</u>**. Here God tells us that wine is pure blood. It is pure because it has not

32

fermented. Once grape juice (wine) has fermented God calls this strong drink. Therefore, Jesus did NOT turn water into alcohol to get people drunk.

The glorious truth of this passage is found in Ephesians 5:25b-27: **Christ also loved the church, and gave himself for it; That he might sanctify and <u>cleanse it with the washing of water by the word</u>, That he might present it to himself a glorious church, not have spot, or wrinkle, or any such thing; but that it should be holy and without blemish.** Jesus turned the nasty, dirty water that was meant for washing your hands and feet into something pure. All this was simply done by His spoken word, and by His word (the holy Bible) He will cleanse and sanctify you from your sin if you will simply believe in Him.

The book of Romans proclaims that **faith cometh by hearing, and hearing by the word of God** and **the word of faith, which we preach; that if thou shalt confess with thy mouth the Lord Jesus, and shalt believe in thine heart that God hath raised him from the dead, thou shalt be saved. For whosoever shall call upon the name of the Lord shall be saved** (Romans 10:8a-9, 13, 17). Have you believed on Him?

[12]After this he went down to Capernaum, he, and his mother, and his brethren, and his disciples: and they continued there not many days. [13]And the Jews' passover was at hand, and Jesus went up to Jerusalem, [14]And found in the temple those that sold oxen and sheep and doves, and the changers of money sitting:

Three times in the year, the men children were to appear before the Lord, offer sacrifices, and partake in different feasts (Exodus 34:22-25). The animals chosen to be sacrificed were supposed to be the best they owned coming from their own herds, not bought for the single purpose of sacrifice. However, the Jews would come to the temple, exchange their money if it was a foreign currency, and simply buy an animal (no matter if it had blemishes or not) to be sacrificed. Their traditions went completely against what God instructed of them, and not to mention they had turned God's house into a marketplace. This was not what God had in mind, nor what he commanded of them!

Even look at verse 13: **the <u>Jews' passover</u> was at hand.** That description tells us exactly what has happened to the relationship between God and the Jews. Every time a feast was mentioned in the Old Testament, it was called **a feast <u>unto the LORD</u>** (Leviticus 23:41, Numbers 29:12). Now this Passover feast is described as belonging to the Jews instead of God. They had completely ignored God and His word.

¹⁵And when he had made a scourge of small cords, he drove them <u>all</u> out of the temple, and the sheep, and the oxen; and poured out the changers' money, and overthrew the tables; ¹⁶And said unto them that sold doves, Take these things hence; make not my Father's house an house of merchandise.

Wal-Mart at Christmas time would be the best scenario possible to compare with this event. Passover is the biggest day of the year for the Jews, and people are coming into town from everywhere to buy animals to be sacrificed, just as people shop to buy gifts at Christmas time. Now, imagine how crazy the shopping centers are, and that is what this scene would look like in the temple. In walks Jesus with a homemade whip, and He drives everyone and everything out. When I think of this event, I do not picture in my mind a skinny, long-haired hippy like so many of the modern Hollywood movies use to portray Jesus. He was a carpenter in an era where machinery did not exist, and His body was not defiled by sin. No doubt He was a man in every form of the word, not to mention God manifest in the flesh because only God could accomplish this task.

¹⁷And his disciples remembered that it was written, The zeal of thine house hath eaten me up.

That scripture comes from Psalm 69:9.

¹⁸Then answered the Jews and said unto him, What sign shewest thou unto us, seeing that thou doest these things?

You mean the performance Jesus just displayed is not sufficient proof for you to listen to Him?

¹⁹Jesus answered and said unto them, Destroy this temple, and in three days I will raise it up. ²⁰Then said the Jews, Forty and six years was this temple in building, and wilt thou rear it up in three days? ²¹But he spake of the temple of his body.

Jesus does not answer their second question because they did not really want an answer. They were simply mocking Him. Therefore, because they did not genuinely want light, the Light would not give it. I understand why they thought He was speaking of the building rather than His body, but if they wanted an explanation to what He meant, they only needed to ask. Instead, they chose to express how ridiculous they thought His statement was.

Also, referencing the other Gospels shows us how truly wicked these Jews are. Jesus pronounces that **an evil and adulterous generation seeketh after a sign** (Matthew 12:39, 16:4, and Luke 11:29).

²²When therefore he was risen from the dead, his disciples remembered that he had said this unto them; and they believed the scripture, and the word which Jesus had said.

Something you should notice upon studying the four Gospels is how often Jesus told His disciples that He would die and resurrect three days later. They would often proclaim to understand Him but this verse, along with all the others, shows that the disciples did not believe Him. They even refused to believe Mary Magdalene's report once she returned from the tomb upon seeing Jesus alive. **Afterward he [Jesus] appeared unto the eleven as they sat at meat, and upbraided⁶ them with <u>their unbelief and hardness of heart, because they believed not them which had seen him after he was risen</u>** (Mark 16:14).

²³Now when he was in Jerusalem at the passover, in the feast day, many believed in his name, when they saw the miracles which he did. ²⁴But Jesus did not commit himself unto them, because he knew all men, ²⁵And needed not that any should testify of man: for he knew what was in man.

Why would Jesus not allow men to testify of the things they saw Him do? There are two simple reasons.

1. There is nothing in man that God can use. **The LORD looketh on the heart** (1 Samuel 16:7b)**, searcheth all hearts, and understandeth all the imaginations of the thoughts** (1 Chronicles 28:9)**,** and **the heart is deceitful above all things, and desperately wicked** (Jeremiah 17:9). Every man is worthless without God for **every man at his best state is altogether vanity** (Psalms 39:5b).
2. It is not until after man has received the Holy Ghost that they are useful because it is He that **will guide you into all truth** (John 16:13). Man must speak and witness to others under the direction of the Holy Ghost to accomplish God's will. This is why the very last chapter of the Bible says **the Spirit <u>and</u> the bride** [the body of believers] **say, come** (Revelation 22:17). The Spirit cannot speak without the believer, and the believer should not speak without the Spirit.

---

⁶ Upbraided means to be charged with something wrong or disgraceful; reproached; reproved.

John 3

For God so loved the world, that he gave his only begotten Son, that whosoever believeth in him should not perish, but have everlasting life – John 3:16: eternal life comes from Jesus Christ

[1]**There was a man of the <u>Pharisees</u>, named Nicodemus, a ruler of the Jews: [2]The same came to Jesus by night, and said unto him, Rabbi, <u>we know</u> that thou art a teacher come from God: for no man can do these miracles that thou doest, except God be with him.**

The Pharisees know that Jesus was a teacher come from God and will eventually reject this truth. Two things are going to happen that inevitably lead them to their rejection:

1. Jesus will make Himself known as being equal with the Father (Chapter 5)
2. The Pharisees will begin to think if they do not stop Jesus and His teachings, they will lose the political power they so desperately crave (Chapter 11). Thus, they will do anything necessary to kill Him.

It seems to be, as shown here and throughout history, that most people in powerful positions within religion only care about their positions, not the people they serve. This egotistical nature of man is why God has so much to say in His word about the overseers' (elders/bishops) roles and responsibilities within the New Testament church. **The elders which are <u>among</u>** (not over) **you I exhort, who am also an elder, and a witness of the sufferings of Christ, and also a partaker of the glory that shall be revealed: Feed the flock of God which is <u>among</u> you, taking the oversight thereof, not by constraint, <u>but willingly</u>; not for filthy lucre, but of a ready mind; Neither as being lords over God's heritage, but <u>being ensamples to the flock</u>** (1 Peter 5:1-3). If only all church leaders led such lives where they understood their position of being an example among the church, not lording over it.

[3]**Jesus answered and said unto him, Verily, verily, I say unto thee, Except a man be born again[7], he cannot see the kingdom of God. [4]Nicodemus saith unto him, How can a man be born when he is old? can he enter the second time into his mother's womb, and be born?**

---

[7] See Appendix – *Why ye must be born again.*

Jesus is using a physical situation to explain the spiritual: something He will do several times in this Gospel. It is spiritual because of what Jesus says in verse 6 regarding the Spirit, and because He said you **cannot <u>see</u> the kingdom of God**. The kingdom of God is a spiritual kingdom. **The kingdom of God cometh <u>not</u> with observation for, behold, the kingdom of God is within you** (Luke 17:20b, 21b). It will take an invisible birth to see an invisible kingdom, and you will only see this kingdom when you are in heaven with the Lord.

Also, when you think about this statement by Jesus, it sounds like an impossible task, just like the task of rebuilding a temple in three days. You might expect Nicodemus to respond with sarcasm like the Pharisees in the previous chapter. However, notice his response. He immediately thinks of his physical birth and how a rebirth could be achieved. I would say it is a natural thought to have based on Jesus' statement. Ultimately though, Nicodemus truly wants to know and understand the truth Jesus is presenting, therefore Jesus will provide him with the answer.

[5]Jesus answered, Verily, verily, I say unto thee, Except a man be born of <u>water</u> and of the Spirit, he cannot enter into the kingdom of God.

Some will argue that water in this verse refers to water baptism,[8] but baptism is not mentioned in the immediate context. The context is two births: one physical (v.4) and one spiritual (v.6). Thus, water speaks of the physical birth, and the Spirit speaks of the spiritual birth.

Now, if we expand our view of this passage outside its immediate context, there are only two biblical ways to look at the word water in verse five as it relates to a birth.

1. As already discussed, water represents the physical birth. This position is the most logical considering the immediate context of the passage.
   When a baby is born from the mother's womb, water is most definitely present. My wife gave birth to our second child in the car while in route to the birth clinic so just take my word for it if you have never witnessed the birth of a child.

2. Water represents the word of God and/or the Spirit of God, present at one's spiritual birth.
   For someone to be born again they must repent and believe the gospel of the Lord Jesus Christ as stated in the word of God. At that moment the Holy Ghost takes residence inside their body (1 Corinthians 6:19).

---

[8] See chapter 4 for more on baptism.

Both the word of God and the Holy Spirit are often pictured in the Bible as water. **Not by works of righteousness which we have done, but according to his mercy he saved us, by the <u>washing of regeneration</u>, and renewing of the Holy Ghost** (Titus 3:5). Regeneration is a new birth – a new creation. See also 2 Corinthians 5:17, Ephesians 5:25-26, and John 7:38-39.

I will not argue with anyone taking either of the above positions on the word water. I must again stress however, the immediate context supports the first position, while the second position has biblical support. Regardless of your interpretation, you must recognize the passage expresses that a new birth is absolutely necessary for someone to enter the kingdom of God.

[6]That which is born of the flesh <u>is</u> flesh; and that which is born of the Spirit <u>is</u> spirit.

Obviously, we have two scenarios: that which is born of the flesh, and that which is born of the Spirit. The first comes from your physical generation, and the other comes from a spiritual generation.

I hope you see that even though someone has been born of the Spirit (reborn/regenerated), that person is still flesh. Whatever that person's flesh desired before salvation, it will still desire after salvation. Whatever that person's temptations were before salvation will still be the same temptations after salvation. **For the good that I would I do not: but the evil which I would not, that I do. Now if I do that I would not, it is no more I that do it, but sin that dwelleth in me. I find then a law, that, when I would do good, evil is present with me** (Romans 7:19-21). A saved child of God <u>is</u> both flesh and spirit, and for that person to ignore his or her old nature requires putting off the old man by the grace of God (Colossians 3:1-17).

[7]Marvel not that I said unto thee, Ye must be born again. [8]The wind bloweth where it listeth, and thou hearest the sound thereof, but canst not tell whence it cometh, and whither it goeth: so is every one that is born of the Spirit.

You will not physically see someone being born of the Spirit. You will only see the results of that birth. It is just like the wind blowing, for you do not see the wind coming or going, only the effect it has upon blowing through.

What effect does this new birth have on a believer? **If any man be in Christ, he is a new creature: old things are passed away; behold, <u>all</u>**

things are become new (2 Corinthians 5:17). After someone is born again, a change will be evident in their life.

⁹**Nicodemus answered and said unto him, How can these things be?** ¹⁰**Jesus answered and said unto him, Art thou a master of Israel, and knowest not these things?**

He is a master of Israel and is supposed to know **these things**. God in various places in the Old Testament scriptures described instances where He would do a work spiritually on the inside of an individual.

I will give them one heart, and one way, that they may fear me for ever, for the good of them, and of their children after them: And I will make an everlasting covenant with them, that I will not turn away from them, to do them good; but I will put my fear in their hearts, that they shall not depart from me (Jeremiah 32:39-40).

And I will give them one heart, and I will put a new spirit within you; and I will take a stony heart out of their flesh, and will give them an heart of flesh: That they may walk in my statutes, and keep mine ordinances, and do them: and they shall be my people, and I will be their God (Ezekiel 11:19-20).

These Pharisees (masters) are supposed to know the scriptures, but the only things they truly knew were the physical aspects of God's word: taste not, touch not, handle not, etc. They missed the spiritual workings of God found in scripture.

¹¹**Verily, verily, I say unto thee, We speak that we do know, and testify that we have seen; and ye receive not our witness.**

Jesus, Nicodemus, and the Pharisees (v.2) all claimed to know the scriptures, and that they had seen the truths found within. But Nicodemus and the Pharisees had not received the witness – John the Baptist (John 1:7) who for months has proclaimed one to come after him that will baptize WITH THE SPIRIT. Nicodemus should have searched the scriptures to find out exactly what John was proclaiming, but he did not. Now, standing in front of him is the God of Jeremiah and Ezekiel proclaiming that He is the one who will give this new birth.

¹²**If I have told you earthly things, and ye believe not, how shall ye believe, if I tell you of heavenly things?**

Again, Jesus is using earthly, physical things to tell this man that he must believe. We all just simply need to believe.

¹³And no man hath ascended up to heaven, but he that came down from heaven, even the Son of man which is in heaven. ¹⁴And as Moses lifted up the serpent in the wilderness, even so must the Son of man be lifted up: ¹⁵That whosoever believeth in him should not perish, but have <u>eternal life</u>. ¹⁶For God so loved the world, that he gave his only begotten Son, that whosoever believeth in him should not perish, but have <u>everlasting life</u>.

In Numbers 21, the Israelites spoke against Moses and the LORD while in the wilderness. Despite all God had provided and done for them, they continually groaned and complained. Therefore, God sent fiery serpents in among them and many perished. Afterward, God commanded Moses to put a brass serpent on top of a pole, and any who were bitten needed only to look up at this serpent to live. Jesus just explained that He (the Son of man) MUST BE lifted on a pole that whosoever believes in him would not perish but have eternal/everlasting life. Thanks be unto God!

Why would Jesus do this for us? **For God so loved the world.** Hallelujah!

¹⁷For God sent not his Son into the world to condemn the world; but that the world through him might be saved. ¹⁸He that believeth on him is not condemned: but he that believeth not is condemned already, because he hath not believed in the name of the only begotten Son of God.

According to verses 16 and 17, God is love and salvation. OR, according to verses 18 and 36, God is condemnation and wrath. It is all a matter of someone believing in response to the light that has been given to them by God.

Why do people choose not to believe? The answer is given in the next verses.

¹⁹And this is the condemnation, that <u>light</u> is come into the world, and men loved darkness rather than light, because their deeds were evil. ²⁰For every one that doeth evil hateth the light, neither cometh to the light, lest his deeds should be reproved. ²¹But he that doeth truth cometh to the light, that his deeds may be made manifest, that they are wrought in God.

They do not like the light illuminating their evil deeds, so it is easier to ignore truth rather than face it and have their evil ways reproved. **They are of those that rebel against the light; they know not the ways thereof, nor abide in the paths thereof** (Job 24:13). Since they do not want light, they will not receive the Light (John 1:7-10), and only one thing is certain: **He that believeth on the Son hath everlasting life: and <u>he that believeth not the Son shall not see life; but the wrath of God abideth on him</u>** (John 3:36).

[22]After these things came Jesus and his disciples into the land of Judaea; and there he tarried with them, and baptized.

Please reference verses 22 and 26, along with John 4:1-2. They do not contradict one another as someone might think. The Holy Spirit obviously instructed John to record exactly what *the people* were claiming about Jesus. Their claims were that Jesus baptized even though He did not.

[23]And John also was baptizing in AEnon near to Salim, because there was much water there: and they came, and were baptized. [24]For John was not yet cast into prison.

See Matthew 14 and Mark 6 for the details of John the Baptist being cast into prison.

[25]Then there arose a question between some of John's disciples and the Jews about purifying. [26]And they came unto John, and said unto him, Rabbi, he that was with thee beyond Jordan, to whom thou barest witness, behold, the same baptizeth, and all men come to him. [27]John answered and said, A man can receive nothing, except it be given him from heaven. [28]Ye yourselves bear me witness, that I said, I am not the Christ, but that I am sent before him. [29]He that hath the bride is the bridegroom: but the friend of the bridegroom, which standeth and heareth him, rejoiceth greatly because of the bridegroom's voice: this my joy therefore is fulfilled.

John simply stated his insignificance compared to Jesus. Jesus is the bridegroom. John is His friend, and all John can do is rejoice. Christ is here! He has come! John has prepared the way of the Lord as he was supposed to, and now his joy is fulfilled.

[30]He must increase, but I must decrease

Oh, what a true statement! The more we realize that we need Him, the better off we will be. Also, note the prevalence of the word *must* in this chapter and the next.

- Ye <u>must</u> be born again (v.7)
- The Son of man <u>must</u> be lifted up (v.14)
- Christ <u>must</u> increase (v.30)

- John (servant) <u>must</u> decrease (v.30)
- God <u>must</u> be worshipped in spirit and in truth (John 4:24)

[31]He that cometh from above is above all: he that is of the earth is earthly, and speaketh of the earth: <u>he that cometh from heaven is above all</u>.

John just admitted that Jesus is from above, from Heaven, descended from the Father, and is above all. What a grand truth!

[32]And what he hath seen and heard, that he testifieth; and now man receiveth his testimony. [33]He that hath received his testimony hath set to his <u>seal</u> that God is true.

This goes hand in hand with what we just discussed about being born again. When you are in Christ, it is something that cannot be lost. According to verse 33 above, those that have received Christ have set to their SEAL that God is true, and according to Ephesians 4:30, it is by the **holy Spirit of God, whereby ye are <u>sealed</u> unto the day of redemption**.

[34]For he whom God hath sent speaketh the words of God: for God giveth not the Spirit by measure unto him. [35]The Father loveth the Son, and hath given all things into his hand. [36]He that believeth on the Son hath everlasting life: and he that believeth not the Son shall not see life; but the wrath of God abideth on him.

Believing on the Son of God is the difference between life and wrath.

John 4

Jesus saith unto her, I that speak unto thee am he – John 4:26: Jesus
claims to be the promised Messiah

[1]**When therefore the Lord knew how the Pharisees had heard that Jesus
made and baptized more disciples than John.** [2]**(Though <u>Jesus himself
baptized not</u>, but his disciples,)** [3]**He left Judaea, and departed again into
Galilee.**

Just as we discussed in the previous chapter (3:22), Jesus did not
baptize.

Also, here are a few notes on why baptism does NOT save you.

1. Salvation and baptism are opposites. Baptism is representative of death
   (Romans 6:1-4), and salvation is a new birth unto life.
2. If baptism saves, nobody in the Old Testament was saved for there is no
   evidence those of old baptized.
3. Baptism is a visible human work. **For by grace are ye saved <u>through
   faith</u>; and that not of yourselves: it is the gift of God: <u>Not of works</u>,
   lest any man should boast** (Ephesians 2:8-9). Compare that with
   Hebrews 11:1: **Now faith is the substance of things hoped for, the
   evidence of things <u>not seen</u>**. Therefore, baptism as grounds for
   obtaining salvation does not line up with biblical salvation through
   faith.
4. Jesus said of Himself in Luke 19:10: **For the Son of man is come to
   seek and to save that which is lost**. Therefore, if baptism saves, Jesus
   is a liar considering He did not baptize.
5. Baptism is not part of the gospel message. 1 Corinthians 1:17a: **For
   Christ sent me [Paul] not to baptize, but to preach the gospel**.

Before we move on, we might as well address the two verses many
salvation by water baptism supporters want to reference. They are 1
Corinthians 10:1-4 and 1 Peter 3:20-21. Before we do, please recall Hebrews
6:1-2 that we referenced back in John 1:30-31.

**Therefore leaving the principles of the doctrine of Christ, let us
go on unto perfection; not laying again the foundation of repentance from
dead works, and of faith toward God, Of the doctrine of baptisms, and of
laying on of hands, and of resurrection of the dead, and of eternal
judgment**. There are several different baptisms in scripture. You have the
baptism of John the Baptist (Luke 7:29, Acts 18:25, 19:2-4), the baptism of
the Holy Ghost (Matthew 3:11, Acts 1:5, 1 Corinthians 12:13), the baptism of

fire (Matthew 3:11), water baptism (Acts 8:36-38), Jesus and sons of Zebedee's baptism speaking of torture and even death (Mark 10:38-40), the baptism unto Moses (1 Corinthians 10:1-4), and what I will call the baptism of Noah (1 Peter 3:20-21). These last two are what we need to examine.

1 Corinthians 10:1-4: **Moreover, brethren, I would not that ye should be ignorant, how that all our fathers were under the cloud, and all passed through the sea; And were all <u>baptized</u> unto Moses <u>in the cloud and in the sea</u>; And did all eat the same spiritual meat; And did all drink the same spiritual drink: for they drank of that spiritual Rock that followed them: and that Rock was Christ**. This takes us back to Exodus when Moses leads the Israelites out of Egyptian bondage by the hand of God and were surrounded or submerged (baptism) in the pillar of <u>a cloud</u> by day and a pillar of fire by night. That was God leading them through the wilderness unto the Promised Land. Also, God parted the Red Sea for them to walk through the sea being surrounded (baptism) by walls of water while they walked on dry ground.

Many people want to stretch the truth of this baptism to be like that of water baptism. Considering Christ is mentioned in the verses they try to claim water baptism as a necessity for salvation. This is my only question. If this baptism is like that of water baptism, then when did these Israelites get wet? The answer is they did not. Thus, this is a poor cross reference to use as support for water baptism as a necessity for salvation.

1 Peter 3:20-21: [20]**when once the longsuffering of God waited in the days of Noah, while the ark was a preparing, wherein few, that is, eight souls were saved by water.** [21]**The like figure whereunto even <u>baptism</u> doth also now save us (not the putting away of the filth of the flesh, but the answer of a good conscience toward God,) by the resurrection of Jesus Christ**. Again, some people like to use these verses to support baptism as a necessity for salvation, but I must ask the same question as above. When did the eight souls on the boat get wet? The answer is still the same. They did not get into the water. All the souls who were outside the boat and in the water drowned. So, we must rightly divide to understand this baptism.

In simple terms, the saving of Noah and his family (v.20) is a figure (v.21), in other words a representation, of a baptism that saves us. The only baptism immediately connected with salvation is the baptism of the Holy Ghost. For the moment someone puts their faith and trust in the finished work of Christ on Calvary, their souls are saved by God's grace through their faith (John 3:16, and Ephesians 2:8-9) and they immediately receive the Holy Spirit

44

of God who takes residence inside them (Ephesians 1:13-14, and 1 Corinthians 6:19). Their flesh, however, is still filthy (v.21) and awaits the redemption of the body (Romans 8:23-25, Ephesians 1:13-14, 1 Corinthians 15:51-54).

⁴And he must needs go through Samaria.

We are about to read of a woman at a well that He needed to talk to. Why the necessity? She wanted light, so the Light goes to give it.

⁵Then cometh he to a city of Samaria, which is called Sychar, near to the parcel of ground that Jacob gave to his son Joseph. ⁶Now Jacob's well was there, Jesus therefore, being wearied with his journey, sat thus on the well: and it was about the sixth hour.

It is midday and Jesus is wearied. Although Christ's deity is the primary focus of the Gospel John, here is one of the few times we read of His humanity. His humanity is mainly themed inside the Gospel of Luke where you consistently read of Him being tired, thirsty, hungry, sad, etc. Nonetheless, there is one important fact relevant here: **We have not an high priest which cannot be touched with the feeling of our infirmities; but was in all points tempted like as we are, yet without sin** (Hebrews 4:15). When we call on God, no matter the situation, nor the degree of discomfort we are experiencing, Christ has experienced it Himself. God, the creator of the universe and all that is in existence can say, "Son, I've been there, and I'll give you enough grace to overcome. My grace is sufficient" (2 Corinthians 12:9). Praise the Lord!

⁷There cometh a woman of Samaria to draw water: Jesus saith unto her, Give me to drink.

Only two times in this Gospel will Christ ask for a favor, and both times he requested something to drink. The second time occurs while hanging on the cross where He said, **I thirst** (John 19:28). Both times unfortunately, He did not get what He asked for. Here, no water was drawn, and on the cross they gave Him vinegar: not a good substance to quench one's thirst.

⁸(For his disciples were gone away unto the city to buy meat.) ⁹Then saith the woman of Samaria unto him, How is it that thou, being a Jew, askest drink of me, which am a woman of Samaria? for the Jews have no dealings with the Samaritans.

45

Based on these verses, the Jews and the Samaritans did not get along. Luke 9:51-54 gives us another example. **And it came to pass, when the time was come that he [Jesus] should be received up, he stedfastly set his face to go to Jerusalem, And sent messengers before his face: and they went, and entered into a village of the <u>Samaritans</u>, to make ready for him. And they did not receive him, because his face was as though he would go to Jerusalem. And when his disciples James and John saw this, they said, Lord, wilt thou that we command fire to come down from heaven, and consume them, even as Elias did?** This is the only account where the disciples desired to destroy those that rejected their message even though the Gospels proclaim repeatedly that many rejected. James and John's desire to destroy them no doubt spawned from the Jews' disapproval of the inhabitants of Samaria.

This distasteful attitude toward these people dates back hundreds of years when Nebuchadnezzar invaded Judah. He carried away the Jews captive into Babylon but left many poor and afflicted people to work the land while also bringing in men from Babylon to possess the land. This was the land of Samaria and intermarrying of the Jews and Babylonians eventually occurred. Therefore, the people born from this *bad-blooded* race were naturally disliked by the more *pure-blooded* Jews.

[10]**Jesus answered and said unto her, <u>If thou knewest</u> the gift of God, and <u>who</u> it is that saith to thee, Give me to drink; thou wouldest have asked of him, and he would have given thee living water.**

There are eight gifts[9] mentioned in the book of John that are available to us. The gift He is referring to **is eternal life through Jesus Christ our Lord** (Romans 6:23b).

This conversation is like the one Jesus had with Nicodemus. He will use the physical to talk about the spiritual. Nicodemus should have known the truth of God's word but did not, and this woman too does not know all of God's word because the Jews forsook God and did not send forth the light they had to others as they were supposed to.

How can Christ give living water? He can because He is the fountain of living waters. **For my people have committed two evils; they have forsaken me <u>the fountain of living waters</u>, and hewed them out cisterns, broken cisterns, that can hold no water** (Jeremiah 2:13). **O, LORD, the hope of Israel, all that forsake thee shall be ashamed, and they that**

---

[9] 1. Living water (4:10), 2. Life for sheep (10:11), 3. Example (13:15), 4. Holy Spirit (14:15), 5. Peace (14:27), 6. Words (17:8), 7. Himself (17:14), 8. Glory (17:22)

depart from me shall be written in the earth, because they have forsaken the LORD, the fountain of living waters (Jeremiah 17:13).

The true and living God of Jeremiah is standing in front of this woman, and He could offer her living waters. If only she knew who Jesus was. If only she knew that Jesus is God. Nonetheless, she responds with a desire to know what Jesus is talking about and will be presented with that very truth.

¹¹The woman saith unto him, Sir, thou hast nothing to draw with, and the well is deep: from whence then hast thou that living water?

An honest question, but the water He has to offer is not in the well. She is thinking of the physical just like Nicodemus did, but Jesus is speaking of the spiritual. Behold, God is my salvation; I will trust, and not be afraid: for the LORD JEHOVAH is my strength and my song; he also is become my salvation. Therefore with joy shall ye draw water out of the wells of salvation (Isaiah 12:2-3). That is how the water Jesus speaks of will be drawn.

¹²Art thou greater than our father Jacob, which gave us the well, and drank thereof himself, and his children, and his cattle?

If only she knew what she just asked. Of course, He is greater than Jacob.

This statement also begins to let us know what it is she trusts in. It's not God. She trusts in her heritage, in the land that was owned by Jacob, and her connection with God's chosen people.

¹³Jesus answered and said unto her, Whosoever drinketh of this water shall thirst again: ¹⁴But whosoever drinketh of the water that I shall give him shall never thirst; but the water that I shall give him shall be in him a well of water springing up into everlasting life.

Drinking of the water Jesus has to offer means you will never thirst spiritually again because whoever drinks of that water will have an eternal life spring within them.

¹⁵The woman saith unto him, Sir, give me this water, that I thirst not, neither come hither to draw. ¹⁶Jesus saith unto her, Go, call thy husband, and come hither.

She wants more truth and now Jesus will truly begin to reveal who He is. He knows exactly who she is, what she has done in her past, everything about her. He is God.

[17]The woman answered and said, I have no husband. Jesus said unto her, Thou hast well said, I have no husband: [18]For thou hast had five husbands; and he whom thou now hast is not thy husband: in that saidest thou truly.

This is a perfect example of what the Bible calls guile. She told Him truth, but it was not all the truth. Apparently, she spends time with a man in such a way that a husband and wife would spend time together even though she is not married to the man.

[19]The woman saith unto him, Sir, I perceive that thou art a prophet.

Here comes a stranger into town and sits on a well that is thousands of years old, and He begins to speak to this woman as if He has known her for years. She begins to slowly gain an idea of His importance, for who else could know such things about her?

[20]Our fathers worshipped in this mountain; and ye say, that in Jerusalem is the place where men ought to worship.

Notice again what she trusts in. She mentioned Jacob, her fathers, the well on the land given to Jacob (which speaks of the Promised Land to Israel), and even the mountain where her fathers worshipped. This mountain is probably Mt. Gerizim where the people shouted Amen upon hearing blessings and cursing read from the word of God (Deuteronomy 11:29, 27:12-16, Joshua 8:33-35).

What Jesus is about to tell her is a truth that everybody must face: if you trust in anything else other than Jesus Christ, you are trusting in the wrong thing.

[21]Jesus saith unto her, Woman,[10] believe me, the hour cometh, when ye shall neither in this mountain, nor yet at Jerusalem, worship the Father. [22]Ye worship ye know not what: we know what we worship: for salvation is of the Jews.

---

[10] This is the same way Jesus addressed Mary in John 2. He puts Mary on the same level, so to speak, as a five-time divorced woman that is more than likely living with a man she is not married to.

This woman, like so many others, is apparently worshipping, but it is not enough just to worship. According to this verse, it is possible for people to worship while being ignorant of what it is they are worshipping. I wonder how many people participate in worship services and have no idea why they are doing the things they do? They just go with the flow and do as everyone else without any thought or regard for what the scripture says. Christmas, Easter, Halloween, etc., are all prime examples.

Lastly, pay close attention to what Christ said. **Ye worship ye know not what**. A "what" cannot get someone to heaven nor restore the lost fellowship between God and man, but a "who" can. That who is Jesus Christ.

[23]But the hour cometh, and now is, when the true worshippers shall worship the Father in spirit and in truth: for the Father seeketh such to worship him. [24]God is a Spirit: and they that worship him must worship him in spirit and in truth.

This is why Jesus went to Samaria (v.4). He was seeking after such to worship Him. If you are going to worship Him, it MUST be done in spirit and in truth, and NOW IS the time. God has given us His holy, perfect word that is inerrant and infallible. God has also given us a spirit capable to retain knowledge and understanding. We must worship Him in both spirit and in truth.

Why churches all over America ignore the word of God week in and week out I will never fully understand. They operate and function based on opinion or tradition, instead of on understanding and knowledge founded on the truth of God's word. God and His word are all the truth we need, and He expects us to worship Him as His word defines.

[25]The woman saith unto him, I know that Messias cometh, which is called Christ: when he is come, he will tell us all things.

I do not want to get too far ahead, but she has been given light by someone because she holds this truth about the Messiah. Even Jesus is about to tell His disciples they entered into other people's labors (v.38), so obviously someone has come with truth to Samaria proclaiming God's word before them. She responded well to the light about the Messiah, but how will she respond to the light Jesus is about to give her?

[26]Jesus saith unto her, I that speak unto thee am he.

This woman must know who Jesus is now. He is the Christ, the savior of the world (v. 42). He has told her all things about herself that no ordinary stranger coming into town should know. Now there is just one thing she must do, and that is to trust in Him.

²⁷And upon this came his disciples, and marveled that he talked with the woman: yet no man said, What seekest thou? or, Why talkest thou with her?

Not only is He, a Jew, speaking with a Samaritan, but according to Jewish tradition, a Rabbi is not supposed to speak with any woman alone; not even if He is teaching on the scripture. However, Jesus is only bound to God's word (His word), not man's tradition.

²⁸The woman then left her waterpot, and went her way into the city, and saith to the men, ²⁹Come, see a man, which told me all things that ever I did: is not this the Christ? ³⁰Then they went out of the city, and came unto him.

She indeed does now know that Jesus is the Christ and has received the light Jesus came to give her.

³¹In the mean while his disciples prayed him, saying, Master, eat. ³²But he said unto them, I have meat to eat that ye know not of. ³³Therefore said the disciples one to another, Hath any man brought him ought to eat?

Once again, as we have so often seen up to this point in John, Jesus is using the physical to explain the spiritual. Naturally, the disciples think Jesus is referring to some physical food He possesses, but that is not what He meant.

³⁴Jesus saith unto them, My meat is to do the will of him that sent me, and to finish his work.

The hour will come when He goes to the cross to die in order to pay the sin debt for the whole world, and there on the cross He will cry, **It is finished** (John 19:30). That is what He came to do according to the will of the Father, and He will accomplish it.

³⁵Say not ye, There are yet four months, and then cometh harvest? behold, I say unto you, Lift up your eyes, and look on the fields; for they are white already to harvest. ³⁶And he that reapeth receiveth wages, and gathereth fruit unto life eternal: that both he that soweth and he that reapeth may rejoice together. ³⁷And herein is that saying true, One

soweth, and another reapeth. [38]**I sent you to reap that whereon ye bestowed no labour: other men labored, and ye are entered into their labours.**

As briefly discussed earlier (v.25), the disciples have entered an area to reap a harvest where they bestowed no labor. Ultimately, it makes no difference whether you are the original sower or the one who reaps the harvest. Either way, both will rejoice together once the harvest is complete.

Also, God is the one that makes the results and accomplishments of the word possible. So, before men and women begin to boast of the work they are doing for God, they ought to consider 1 Corinthians 3:5-8: **Who then is Paul, and who is Apollos, but ministers by whom ye believed, even as <u>the Lord gave to every man</u>? I have planted, Apollos watered; but <u>God gave the increase</u>. So then <u>neither is he that planteth any thing, neither he that watereth</u>; but God giveth the increase. Now he that planteth and he that waterth are one: and every man shall receive his own reward according to his own labour.** We should all labor as God has given us the ability, but we must understand that we can do nothing without Christ (John 15:5).

[39]**And many of the Samaritans of that city believed on him for the saying of the woman, which testified, He told me all that ever I did.** [40]**So when the Samaritans were come unto him, they besought him that he would tarry with them: and he abode there two days.** [41]**And many more believed because of his own word;** [42]**And said unto the woman, Now we believe, not because of thy saying: for we have heard him ourselves, and know that this is indeed the Christ, the Saviour of the world.**

Here is a good example of the diversities in the amounts of light individuals will need to receive before they fully believe the word of God. Some will only need to hear the testimonies of others on what God has done for them. Others will need to hear those same testimonies along with additional words from scripture. Either way, if people will receive the light that is given, more can be dispensed as needed. This is how God operates, and how individual believers should operate as illustrated by this woman.

Please also do not miss the remarkably simple definitional truth about who Christ is at the end of verse 42. The Christ is the Savior of the world.

[43]**Now after two days he departed thence, and went into Galilee.** [44]**For Jesus himself testified, that a prophet hath no honour in his own country.**

Regarding Jesus Christ, many could not get beyond the fact that He was a carpenter, the supposed son of Joseph (Luke 3:23), and they were astonished upon hearing Him teach considering He had no formal education. **And when he [Jesus] was come into his own country, he taught them in their synagogue, insomuch that they were astonished, and said, Whence hath this man this wisdom, and these mighty works? Is not this the carpenter's son? is not his mother called Mary? and his brethren, James, and Joses, and Simon, and Judas? And his sisters, are they not all with us? Whence then hath this man all these things? And they were offended in him** (Matthew 13:54-57a).

In the similar passage from Mark 6:3, they asked, **Is not this the carpenter?** I am sure for many, Jesus was hired in His town to perform carpentry work, and because of that, some people gave very little credit to His words.

In like manner, when you or I try to prophesy (that is, speaking unto men to edification, and exhortation, and comfort – 1 Corinthians 14:3), oftentimes the more people know about us the less credit they tend to give to God's words spoken through us. An unfortunate truth but true, nonetheless. Now, that is not a blanket statement for all men everywhere, because I am just as sure there have been individuals to preach in their hometowns and the people receive them well. But those situations are minimal at best.

[45]Then when he was come into Galilee, the Galilaeans received him, having seen all the things that he did at Jerusalem at the feast: for they also went unto the feast. [46]So Jesus came again into Cana of Galilee, where he made the water wine. And there was a certain nobleman, whose son was sick at Capernaum. [47]When he heard that Jesus was come out of Judaea into Galilee, he went unto him, and besought him that he would come down, and heal his son: for he was at the point of death. [48]Then said Jesus unto him, Except ye see signs and wonders, ye will not believe.

All throughout Israel's history the Jews have required signs and wonders to believe God. This was true when Moses brought them the law from God. It was also true when God turned to the first prophets, Elijah and Elisha, to turn the people back to Him. Even 1 Corinthians 1:22a states, **For the Jews require a sign.** Therefore, Jesus is providing this man an opportunity to believe, only by faith, without the prerequisite of signs and wonders the Jews so often require.

49The nobleman saith unto him, Sir, come down ere my child die. **50**Jesus saith unto him, Go thy way; thy son liveth. And the man believed the word that Jesus had spoken unto him, and he went his way.

The nobleman did indeed believe by faith, and faith is the only way to please God. **But without faith it is impossible to please him: for he that cometh to God must believe that he is, and that he is a rewarder of them that diligently seek him** (Hebrews 11:6).

51And as he was now going down, his servants met him, and told him, saying, Thy son liveth. **52**Then enquired he of them the hour when he began to amend. And they said unto him, Yesterday at the seventh hour the fever left him. **53**So the father knew that it was at the same hour, in the which Jesus said unto him, Thy son liveth: and himself believed, and his whole house. **54**This is again the second miracle that Jesus did, when he was come out of Judaea into Galilee.

This is the second miracle performed by Jesus as recorded by John, and both miracles have seven things in common:

1. Both happened in Cana of Galilee
2. Both happened on the third day (2:1, and 4:43)
3. Jesus rebuked someone before the miracle was performed in both cases (Mary – 2:4, and the nobleman – 4:48)
4. Both miracles showed obedience to Jesus' words
5. Both miracles illustrated God's work by His spoken word
6. Both miracles mentioned servants
7. Both miracles followed with witnesses believing –illustrating the theme of John (John 20:30-31).

John 5

But Jesus answered them, My Father worketh hitherto, and I work
– John 5:17: Jesus made Himself equal with God

[1]**After this there was a <u>feast of the Jews</u>; and Jesus went up to Jerusalem.**

There are multiple feasts instituted by God for the Jews to observe. Most of them can be found in Leviticus 23.

- Passover Feast – observed on 14th day of first month, Nisan.[11]
- *Unleavened Bread Feast* – observed Nisan 15-21.
- Firstfruits Feast – observed the day after the first weekly Sabbath following Passover.[12]
- *Feast of Weeks (Pentecost)* – observed the Sunday following the seventh weekly Sabbath (50 days) after Passover.
- Feast of Trumpets – observed on the 1st day of seventh month, Tishri.
- Day of Atonement – observed Tishri 10.
- *Feast of Tabernacles* – observed Tishri 15-22.

The three feasts identified in italic above are known as pilgrim feasts. Every Jewish male was required to present himself before the Lord three times annually during those feast days (Exodus 23:14-17; 34:18-23; Deuteronomy 16:16 and 2 Chronicles 8:13). This was practiced for all males twelve years old and up (Luke 2:40-52).

Four more feasts that God instituted for His people to observe were:

- Sabbath feasts – observed every Saturday (day of rest)
- New Moon feasts – observed at the beginning of each month.
- Sabbath Year Feasts – observed every 7th year (year of rest).
- Jubilee Feasts – observed every 50th year (year of rest).

Additionally, there were two other feasts that the Jews decided amongst themselves to observe every year.

- Purim – observed Adar 14. Started after Esther helped save her people from Haman's evil plot to destroy the Jews (Esther 9).
- Hanukkah – observed in ninth month, Kislev. Started after the Maccabean revolt in the second century B.C. between the writing of Malachi and Matthew.

---

[11] See Appendix – *Biblical Calendar*
[12] This feast occurred on Sunday and is the day Christ's body was discovered missing from the tomb. This is why He is called the **firstfruits of them that slept** (1 Corinthians 15:20).

Lastly, there were also a few feasts added to their list of holy days known as dedications.

- Dedication of the altar (Numbers 7:84-88, 2 Chronicles 1:10, 1 Kings 8:2). This happened on the twenty-third day of the seventh month, Tishri.
- Feast in remembrance of the house of God being completed on the third day of the month Adar under the reign of king Darius (Ezra 6:15-17).

All these feasts are presented here because it is unclear which one is being observed at the beginning of this chapter. Based on the context, I would conclude it is a Sabbath feast (vs. 9), but that cannot be guaranteed.

²Now there is at Jerusalem by the sheep market a pool, which is called in the Hebrew tongue Bethesda, having five porches. ³In these lay a great multitude of impotent folk, of blind, halt, withered, waiting for the moving of the water. ⁴For an angel went down at a certain season into the pool, and troubled the water: whosoever then first after the troubling of the water stepped in was made whole of whatsoever disease he had.

There are just a couple of things to mention about the passage thus far. Apparently, the impotent folk gathered around this pool with hopes of having their infirmities healed. These people were blind, halt (unable to walk), and withered. They desired to be the first to step into the pool IF an angel was to trouble the waters as had happened before. There is no need to question whether this happened in the past for the Bible plainly stated it did.

My questions are …
1. How would the blind know the water was troubled without help?
2. How would these halt and withered individuals get into the water without help?

These people want to be made whole, and they cannot help themselves. They need a man to help them. A man must help them. Here comes the man Christ Jesus (1 Timothy 2:5b).

⁵And a certain man was there, which had an infirmity <u>thirty and eight years</u>.

Thirty-eight years is the exact amount of time the Israelites spent wandering in the wilderness after their exodus from Egypt (Deuteronomy 2:14).

This man is going to be the only individual made whole out of all these gathered at Bethesda. Why did Jesus not make them all whole? Perhaps the simplest answer is derived from the context of the passage. When an angel stirs the water, the first and only the first person to get in is made whole. In like manner, the first person Jesus meets at this pool is healed. This simply shows that help and healing of infirmities comes from Jesus. Stop waiting on an angel that may or may not come. Jesus is here!

[6]When Jesus saw him lie, and knew that he had been now a long time in that case, he saith unto him, Wilt thou be made whole? [7]The impotent man answered him, Sir, I have no man, when the water is troubled, to put me into the pool: but while I am coming, another steppeth down before me.

Just as we previously discussed, this man is completely helpless and hopeless. He cannot do this by himself. He must be helped.

[8]Jesus saith unto him, Rise, take up thy bed, and walk. [9]And immediately the man was made whole, and took up his bed, and walked: and on the same day was the sabbath.

This man did not need an angel. He needed Jesus Christ. The point is that an angel could not meet every need because even if the waters were stirred, someone else would still have to aid him into the pool.

To make further application, the preaching of the gospel is what every man, woman, and child needs on this earth. 1 Peter 1:12 says that is something the angels desire to investigate because they do not fully understand it. Thus, again, no angel can meet every need man has. See Acts 10:1-6 for an example. **There was a certain man in Caesarea called Cornelius, a centurion of the band called the Italian band, A devout man, and one that feared God with all his house, which gave much alms to the people, and prayed to God always. He saw in a vision evidently about the ninth hour of the day an angel of God coming in to him, and saying unto him, Cornelius. And when he looked on him, he was afraid, and said, What is it, Lord? And he said unto him, Thy prayers and thine alms are come up for a memorial before God. And now send men to Joppa, and call for one Simon, whose surname is Peter: He lodgeth with one Simon a tanner, whose house is by the sea side: he shall tell thee what thou oughtest to do.** This angel could not give the gospel. He could only point Cornelius in the right direction to receive the gospel from Peter in verses 34-43.

[10]The Jews therefore said unto him that was cured, It is the sabbath day: it is not lawful for thee to carry thy bed.

What!? This man is simply carrying a blanket down the street, so what is the problem? The law states, **six days shalt thou labour, and do all thy work: But the seventh day is the sabbath of the LORD thy God: in it thou shalt not do any work** (Exodus 20:9-10a). How is a man carrying his blanket down the road considered a work?

This is one example of how the Pharisees misused and perverted God's law. **Thus saith the LORD; Take heed to yourselves, and <u>bear no burden</u> on the sabbath day, nor bring it in by the gates of Jerusalem; Neither <u>carry forth a burden</u> out of your houses on the Sabbath day, neither do ye any work, but hallow ye the sabbath day, as I commanded your fathers** (Jeremiah 17:21-22). This man's burden is gone so he is in no way, shape, or form breaking the Sabbath.

[11]He answered them, He that made me whole, the same said unto me, Take up thy bed, and walk. [12]Then asked they him, What man is that which said unto thee, Take up thy bed, and walk? [13]And he that was healed wist not who it was: for Jesus had conveyed himself away, a multitude being in that place. [14]Afterward Jesus findeth him in the temple, and said unto him, Behold, thou art made whole: <u>sin no more</u>, lest a worse thing come unto thee.

Jesus does not ignore this man's sin. Something else to note is when a miracle is performed in scripture, repentance from sin is expected to follow. Why? It is because a worse thing could come as a result. This impotent man had a rough life for thirty-eight years, but there are indeed worse things in this life than not being able to walk. Death being the most obvious example.

Plenty of people in this life have decided to live a life of sin and now must suffer the consequences. A person decides to become drunken with alcohol and get behind the wheel of a car thinking everything will be ok. The next thing he or she experiences is hitting another car head on carrying a family of four killing the two children in the back seat. That is something which cannot be fixed or corrected. The drunkard has to live with those consequences for the rest of his or her life.

[15]The man departed, and told the Jews that it was Jesus, which had made him whole. [16]And therefore did the Jews persecute Jesus, and sought to slay him, because he had done these things on the sabbath day.

It is obvious that these Jews cared extraordinarily little about the people. They should be happy an impotent man has been healed. Instead, they wanted to kill Jesus for healing him. Their only concern was for their interpretation of the law and the power it gave them. This jealousy toward Jesus will only worsen as we progress through this Gospel.

[17]But Jesus answered them, <u>My Father</u> worketh hitherto, and I work.

In short, Jesus just announced that He works on the Sabbath just as God does. God rested the seventh day of creation, but once sin entered the world in the Garden of Eden, He has not rested since.

The fact that Jesus proclaimed to work on the Sabbath day does not violate the law. **The sabbath was made <u>for man</u>, and not man for the sabbath: Therefore the Son of man is Lord also of the sabbath** (Mark 2:27b-28). Considering Jesus is God, it is only natural He works on the Sabbath day as His Father does.

[18]Therefore the Jews sought the more to kill him, because he not only had broken the sabbath, but said also that God was his Father, <u>making himself equal with God</u>.

First thing to note is the scriptural support for wanting to kill a man who makes such a proclamation as Jesus did. See Deuteronomy 13:1-11. However, take careful note of what Deuteronomy actually says. **If there arise among you a prophet, or a dreamer of dreams, and giveth thee a sign or a wonder. And the sign or the wonder come to pass, whereof he spake unto thee, saying, <u>Let us go after other gods</u>, which thou hast not known, and let us serve them; Thou shalt not hearken unto the words of that prophet, or that dreamer of dreams…And that prophet, or that dreamer of dreams, shall be put to death** (Deuteronomy 13:1-3a, 5a). Jesus is not trying to turn them away unto other gods; therefore, He does not deserve the death penalty. He is simply trying to turn them BACK unto the true and living God they have long ignored.

Secondly, I am sure you have heard people say on occasion, as I have, that Jesus never claimed to be God. He only claimed to be the Son of God. The response to such a statement is John 5:17-18. Every time Jesus used the words: "My Father," He was claiming His deity.[13] The statement meant He was equal with God and the Jews understood that meaning. That is why they wanted to kill Him. No matter what different denominations or cults teach regarding the deity of Jesus Christ, He is indeed equal with the Father. See also John 10:33-34.

---

[13] There are four statements by Jesus in John that declare His deity: John 3:13; 5:17; 8:58; and 10:30.

¹⁹**Then answered Jesus and said unto them, Verily, verily, I say unto you, The Son can do nothing of himself, but what he seeth the Father do: for what things soever he doeth, these also doeth the Son likewise.**

There is an agreement between God the Father and God the Son. Whatever the Father does, the Son does likewise. They are NOT independent of one another but equal, just as verse 18 stated.

²⁰**For the Father loveth the Son, and sheweth him all things that himself doeth: and he will shew him greater works than these, that ye may marvel. ²¹For as the Father raiseth up the dead, and quickeneth them; even so the Son quickeneth whom he will.**

Jesus just said that God the Father will show Him greater works than healing an impotent man THAT these Jews may marvel. Not only does Jesus have the power to give an individual a spiritual birth (John 3), but He has the power to raise someone from the dead. That is a marvelous thing!

These Jews are going to behold Jesus raising Lazarus from the dead in John 11, and some of them will not know what to do (see John 11:46-47). They will only continue to stick to the same conclusion they have made here: He must die. Then, Jesus Himself will rise from the dead after three days, and after **many infallible proofs** (Acts 1:3), yet they still will not believe on Him. What a marvel that is!

²²**For the Father judgeth no man, but hath committed all judgment unto the Son: ²³That all men should honour the Son, even as they honour the Father. He that honoureth not the Son honoureth not the Father which hath sent him.**

If some of these Jews did not want to kill Him before, they do now. He boldly stated that He, not the Father, would be the one to judge every man, and He did not stop there. He continued by saying the Father committed all judgment unto Him that all men should honor the Son just as they honor the Father. WOW!

When I hear people testify to their belief that Jesus was just a good man, it tells me they really have not read their Bible. If His statements are not true, He is the biggest liar on the face of the planet. How can someone believe that Jesus is not God and at the same time believe Him to be a good man? No way that is possible.

²⁴Verily, verily, I say unto you, He that heareth my word, and believeth on him that sent me, hath everlasting life, and shall not come into condemnation; but is passed from death unto life.

The Bible is so clear. To have everlasting life, you must hear Jesus' words and believe on the Father that sent Him (v. 24). That means you must believe Jesus and the Father are equal (v.18). You must believe that Jesus is the one who gives life (v. 20). You must believe that Jesus deserves the same honor that is given to the Father (v. 23). You must believe that Jesus is God (v. 18-21).

Oh, how I love this Gospel. Jesus is, without a doubt, God manifest in the flesh.

²⁵Verily, verily, I say unto you, The hour is coming, <u>and now is</u>, when the dead shall hear the voice of the Son of God: and they that hear shall live.

I hope it is becoming very evident to you as to why these religious people sought to kill Jesus (vs.16-18). Not only has He made extremely bold statements regarding His deity, but now He is pronouncing them to be dead. A true and accurate statement when considering Ephesians 2:1 which states we are **dead in trespasses and sins** before we hear and believe God's word. However, the truth presented here, in Ephesians 2, and throughout John is that to live you must hear Jesus' words. The only way you will hear is when you desire truth while being willing to receive it (John 1:11-13). These people simply do not want truth; thus, they do not hear.

²⁶For as the Father hath life in himself; so hath he given to the Son to have life in himself; ²⁷And hath given him authority to execute judgment also, because he is the Son of man.

Jesus can give life unto those that hear Him because the Father hath given Him life to have in Himself. This takes us back to John 1:4: **in him was life**, and John 1:12-13(a): **as many as received him to them gave he power to become the sons of God, even to them that believe on his name: which were born…of God**. Jesus must indeed be equal with God! As God, He gives both physical and spiritual life and has the authority to execute judgment.

²⁸Marvel not at this: for the hour is coming, in the which <u>all</u> that are in the graves shall hear his voice, ²⁹And shall come forth; they that have done good, unto the resurrection of life; and they that have done evil, unto the resurrection of damnation.

So, not only will Christ raise individual men from the grave (v.21), but one day <u>all</u> that are in the graves will resurrect. Those that have done good, unto the resurrection of life, and those that have done evil, unto the resurrection of damnation. Why? John 3:18-21: **He that believeth on him is not condemned: but he that believeth not is condemned already...For <u>everyone that doeth evil hateth the light, neither cometh to the light,</u> lest his deeds should be reproved. But <u>he that doeth truth cometh to the light,</u> that his deeds may be made manifest, that they are wrought in God**.

Doing good verses doing evil is simply making a choice between believing and not believing in Jesus Christ. Those that chose not to believe were evil because their deeds are evil, and they love darkness. As a result, they are condemned already, and once God empties the graves they will resurrect unto damnation (Revelation 20:11-15).

[30]I can of mine own self do nothing: as I hear, I judge: and my judgment is just; because I seek not mine own will, but the will of the Father which hath sent me.

I hope you realize how truly bold Jesus is being by making all these statements, for only God can do these things. Not only has He proclaimed to be able to give life unto whom He will, and to resurrect <u>all</u> that are in the graves unto judgment where He will be the judge, but He proclaims that His judgments are correct and just! Can you see the boldness Jesus has? To be able to do what He claims would mean that He has been around since Adam in the garden. There is no other way He would be able to accurately judge every man's work. He had to be around to see their work. John 1:1 proves He was. Hallelujah!

[31]If I bear witness of myself, my witness is not true. [32]There is another that beareth witness of me; and I know that the witness which he witnesseth of me is true.

How can someone be sure that Jesus is telling the truth, and that He is indeed equal with the Father? The Bible explains that **in the mouth of two or three witnesses shall every word be established** (2 Corinthians 13:1(b); see also Deuteronomy 17:6, 19:15, and Matthew 18:16). Before this chapter closes, Jesus will reveal not two or three witnesses, but a total of four to support His proclamations. Therefore, it is forever settled that Jesus is telling the truth based on the word of God!

³³Ye sent unto <u>John</u>, and he bare witness unto the truth. ³⁴But I receive not testimony from man: but these things I say, that ye might be saved. ³⁵He was a burning and a shining light: and ye were willing for a season to rejoice in his light.

The first witness is John the Baptist. He prepared the way of the Lord (Matthew 3:3, Mark 1:3, Luke 3:4, John 1:23) by telling the multitudes that Christ was coming (Matthew 3:11, John 1:15), and all Jerusalem, Judaea, and the region round about Jordan went to hear him (Matthew 3:5).

Even though **among them that are born of women there hath not risen a greater than John the Baptist** (Matthew 11:11), Jesus does not need testimony from man because there is a greater witness than John.

³⁶But I have greater witness than that of John: for the works which the Father hath given me to finish, the same <u>works that I do</u>, bear witness of me, that the Father hath sent me.

Witness number two provided to prove Christ is God is His own works that the Father hath given Him to finish. He set out to do **always those things that please him** (John 8:29), and in John 17:4 while in the upper room with His disciples He announces that He finished the work the Father gave Him. Finally on the cross He cried **it is finished** (John 19:30).

³⁷And <u>the Father</u> himself, which hath sent me, hath borne witness of me. Ye have neither heard his voice at any time, nor seen his shape. ³⁸And ye have not his word abiding in you: for whom he hath sent, him ye believe not.

The Father is the third witness. God the Father spoke audibly in Matthew 3:17 saying **This is my beloved Son, in whom I am well pleased** (see also Hebrews 1:5, Psalm 2:7).

The Father's shape is exactly what we discussed in John 1:18. Seeing the Son is the same as seeing the Father. Unfortunately, these people would not believe the words of the people God sent (v. 38), they did not hear the prophets who declared Jesus (Romans 1:1-3), they did not completely believe John the Baptist who bore witness of Jesus (John 1), and they did not believe the Son of God whom the Father sent. It is no wonder they have not heard God's voice. They refuse to listen.

³⁹Search <u>the scriptures</u>; for in them ye think ye have eternal life: and they are they which testify of me.

The last witness is the scripture.

Romans 1:1-3 declares that the gospel of God was promised afore by His prophets in the holy scriptures, and the gospel of God is concerning his Son Jesus Christ our Lord! So, not only do we have the gospel in the New Testament, but it was declared before in the scriptures by the prophets. Jesus Christ is the gospel. He is the good news, and the prophets spoke of Him.

[40] And ye will not come to me, that ye might have life. [41] I receive not honour from men. [42] But I know you, that ye have not the love of God in you. [43] I am come in my Father's name, and ye receive me not: if another shall come in his own name, him ye will receive. [44] How can ye believe, which receive honour one of another, and see not the honour that cometh from God only? [45] Do not think that I will accuse you to the Father: <u>there is one that accuseth you, even Moses, in whom ye trust</u>.

At the end of this speech, Christ is going to hit these Pharisees at their very core. They boast of being Abraham's seed: the chosen people (Matthew 3:9, Luke 3:8, John 8:33), and of being Moses' disciples (John 9:28). However, the very thing they trust in is going to accuse them of their guilt for not believing on Him.

[46] For had ye believed Moses, ye would have believed me; for he wrote of me. [47] <u>But if ye believe not his writings, how shall ye believe my words</u>?

Moses wrote the first five books of the Bible, and those books speak of Jesus Christ. The Pharisees need to stop trusting in Moses and start trusting in what he wrote.

This is one of the most powerful verses concerning our school systems in America today. Ever since the Scopes Trial (Tennessee, 1925), evolution began to be increasingly accepted within the public-school science curriculum. By the 1960's, Creationism (as stated in the creation account of Genesis) practically ceased to exist within the curriculum. As a result, children have been taught for decades a *theory* in place of Bible truth, and we wonder why people are not getting saved the way they used to. **If ye believe not his** [Moses] **writings** (Genesis account of creation)**, how shall ye believe my words**? When people do not believe **God created the heaven and the earth** (Genesis 1:1), it's as if God does not exist. So, why would someone believe Jesus is God? How can they believe Jesus is God? The proofs He provided (John the Baptist, Jesus' works, the Father, and the scriptures) have been ignored for generations.

John 6

For I came down from heaven, not to do mine own will, but the will of him that sent me – John 6:38: Jesus claimed to have come down from heaven

[1]After these things Jesus went over the sea of Galilee, which is the sea of Tiberias. [2]And a great multitude followed him, because they saw his miracles which he did on them that were diseased.

I would say these people are curious and want to see what Jesus might do next. If you think about it, when someone does something *miraculous* everyone's first reaction is to say, "Do it again." These people are no different.

[3]And Jesus went up into a mountain, and there he sat with his disciples. [4]And the passover, a feast of the Jews, was nigh.

See Exodus 12 and Leviticus 23 for details regarding the Passover feast. [14]

[5]When Jesus then lifted up his eyes, and saw a great company come unto him, he saith unto Philip, Whence shall we buy bread, that these may eat? [6]And this he said to prove him: for he himself knew what he would do.

Throughout the Bible you will read of God asking questions you know He knows the answers to. So, why ask the question?

When every person stands before Christ, on the Day of Judgment, you will be judged by your very own words. **Every idle word that men shall speak, they shall give account thereof in the day of judgment. For <u>by thy words thou shalt be justified</u>, and <u>by thy words thou shalt be condemned</u>** (Matthew 12:36-37).

[7]Philip answered him, Two hundred pennyworth of bread is not sufficient for them, that every one of them may take a little. [8]One of his disciples, Andrew, Simon Peter's brother, saith unto him, [9]There is a lad here, which hath five barley loaves, and two small fishes: but what are they among so many?

An interesting note in John is that every time Andrew is mentioned, he is bringing someone to Christ (1:40-41; 6:8-9; 12:21-22).

---

[14] See Appendix – *How long was Jesus' ministry?*

[10]**And Jesus said, Make the men sit down. Now there was much grass in the place. So the men sat down, in number about five thousand.**

Here are two things you need to understand.

1. Matthew 14:13 and 6:35 call this a desert place. Here we get an important detail (as well as in the other Gospels) that this desert place has much grass. I bring this to your attention because many movies regarding Israel's wanderings in the desert places of the wilderness show the scene as being dry, hot, rocky, and completely barren of vegetation. If everywhere they went were that way, how would they have kept their livestock fed? A wilderness or a desert place is simply a place that is uninhabited or deserted: nobody lives there.

2. Matthew 14:21 gives us a little more insight into this scene. **And they that had eaten were about five thousand men, <u>beside women and children</u>**. So, we know there were 5,000 men but we do not know the total number of people because the number of women and children is not given. Thus, there could have been as many as ten or fifteen thousand people present.

[11]**And Jesus took the loaves; and when he had given thanks, he distributed to the disciples, and the disciples to them that were set down; and likewise of the fishes <u>as much as they would</u>.**

So, they ate as much as they wanted.

[12]**When they were filled, he said unto his disciples, Gather up the fragments that remain, that nothing be lost.**

I sure would like to know exactly what the disciples were thinking at this moment. Surely, they had to be in a state of bewilderment.

[13]**Therefore they gathered them together, and filled twelve baskets with the fragments of the five barley loaves, which remained over and above unto them that had eaten.**

There are twelve baskets because there are twelve disciples gathering up the fragments that remained. Also, take note that Jesus wasted nothing. He believes in leftovers. I just thought I would point that out to you just in case you do not like the idea of eating the same thing for two days in a row.

The point of this miracle is two-fold. In the Old Testament, it was God who fed the Israelites in the wilderness with bread from heaven (manna). Here God the Son is doing the same thing He did years ago, thus proving His deity.

The second point is an application for us today. The five loaves and two fish were not enough to meet the need of the hour. Therefore, they gave what they had to Jesus. He broke it, blessed it, and gave it back to them to meet the need. We need to be disciplined enough to understand that what we have to offer is insufficient to meet any need. Thus, we should give what we have to Jesus and allow Him to break it. Once it is broken, we must not quit because only then are we truly able to meet the need.

Let me put it this way using scripture. **He that abideth in me, and I in him, the same bringeth forth much fruit: <u>for without me ye can do nothing</u>** (John 15:5). Understanding that fact and allowing God to work through us makes Philippians 4:9, 13 true. **Those things, which ye have both learned, and received, and heard, and seen in me, <u>do</u>: and the God of peace shall be with you.** We can do those things because **<u>I can do all things through Christ which strengtheneth me</u>**.

[14]**Then those men, when they had seen the miracle that Jesus did, said, This is of a truth that prophet that should come into the world. [15]When Jesus therefore perceived that they would come and take him by force, to <u>make him</u> a king, he departed again into a mountain himself alone.**

There is no need to *make him* a king because He is the King. Israel simply needs to receive that truth, but we will find out later in this Gospel that they will not. What also needs to be understood is that Christ did not come to set up the earthly kingdom[15] at His first coming. It is not until His second coming that He will rule and reign from David's throne at Jerusalem.

[16]**And when even was now come, his disciples went down unto the sea, [17]And entered into a ship, and went over the sea toward Capernaum. And it was now dark, and Jesus was not come to them.**

Some people might have two questions because of reading this.

1. Why did the disciples leave without Jesus? Matthew 14:22 tells us that Jesus told them to. **And straightway Jesus <u>constrained</u> his disciples to get into a ship, and to go before him unto the other side, while he sent the multitudes away.** The reason Jesus had to constrain them to go without Him is because the last time they were out at sea a mighty storm arose making them fear for their very lives. That was when Jesus

---

[15] See Author's work: <u>Matthew</u> for additional commentary on the kingdom of heaven vs. the kingdom of God.

calmed the storm by His spoken word (Matthew 8:23-27 and Mark 4:35-41).

2. How would Jesus meet back up with His disciples if not by walking on water, as told by the next verses? The answer is simply walking on land like the multitude did to get to this desert place. **When Jesus heard of it, he departed thence by ship into a desert place apart: and when the people had heard thereof, they followed him on foot out of the cities** (Matthew 14:13).

[18]And the sea arose by reason of a great wind that blew. [19]So when they had rowed about five and twenty or thirty furlongs,[16] they see Jesus walking on the sea[17], and drawing nigh unto the ship: and they were afraid. [20]But he saith unto them, It is I; be not afraid.

Apparently, the disciples did not realize this was Jesus. Mark 6:49 tells us **they supposed it to be a spirit**. The sea giving them trouble, like the last time, is bad enough, and now they see someone walking on the water they do not recognize. Say what you want, but I think anybody would be afraid at this point.

[21]Then they willingly received him into the ship: and immediately the ship was at the land whither they went.

This is an amazing event that is never discussed simply because it gets lost in the context of Jesus walking on water. When Jesus gets in this boat, immediately they arrive at their destination. All night long (Mark 6:48) the disciples have been toiling and rowing against this sea, and within a moment their struggles are over. That is a fantastic picture of what Jesus does for believers, is it not? You will face trials and struggles in this life (John 16:33, 1 Thessalonians 3:3), but at least we can have confidence that Jesus will be right there with us along the way (Hebrews 13:5-6).

[22]The day following, when the people which stood on the other side of the sea saw that there was none other boat there, save that one whereinto his disciples were entered, and that Jesus went not with his disciples into the boat, but that his disciples were gone away alone; [23](Howbeit there came other boats from Tiberias nigh unto the place where they did eat bread, after that the Lord had given thanks:) [24]When the people therefore saw that Jesus was not there, neither his disciples, they also took shipping,

---

[16] One furlong is approximately one-eighth of a mile.
[17] See Appendix: *Jesus walks on water.*

and came to Capernaum, seeking for Jesus. **²⁵And when they had found him on the other side of the sea, they said unto him, Rabbi, when camest thou hither? ²⁶Jesus answered them and said, Verily, verily, I say unto you, Ye seek me, not because ye saw the miracles, but because ye did eat of the loaves, and were filled.**

Jesus did not answer their question. He just simply tells them the thoughts and intents of their hearts (Hebrews 4:12). He is basically a meal ticket to these people and that is the only reason they wanted to know when He came to Capernaum. They do not want Him; they only want what He has to offer. This is no different than many so-called Christians today who want God's air, God's water, God's food, raiment, blessings, and abundance but they do not want the Bible to tell them what to do or how to live.

²⁷Labour not for the <u>meat</u> which perisheth, but for that meat which endureth unto everlasting life, which the Son of man shall give unto you: for him hath God the Father sealed.

Jesus is again using a physical situation to explain the spiritual. These people just labored to row their boats across the sea to get to Him, and for what? Another free meal? Jesus is simply telling them to labor for the things of everlasting life (spiritual) as hard as they do for the things that perish (physical).

²⁸Then said they unto him, <u>What shall we do</u>, that we might work the works of God? ²⁹Jesus answered and said unto them, <u>This is the work of God, that ye believe on him whom he hath sent.</u>

Recall John 4:34: **My meat is to do the will of him that sent me, and to finish his work**. Jesus Christ is going to finish the work of God the Father on the cross at Calvary (John 19:30). Once that work is finished, the only labor/work that is left for you and me to do it is to believe on Jesus Christ whom God the Father sent. You cannot earn salvation, nor can you work for it. It only comes by faith in Jesus Christ. **For by grace are ye saved through faith; and that not of yourselves: it is the gift of God: <u>Not of works</u>, lest any man should boast** (Ephesians 2:8-9). It is that simple, yet so many struggle with receiving this truth. **But I fear, lest by any means, as the serpent beguiled Eve through his subtilty, so your mind should be corrupted from the simplicity that is in Christ** (2 Corinthians 11:3).

The next verses I want to reference explain thoroughly that you cannot save yourself by works. According to your Bible, there is a way to save yourself by works, but in truth, the work is impossible to complete. **Deck** thyself now with majesty and excellency; and array thyself with glory and beauty. Cast abroad the rage of thy wrath: and behold every one that is proud, and abase him. Look on every one that is proud, and bring him low; and tread down the wicked in their place. Hide them in the dust together; and bind their faces in secret. **Then** will I [God] also confess unto thee **that thine own right hand can save thee** (Job 40:10-14).

Even if you could array yourself with glory and beauty (your glory would have to match Christ's glory being full of grace and truth: John 1:14), there is no way possible to abase every proud person in the world. Even someone reading that scripture and thinking, "I can do that" is guilty of pride. Thus, the only way possible to be saved is through faith in Jesus Christ.

[30]**They said therefore unto him, What sign shewest thou then, that we may see, and believe thee? what dost thou work?**

Really! You mean Jesus feeding 5,000 men plus women and children while only using a little boy's lunch is not enough evidence for you to believe? Truly these people REQUIRE a sign as the scripture says (1 Corinthians 1:22).

[31]**Our fathers did eat manna in the desert; as it is written, He gave them bread from heaven to eat.**

The word manna tells us a lot about these Israelites. When the Israelites wandered in the wilderness, they began complaining and murmuring against Moses and Aaron in Exodus 16. **Would to God we had died by the hand of the LORD in the land of Egypt, when we sat by the flesh pots, and when we did eat bread to the full; for ye have brought us forth into this wilderness, to kill this whole assembly with hunger** (Exodus 16:3). They wanted and desired bread and God gave them what they desired. In the evening, He gave them quail, and during the morning dew He provided them with bread.

What you need to notice about those Israelites is how they still complained despite God giving them the desires of their hearts.

[32]**Then Jesus said unto them, Verily, verily, I say unto you, Moses gave you not that bread from heaven; but my Father giveth you the true bread from heaven. [33]For the bread of God is he which cometh[18] down from heaven, and giveth life unto the world.**

---

[18] The phrase **came** or **cometh down from heaven** occurs 7 times in this chapter.

69

The bread of God is He: Jesus Christ that came down from heaven and giveth life unto the world.

³⁴Then said they unto him, Lord, evermore give us this bread.

They completely missed what He just said. Jesus is the bread!

³⁵And Jesus said unto them, <u>I am the bread of life</u>: he that cometh to me shall never hunger; and he that <u>believeth on me</u> shall never thirst.

This is an identical statement He made to the woman at the well in chapter four: "You must believe." Upon believing you will never hunger or thirst again.

³⁶But I said unto you, That ye also have seen me, and believe not.

Not believing is their problem.

³⁷All that the Father giveth me shall come to me; and him that cometh to me I will in no wise cast out. ³⁸For <u>I came down from heaven</u>, not to do mine own will, but the will of him that sent me.

In verses 29, 33, and now again in 38, Jesus made the proclamation that God sent the true bread of life down from heaven. Now, without controversy, He just stated that He is the one who came down from heaven being sent from the Father. Plus, He stated that He is in accord with the Father's will. It is the reason the Father sent Him, and that is what He came to do. All I can say is "Praise God!"

³⁹And this is the Father's will which hath sent me, that of all which he hath given me <u>I should lose nothing</u>, but should raise it up again at the last day. ⁴⁰And this is the will of him that sent me, that every one which seeth the Son, and believeth on him, may have everlasting life: and I will raise him up at the last day.

If Jesus will lose nothing, where do certain *Bible teachers* find support for losing one's salvation?

⁴¹The Jews then murmured at him, because he said, I am the bread which came down from heaven. ⁴²And they said, Is not this Jesus, the son of Joseph, whose father and mother we know? how is it then that he saith, I came down from heaven?

It is a very bold statement Jesus just made. He is essentially claiming that His beginning did not start at His birth: a very true statement, as we have already seen in John. Next, He said that He would raise up those that believe on Him at the last day. These Jews have a ridiculously hard time receiving that truth and considering their unbelief I understand their murmuring.

Please take some time to consider exactly what Jesus just said. He existed before His birth in Bethlehem, came down from heaven to be born, and will be around at the last day to raise up those that believe on Him. He must be God for all that to be possible!

43Jesus therefore answered and said unto them, Murmur not among yourselves. 44No man can come to me, except the Father which hath sent me draw him: and I will raise him up at the last day.

This is a particularly important fact that we must be careful not to distort from what the Bible is saying. The fact is God must draw you to Him. Where the distortion comes into play is when the Calvinists teach that only an *elect* or *chosen* group will be drawn to God. If you are not in that group, then you will not be drawn by God, and you will not be saved. However, the very next verse proves that thinking to be false.

45It is written in the prophets, And they shall be all taught of God. Every man therefore that hath heard, and hath learned of the Father, cometh unto me.

ALL will be taught of God; therefore, the Calvinists are wrong. God gives light to every man that comes into the world (John 1:9) and then He proceeds to give more truth. If the recipient continues to hear AND learn of the Father by the word of God, he or she will come unto Christ and get saved by believing on Him (v. 29). Salvation is an amazingly simple thing (as easy as eating and drinking – what we will see in the upcoming verses), but salvation requires belief.

46Not that any man hath seen the Father, save he which is of God, he hath seen the Father. 47Verily, verily, I say unto you, He that believeth on me hath everlasting life.

See! Once you believe the truth of God's word, you have everlasting life. It is everlasting (never ending) because Jesus just said that He will raise them up at the last day. It's guaranteed. The problem with these Jews and every lost person we encounter during our day-to-day endeavors is that they refuse to believe God's word.

48I am the bread of life.

He is restating what He already said in verses 32 and 33. He will go on to refer to Himself as the bread of life 7 times in this chapter.

[49]Your fathers did eat manna in the wilderness, and are dead. [50]This is the bread which cometh down from heaven, that a man may eat thereof, and not die. [51]<u>I am the living bread</u> which came down from heaven: if any man eat of this bread, he shall live for ever: and the bread that I will give is my flesh, which I will give for the life of the world. [52]The Jews therefore strove among themselves, saying, How can this man give us his flesh to eat?

These Jews, just like we saw with Nicodemus and the woman at the well, are only thinking about the physical: literally eating His flesh.

[53]Then Jesus said unto them, Verily, verily, I say unto you, Except ye eat the flesh of the Son of man, and drink his blood, ye have no life in you. [54]Whoso eateth my flesh and drinketh my blood, <u>dwelleth in me, and I in him</u>. [55]For my flesh is meat indeed, and my blood is drink indeed. [56]He that eateth my flesh, and drinketh my blood, <u>dwelleth in me, and I in him</u>.

This is where the Catholic Church comes in and tries to support their doctrine of transubstantiation: the teaching that the wafer eaten during mass literally turns into the body of Jesus. They have the same problem that these Jews have. They are thinking about the physical and not the spiritual.

If you go to mass, I doubt very seriously you will hear any teaching on you being in Christ as these verses explain. You will hear plenty about Christ being in you, considering their teaching that you literally ate His flesh, but the verses themselves show a contradiction in their doctrine.

Here are a few biblical reasons why Jesus is NOT talking about someone physically eating His flesh.

1. Deuteronomy 8:3b: **man doth not live by bread only, but by every word that proceedeth out of the mouth of the LORD doth man live** (see also Matthew 4:4, Luke 4:4). It is an accurate statement to say that one must consume or eat the word of the Lord in order to live.

2. Ezekiel 2:7-8: **And thou shalt speak my words unto them, whether they will hear, or whether they will forbear: for they are most rebellious. But thou, son of man, hear what I say unto thee; Be not thou rebellious like that rebellious house: <u>open they mouth, and eat</u> that I give thee.** Eating the word of God should not be a new concept for these Jews. The very idea was written by the prophets of old. See also Jeremiah 15:16, Ecclesiastes 5:19 and 6:2.

3. The Ezekiel passage leads us right into what Christ is saying about Himself. John 1:1 and 14 tell us that Christ is the Word, and the Word became flesh and dwelt among us. Since He is the Word, and you must eat the word to live, these statements by Jesus should not be that difficult to understand only if we look at it spiritually instead of physically.

4. Here is what David said in 2 Samuel 23:15-17: **And David longed, and said, Oh that one would give me drink of the water of the well of Bethlehem, which is by the gate! And the three mighty men brake through the host of the Philistines, and drew water out of the well of Bethlehem, that was by the gate, and took it, and brought it to David: nevertheless he would not drink thereof, but poured it out unto the LORD. And he said, Be it far from me, O LORD, that I should do this: <u>is not this the blood of the men</u> that went in jeopardy of their lives?** That water from the well of Bethlehem was not literally the blood of those three men who went to fetch it. Not a single person reading those words would think it was. So, why someone would think that Christ is literally telling those people to drink His blood and eat His flesh[19] is a mystery to me.

[57]As the living Father hath sent me, and I live by the Father: so he that eateth me, even he shall live by me.

Once again, *eating Jesus* means to live by Him – live by His words for He is the Word (John 1:1, 14). Receive the word, trust the word, and believe the word.

[58]This is that bread which came down from heaven: not as your fathers did eat manna, and are dead: he that eateth of this bread shall live for ever.

These verses tell the whole story. The Jews once ate manna that came down from heaven but would later die. Now, this bread (Jesus Christ) has also come down from heaven, but whosoever eats it shall live forever.

Look at verse 57 again. Christ lives by the Father, and those that receive Him will live by Him. In other words, we can have the same everlasting relationship with Christ that Christ has with the Father if you will simply believe.

---

[19] If you would like to do a little more study on this subject, search out how often God uses eating terms like consume or devour when the context of the remark has nothing to do with physically eating.

[59]**These things said he in the synagogue, as he taught in Capernaum.** [60]**Many therefore of his disciples, when they had heard this, said, This is an hard saying; who can hear it?**

No surprise. The disciples are thinking just like the Pharisees: physical and not spiritual.

[61]**When Jesus knew in himself that his disciples murmured at it, he said unto them, Doth this offend you?** [62]**What and if ye shall see the Son of man ascend up where he was before?** [63]**It is the spirit that quickeneth; the flesh profiteth nothing: <u>the words that I speak</u> unto you, <u>they are spirit</u>, and they are life.**

See!? The context is spiritual, not physical!

Jesus has just compared Himself with manna that was once given from heaven back in the Old Testament. Therefore, it might help us to answer the following question: Why was the manna given in the first place? Deuteronomy 8:3 supplies us with that answer.

And he humbled thee, and suffered thee to hunger, and <u>fed thee with manna</u>, which thou knewest not, neither did thy fathers know; <u>that he might make thee know</u> that man doth not live by bread only, but by every word that proceedeth out of the mouth of the LORD doth man live. Do you see? God wants us to know that we cannot live by bread only. We need every word of God to have life (John 20:31). Stop laboring for the meat that perisheth (v.27), and work for the meat that endureth to everlasting life by believing on Jesus Christ (v.29).

[64]**But there are some of you that believe not. For Jesus knew from the beginning who they were that believed not, and who should betray him.** [65]**And he said, Therefore said I unto you, that no man can come unto me, except it were given unto him of my Father.** [66]**From that time many of his disciples went back, and walked no more with him.**

Christ is called a rock of offence (1 Peter 2:8, Romans 9:32), and a stumbling stone (1 Peter 2:8). He is the truth (John 14:6), and often the truth is offensive when heard. The disciples in these verses are proof of this, and Matthew 15:8-12 also illustrates how the Pharisees were offended at His words.

The reason people become offended when someone speaks truth is because of the flesh. People get angry, upset, defensive, or even feel defeated, and usually someone in that position will think, "I don't understand it, so I don't want to hear it." **It is the spirit that quickeneth; the flesh profiteth nothing** (v. 63), so we must get beyond our thoughts, inclinations, and feelings because they profit us nothing. Get beyond how you feel about what God says, and just believe Him. I praise the Lord that His word does not say UNDERSTAND the Lord Jesus Christ and thou shalt be saved, but accurately says **believe on the Lord Jesus Christ, and thou shalt be saved** (Acts 16:31). There is plenty about the word of God I do not understand, but thanks be to God I only have to believe it, not understand it.

Also, notice John 6:66. The number six is the number for man, and three sixes is the number of the beast from Revelation 13:18. This verse speaks of man doing what Satan desires for all men, and that is to not follow Jesus Christ.

⁶⁷Then said Jesus unto the twelve, Will ye also go away? ⁶⁸Then Simon Peter answered him, Lord, to whom shall we go? thou hast the words of eternal life.

Hallelujah, Peter gets it! Throughout the Gospels, Peter will often make statements where he would have been better off inserting his foot into his mouth. However, everything he just said here is absolutely true.

⁶⁹And we believe and are sure that thou art that Christ, the Son of the living God.

Belief is what matters!

⁷⁰Jesus answered them, Have not I chosen you twelve, and one of you is a devil? ⁷¹He spake of Judas Iscariot the son of Simon: for he it was that should betray him, being one of the twelve.

Not every one of the twelve believed. Judas Iscariot did not believe and will later betray the Lord for thirty pieces of silver (Matthew 26:14-16).

John 7

He that believeth on me, as the scripture hath said, out of his belly shall flow rivers of living water – John 7:38: *Initial statements of equality between Jesus and the Holy Ghost*

¹After these things Jesus walked in Galilee: for he would not walk in Jewry, because the Jews sought to kill him.

His hour had not yet come (John 2:4), and He will not lay down His life (John 10:15-17) until it has.

²Now the Jew's feast of tabernacles was at hand.

See Leviticus 23:34-36 for the description on this feast.

³His brethren therefore said unto him, Depart hence, and go into Judaea, that thy disciples also may see the works that thou doest. ⁴For there is no man that doeth any thing in secret, and <u>he himself seeketh to be known openly</u>. If thou do these things, shew thyself to the world. ⁵For <u>neither did his brethren believe in him</u>.

The brothers of Jesus did not believe Him to be the Son of God. They respond to His works by telling Him to show the world, but Jesus is not looking for vain glory by performing miracles. He came into this world to save sinners, and going to the cross is the only way to accomplish that.

They probably did not believe because they refuse to see Him as nothing more than a brother. This takes us back to John 4:44: **a prophet hath no honour in his own county**.

⁶Then Jesus said unto them, <u>My time is not yet come</u>: but your time is alway ready.

When the time is right for Him to die (v.1), He will go to the one specific place (the garden of Gethsemane) He knows men will come to look for Him. See John 18:1-4.

As for His brethren, their time is now to believe on Him.

⁷The world cannot hate <u>you</u>; but me it hateth, because I <u>testify</u> of it, that the works thereof are evil.

The world does not hate them, because they are not of the spiritual family of God. They are simply physically related to Jesus and those physical relations do not concern the world.

An example would be a preacher standing up to boldly proclaim the word of God. Those that disapprove do not hate his family. They disagree with the testimony coming from his lips, and therefore they hate him.

[8]**Go ye up unto this feast: I go <u>not up yet</u> unto this feast: for my time is not yet full come. [9]When he had said these words unto them, he abode still in Galilee. [10]But when his brethren were gone up, <u>then went he also up</u> unto the feast, not openly, but as it were in secret.**

Someone might read this passage and think that Christ could not make up His mind on what He was going to do. But read it again carefully. He did not go up <u>yet</u>[20] with his brethren, so that He would be able to come up later in secret. He needed to remain in secret to avoid those Jews seeking to kill Him (v.1) because it was not yet His time to die (v.6).

[11]**Then the Jews sought him at the feast, and said, Where is he? [12]And there was much murmuring among the people concerning him: for some said, He is a good man: others said, Nay; but he deceiveth the people. [13]Howbeit no man spake openly of him for fear of the Jews.**

This is still the argument today. Some will only say He was a good man (we discussed this in chapter 6), and others will profess Him to be a liar. Simply put: God's word divides. **For the word of God is quick, and powerful, and sharper than any twoedged sword, piercing even to the dividing asunder of soul and spirit, and of the joints and marrow, and is a discerner of the thoughts and intents of the heart** (Hebrews 4:12).

[14]**Now about the midst of the feast Jesus went up into the temple, and taught. [15]And the Jews marveled, saying, How knoweth this man letters, having never learned?**

These people know Jesus is the son of a carpenter and should not be able to walk into the temple and teach the way He does. Oh, but there is much more to Jesus than meets the eye. He is the son of God.

[16]**Jesus answered them, and said, My doctrine is not mine, but his that sent me.**

Jesus will testify seven times in John that His words came from the Father: John 7:16, 8:28, 8:46, 12:49, 14:10, 14:24, and 17:8.

---

[20] Many modern versions omit "yet" from the scripture. This results in Christ being a liar. See the author's work: <u>Mark</u> for a more thorough commentary regarding modern versions.

[17]**If any man will do his will, he shall know of the doctrine, whether it be of God, or whether I speak of myself.**

The doctrine Jesus proclaims came from the Father and not from Himself. Jesus said **I came down from heaven, not to do mine own will, but the will of him that sent me** (John 6:38). God's will is to redeem the world **for God so loved the world, that he gave his only begotten Son, that whosoever believeth in him should not perish, but have everlasting life** (John 3:16) because God is **not willing that any should perish, but that all should come to repentance** (2 Peter 3:9).

[18]**He that speaketh of himself seeketh his own glory: but he that seeketh his glory that sent him, the same is true, and no unrighteousness is in him.**

I really would like to see the look on these people's faces when Jesus tells them there is no unrighteousness in Him. After all the things He told them in chapters 5 and 6, He adds this to the list, and I am sure hatred is written on every religious wrinkle in their forehead.

[19]**Did not Moses give you the law, and yet none of you keepeth the law? Why go ye about to kill me?**

Of course, they did not keep the law for nobody ever did, nor ever has other than Jesus. Them desiring to kill Him proves they do not keep it for the law states **Thou shalt not kill** (Exodus 20:13).

[20]**The people answered and said, Thou hast a devil: who goeth about to kill thee?**

This is another example of guile like we discussed in John 4:18. It is when someone makes a statement to skirt answering the question that has been asked and makes those listening think the answer to the question is the opposite of the truth. They did seek to kill Jesus but wanted everyone else to be unaware of it. Try all you want to trick and deceive people into thinking you are someone other than you are. People can see right through you (v. 25).

[21]**Jesus answered and said unto them, I have done one work, and ye all marvel.**

While it is true that Christ came to finish His Father's work (John 4:34), the work Jesus is referring to here, in context, is healing a man on the Sabbath day (chapter 5).

78

[22]**Moses therefore gave unto you circumcision; (not because it is of Moses, but of the fathers;) and ye on the sabbath day circumcise a man.** [23]**If a man on the sabbath day receive circumcision, that the law of Moses should not be broken; are ye angry at me, because I have made a man every whit whole on the sabbath day?**

No, they are not angry because Jesus healed a man. The real reason they are angry is because **the world is gone after Him** (John 12:19), and He is taking the religious authority and position away from the Pharisees that they so desire to have and keep (John 11:47-48).

[24]**Judge not according to the appearance, but judge righteous judgment.**

In today's *modernized preaching*, judging is one of the most misconstrued topics. Most Christians will try to condemn judging other people's actions by proclaiming: "Judge not, lest ye be judged," as if quoting the Bible, but there is just one problem. That phrase is NOT found anywhere in scripture.[21]

The Bible just told us that we are supposed to judge. Why judging makes people so upset is because the average Christian and every unbeliever sets their own standard of judgment. When someone's judgement does not line up with their standard they cry, "Judge not," which really means, "I don't like your standard of judgment." We all need to examine the scripture to see exactly what the Bible says about judging.

Verse 24 states we should judge righteous judgment, so there must be a fine line between what is right and what is wrong. Titus 2:11-12 tells us, **For the grace of God that bringeth salvation hath appeared to all men, Teaching us that, denying ungodliness and wordly lusts, we should live soberly, righteously, and godly, in this present world**. God declares some things are wrong and should be denied (ungodliness and wordly lusts), while other things are right and should be lived in accordance with sobriety, righteousness, and godliness. So, everything I decide to do needs to be examined to determine which category that action will fall under. Is it godly or ungodly? Is it righteous or unrighteous? Everything must be judged that way.

Suppose someone offers me a cigarette. Should I take it? "Well, I think" … it does not matter what you think because what you think is not the standard. You must go by the Bible. 1 Corinthians 3:16-17 tells me that my

---

[21] They try to quote Matthew 7:1: Judge not, <u>that</u> ye be not judged. The context of that statement in Matthew has been vastly ignored and misused by people to condemn judging.

body is the holy temple of the Spirit of God and should not be defiled. Thus, I must say no to the cigarette offer because I should not defile my body.

"That's being critical" cries the ungodly. No, that is not critical. That is righteous judgement.

A teenager extends an invitation to another teenager for a party at a friend's house whose parents are not home. Should the teenager attend? It seems harmless at first until it is made known that alcohol with loose men and women is the theme of the party. Well, the Bible says **woe unto him that giveth his neighbor drink, that puttest thy bottle to him, and makest him drunken also, that thou mayest look on their nakedness!** (Habakkuk 2:15) **It is not good for a man to touch a woman,** and **whosoever looketh on a woman to lust after her hath committed adultery with her already in his heart** (1 Corinthians 7:1, Matthew 5:28). Lastly, Christians should **abstain from all appearance of evil** (1 Thessalonians 5:22). So, according to the Bible, the teenager should decline the invitation.

"That's being narrow minded."

"Children should be allowed to express themselves."

"You're going to ruin his or her self-esteem."

No, that teenager will become a twofold child of hell if ungodliness and worldly lusts continue to go unjudged. Judgement is necessary and must be done if you are a child of God for, **he that is spiritual judgeth all things** (1 Corinthians 2:15).

John 7:24 stated: **Judge not according to the appearance, but judge righteous judgment**. I was jogging while pushing my eldest son (two years old at the time) around the neighborhood at our home, and I noticed a rough looking man walking down the street holding a brown paper bag with something obviously in it. My first thought was, "I need to avoid that drunkard." That is a prime example of wrong judgement according to the appearance. All I knew for certain was I saw a man walking down the street holding a brown paper bag. I had no idea what was in the bag. I did not even know if the man was a drunk or if he had ever tasted alcohol. I could not make such a judgment based on the limited information I had.

My simple point is that every action, every thought, every idle word must be put on trial and judged to determine if it righteously lines up with God's standard of approval, or if it is unrighteous and needs to be denied.

Even what is said in the house of God needs to be judged. **He that prophesieth speaketh unto men to edification, and exhortation, and comfort** (1 Corinthians 14:3). So, prophecy is not just telling the future. It is speaking words of edification, exhortation, and comfort. Later, 1

Corinthians 14:29 says to **Let the prophets speak two or three, and let the other judge**. Every sermon, every testimony, every Sunday school lesson, and every hymn needs to be judged to see if it lines up with God's word.

If you need yet another biblical example of Christian judgement being necessary, read 1 Corinthians, chapters 4 and 5.

25Then said some of them of Jerusalem, Is not this he, whom they seek to kill? 26But, lo, he speaketh boldly, and they say nothing unto him. Do the rulers know indeed that this is the very Christ?

They must know! How much plainer does Jesus have to state that very fact? They just deny it and refuse to believe.

27Howbeit we know this man whence he is: but <u>when Christ cometh, no man knoweth whence he is.</u>

This thought by those of Jerusalem is not accurate according to the Old Testament scriptures. Much of the Old Testament speaks of Christ: where He would to be born, what He would do, who He would be, etc. They must have been taught this contrary to the scriptures, or they are just trying to be argumentative.

28Then cried Jesus in the temple as he taught, saying, Ye both know me, and ye know whence I am: and I am not come of myself, but he that sent me is true, whom ye know not. 29But I know him: for I am from him, and he hath sent me.

They know where Jesus came from physically: He is the adopted son of Joseph and biological child of Mary with at least 6 other siblings (Matthew 13:55-56). However, they do not believe Jesus came from God, therefore they do not know God nor His Son.

30Then they sought to take him: but no man laid hands on him, because <u>his hour was not yet come.</u>

I hope this is being driven into your memory because Jesus is going to lay down His life only when the time is right. Yes, the Jews will play their part along with the Romans playing theirs, but Jesus will die only when He is supposed to and as He is supposed to. That hour will be when all scripture is fulfilled and when He has finished His work (John 4:34, John 19:30).

31And many of the people believed on him, and said, When Christ cometh, will he do more miracles than these which this man hath done? 32The

Pharisees heard that the people murmured such things concerning him; and the Pharisees and the chief priests sent officers to take him.

The Pharisee's hatred toward Jesus will continue to grow as the popularity of Jesus increases. They will stop at nothing until He has been destroyed (Matthew 27:20).

[33]**Then said Jesus unto them, Yet a little while am I with you, and then I go unto him that sent me. [34]Ye shall seek me, and shall not find me: and where I am, thither ye cannot come.**

He is going back to the Father who sent Him, and they cannot come because they refuse to believe. He is the only way to the Father (John 14:6).

[35]**Then said the Jews <u>among themselves</u>, Whither will he go, that we shall not find him? will he go unto the dispersed among the Gentiles, and teach the Gentiles? [36]What manner of saying is this that he said, Ye shall seek me, and shall not find me: and where I am, thither ye cannot come?**

Stop going to your friends and acquaintances with questions they cannot possibly answer! Go to Jesus and His word for the answers. **Let God be true, but every man a liar** (Romans 3:4). That is a tremendous truth I learned the hard way.

As a boy at a summer church youth camp, I was told by our group director after people died, they would be presented to a massive gulf where they would attempt to jump across – think of jumping from one side of the Grand Canyon to the other. If that person believed they could make it, upon jumping they would make it safely across and thus be allowed to enter heaven. If faith was absent, they would fall into the gulf and into hell. If I had consulted the Bible and not my group leader (who apparently loved Indiana Jones movies) I would have known this to be a lie.

A few years later my family and I attended a local church play entitled *Heaven's Gates and Hell's Flames*. Some people were portrayed as living a godly life who entered heaven after death. Others were presented to live an ungodly life who entered hell after death. Upon the close of the play an altar call was given and as a nine-year-old boy I went down wanting to know how I could be one of the people to go to heaven instead of hell. I was handed a green piece of paper and only asked for my name, address, and phone number. Nobody mentioned Jesus to me. Nobody told me I needed to repent. Nobody told me I needed to receive Jesus' sacrificial offer of His life on the cross as the only justifiable payment for my sins. Nobody tried to lead me down the *Roman's Road*. Apparently, they thought me providing them with my information was all God needed for me to go to heaven. If I had consulted the Bible, I would have known this to be a lie.

All I am simply saying is what the Bible declares. **Let God be true, but <u>every man</u> a liar**. Friends will lie. Family members will lie. Acquaintances will lie. Church members, pastors, and religious leaders will lie. The word of God is your only source for one hundred percent truth, one hundred percent of the time.

[37]**In the last day, that great day of the feast, Jesus stood and cried, saying, If any man thirst, let him come unto me, and drink.**

See Leviticus 23:36 for a description of the last day of this feast.

This statement by Jesus is remarkably similar to His discussion with the woman at the well in chapter 4 showing that salvation is as easy as eating and drinking. Also, as we have previously discussed, it proves His deity. **For I [the LORD] will pour water upon him that is thirsty, and floods upon the dry ground: I will pour my spirit upon thy seed, and my blessing upon thine offspring** (Isaiah 44:3).

The Bible also describes the LORD as being **the fountain of living waters** (Jeremiah 2:13). Therefore, Jesus is once again proclaiming Himself to be equal with the Father.

[38]**He that believeth on me, as the scripture hath said, out of his belly shall flow rivers of living water.** [39]**(But this spake he of the Spirit, which they that believe on him should receive: for the Holy Ghost was not yet given; because that Jesus was not yet glorified.)**

The Holy Ghost could not be given until after Christ was glorified: died, buried, resurrected, and ascended. Christ said in John 16:7, **I tell you the truth; It is expedient for you that I go away: for if I go not away, the Comforter will not come unto you; but if I depart, I will send him unto you**. The Comforter is the Holy Ghost (John 14:26).

[40]**Many of the people therefore, when they heard this saying, said, Of a truth this is the Prophet.**

We addressed this in chapters 1 and 6. The Prophet is whom Moses wrote of in Deuteronomy 18:15-19. **The LORD thy god will raise up unto thee a Prophet from the midst of thee, of thy brethren, like unto me; unto him ye shall hearken; According to all that thou desiredst of the LORD thy God in Horeb in the day of the assembly, saying, Let me not hear again the voice of the LORD my God, neither let me see this great fire** any more, that I die not. And the LORD said unto me, They have well spoken that which they have spoken. I will raise them up a Prophet from among their brethren, like unto thee, and will put my words in his mouth; and he shall speak unto them all that I shall command him. And it shall come to pass, that whosoever will not hearken unto my words which he shall speak in my name, I will require it of him.

[41]Others said, This is the Christ. But some said, Shall Christ come out of Galilee? [42]Hath not the scripture said, That Christ cometh of the seed of David, and out of the town of Bethlehem, where David was?

Refer to v. 27. They previously said they did NOT know where Christ was coming from, yet here they are referencing scripture that says exactly where He would be born.

This shows an undeniable truth. When dealing with lost people about believing the gospel (Jesus' death, burial, and resurrection), they will usually contradict themselves during the conversation just as these Jews did here.

"Excuse me sir. Are you going to heaven when you die?"

"Yes I am."

"How do you know sir?"

"Well, I'm a good man who has lived a good life."

"Ok. Are you aware that the Bible says there are none righteous, no not one, and that Ephesians 2:8-9 says salvation is not by works but of faith?"

"Oh yeah, yeah, I know but …" and next follows a contradiction.

[43]So there was a division among the people because of him.

Not believing Jesus' words is why the division exists. Truthfully, believing on Jesus breaks down all types of divisions:

- Jew and Gentile no longer divided (Ephesians 2:11-16)
- No race or socioeconomic divisions (Acts 13:1)
- No political or national divisions (Mark 3:18, Colossians 3:11)
- No gender-based divisions (Galatians 3:28, Colossians 3:11)
- No occupational based divisions (Colossians 3:11)

[44]And some of them would have taken him; but no man laid hands on him. [45]Then came the officers to the chief priests and Pharisees; and they said unto them, Why have ye not brought him? [46]The officers answered, Never man spake like this man. [47]Then answered them the Pharisees, Are ye also deceived? [48]Have any of the rulers or of the Pharisees believed on him?

Yes, Nicodemus believed (John 19:38-39).

[49]**But this people who knoweth not the law are cursed.**

Wrong! **Cursed is every one that continueth not in <u>all things</u> which are written in the book of the law to do them** (Galatians 3:10). You Pharisees are cursed because you do not keep all things written in the law, and there is only one way to deal with this curse: Believe on Jesus Christ. **Christ hath redeemed us from the curse of the law, being made a curse for us: for it is written, Cursed is every one that hangeth on a tree** (Galatians 3:13).

[50]**Nicodemus saith unto them, (he that came to Jesus by night, being one of them,)** [51]**Doth our law judge any man, before it hear him, and know what he doeth?**

The reason Nicodemus probably came to Jesus by night (John 3) is addressed here. The Pharisees (the group Nicodemus was a part) hated Jesus, therefore Nicodemus could not afford being seen talking with Him.

Also, the answer to Nicodemus' question is NO. Deuteronomy 1:16-18, 17:8-9 and 19:15 all show how man should be dealt with according to the law. Jesus should indeed be given a trial. Furthermore, the LORD specifically told Israel **not to be afraid of the face of man; for the judgment is God's** (Deuteronomy 1:17). They do not want to give Jesus a trial because they fear Him, and they want to cast their own judgment, not God's.

[52]**They answered and said unto him, Art thou also of Galilee? <u>Search, and look: for out of Galilee ariseth no prophet.</u>** [53]**And every man went unto his own house.**

Notice, they never answered Nicodemus' question which proves exactly what we just discussed. They fear Jesus, and do not want to judge Him God's way. If they judge Him God's way, He is innocent. He has done nothing contrary to God's law.

The statement by the Pharisees is an interesting one indeed. They said, **Search <u>and</u> look**. You must do both, or you will find yourself erring just as they have by stating **out of Galilee ariseth no prophet**.

If you were to only *look* through the Old Testament scriptures to see if any of the prophets came out of Galilee, it would appear the Pharisees were right. No prophet was ever said to have come out of Galilee. However, if you *search* out the truth you will discover the Pharisees are wrong.

Jonah is a perfect example. *Looking* in 2 Kings 14:25 we are told that he is from Gath-hepher. Now, if we *search* to find where this place is on a map, you will discover that Gath-hepher is in the southern half of the region called Galilee. These Pharisees need to follow their own advice.

John 8

Jesus said unto them, Verily, verily, I say unto you, Before Abraham was, I am – John 8:58: Jesus claims to be the "I am" before Abraham

[1]**Jesus went unto the mount of Olives.** [2]**And early in the morning he came again <u>into the temple</u>, and all the people came unto him; and he sat down, and taught them.**

I would dare say the story we are about to read is well known among the saved and lost alike. Unfortunately, the setting of this story taking place inside the temple is almost always overlooked. It is also the most vital piece of information to understand Jesus' actions and comments in response to these Pharisees.

Secondly, most people who refer to this story usually quote (as closely as possible) verse seven attempting to defend and justify themselves for committing some act of sin. However, to justify sin was not the purpose of the comment. The context of the remark must be examined it order to understand exactly WHY Jesus said that.

[3]**And the scribes and Pharisees brought unto him a woman taken in adultery; and when they had set her in the midst,** [4]**They say unto him, Master, this woman was taken in adultery, in the very act.**

Unbelievable! These religious leaders have the audacity to storm into this holy place of worship and interrupt Jesus' teaching in such a manner. No number of words could accurately depict how ungodly this temple scene must have looked with these men carrying stones in their hands fully prepared to conduct an execution. Furthermore, considering she was taken in the very act of this sexual misconduct, there is no telling how she is dressed. I say that because I doubt they expressed any concern and care for her appearance before dragging her into God's house to create this uproar in front of all the people.

[5]**Now Moses in the law commanded us, that such should be stoned: but what sayest thou?** [6]**This they said, tempting him, that they might have to accuse him.**

My first question is this…If the law clearly states that such should be stoned, why have they taken the time to create this scene in the house of God? If the law justifies stoning the woman, then go stone her.

They do not care about the law, and they do not care about this woman nor the consequences of their disgusting actions. They simply want to tempt Jesus into making a decision that is contrary to God's law.

In truth, their scheme is quite an ingenious plot. If Jesus says yes, He violates the law. If He says no, He still violates the law. **If a man be found lying with a woman married to an husband, then they shall <u>both of them die</u>, both the man that lay with the woman, and the woman: so shalt thou put away evil from Israel. Then ye shall bring them both out <u>unto the gate of that city</u>, and ye shall stone them with stones that they die** (Deuteronomy 22:22 & 24a).

The law clearly states that both the man and the woman are to die at the gate of the city. Why these Pharisees only brought the woman is up for speculation. Maybe the man was involved with concocting the plot, or maybe the man was a scribe or Pharisee, and his religious cohorts wanted to avoid shaming him in the face of the public. The speculations are endless. Nevertheless, If Jesus were to say no, He violates the law because she is supposed to die. If He says yes, He then violates the law on two counts: the man is not being put to death as required, and the execution would be carried out in the wrong place. Just imagine the gossip and murmuring that would occur throughout Jerusalem if this woman was executed in the temple at Jesus' command.

But Jesus stooped down, and with his finger wrote on the ground, as though he heard them not. [7]So when they continued asking him, he lifted up himself, and said unto them, He that is without sin among you, let him first cast a stone at her. [8]And again he stooped down, and wrote on the ground.

What a marvelous response by Jesus! He knows their intent to trap Him and considering He cannot say yes or no without violating the law, He doesn't say anything. Instead, He simply stoops down and writes on the ground. Then, after this mob continues to ask Him what they should do, He completely shifts the attention off Himself putting it on them by saying, **He that is without sin among you** … He knows exactly what they are trying to do and calls them out on it. You will not get anything over on God!

There is much speculation as to what was written on the ground, but what He wrote does not matter. If we needed to know, God would have told us. As a matter a fact, we get all the information we need if we reexamine the law once more to see why this story taking place in the temple is so vital to our discussion.

88

Numbers 5:12-30: **If any man's wife go aside, and commit a trespass against him, and a man lie with her carnally, and it be hid from the eyes of her husband, and be kept close, and she be defiled, and there be no witness against her, neither she be taken with the manner** (i.e. pregnant)**; And the spirit of jealousy come upon him, and he be jealous of his wife, and she be defiled: or if the spirit of jealousy come upon him, and he be jealous of his wife, and she be not defiled: Then shall the man bring his wife unto the priest, and he shall bring her offering for her, the tenth part of an ephah of barley meal; he shall pour no oil upon it, nor put frankincense theron; for it is an offering of jealousy, and offering of memorial, bringing iniquity to remembrance. And the priest shall bring her near, and <u>set her before the LORD</u>: And the priest shall take holy water in an earthen vessel; and of <u>the dust that is in the floor of the tabernacle the priest shall take, and put it into the water</u>. And the priest shall set the woman before the LORD, and uncover the woman's head, and put the offering of memorial in her hands, which is the jealousy offering: and the priest shall have in his hand the bitter water that causeth the curse: And the priest shall charge her by an oath, and say unto the woman, If no man have lain with thee, and if thou hast not gone aside to uncleanness with another instead of thy husband, be thou free from this bitter water that causeth the curse: But if thou hast gone aside to another instead of thy husband, and if thou be defiled, and some man have lain with thee beside thine husband: Then the priest shall charge the woman with an oath of cursing, and the priest shall say unto the woman, The LORD make thee a curse and an oath among thy people, when the LORD doth make thy thigh to rot, and thy belly to swell; And this water that causeth the curse shall go into thy bowels, to make thy belly to swell, and thy thigh to rot: And the woman shall say, Amen, amen. And the priest shall write these curses in a book, and he shall blot them out with the bitter water: And he shall cause the woman to drink the bitter water that causeth the curse: and the water that causeth the curse shall enter into her, and become bitter. Then the priest shall take the jealousy offering out of the woman's hand, and shall wave the offering before the LORD, and offer it upon the altar: And the priest shall take an handful of the offering, even the memorial thereof, and burn it upon the altar, and afterward shall cause the woman to drink the water. And when he hath made her <u>to drink the water</u>, then it shall come to pass, that, if she be defiled, and have done trespass against her husband, that the water that causeth the curse shall enter into her, and**

become bitter, and her belly shall swell, and the thigh shall rot: and the woman shall be a curse among her people. And if the woman be not defiled, but be clean; then she shall be free, and shall conceive seed. This is the law of jealousies, when a wife goeth aside to another instead of her husband, and is defiled; Or when the spirit of jealousy cometh upon him, and he be jealous over his wife, and shall <u>set the woman before the LORD</u>, and the priest shall execute upon her all this law.

Quite a lengthy passage, but it was necessary to gather all the information. In summary, if a man suspects that his wife has committed adultery but there is no proof of the incident, he is supposed to bring her to the temple (the temple replaced the tabernacle) to be set before the LORD and be made to drink water that has been mixed with the dirt of the temple floor. Then the LORD will pronounce judgment with or without a curse.

Have you figured out why Jesus wrote on the ground yet? By stooping down and writing on the ground He acknowledged to them that the ground on which they were standing is only meant for jealousy trespasses. That ground would be mixed with water for a woman to drink when she is suspected of committing adultery, not when her guilt is openly known. Then Jesus stood up, called them sinners, and stoops back down to continue writing on the ground to reiterate His point. What a perfect response to their trap!

Also, did you notice what else the Numbers passage told us? When a woman was brought to the temple under the jealousy trespass, she was supposed to be set before the LORD. That is exactly who these Pharisees set her before! They wanted to discredit Jesus by trying to tempt Him with the very law He wrote but failed. On top of that, their actions proved exactly what they wanted to disprove: Jesus is God!

Hallelujah. Don't you just love the Bible?

[9]**And they which heard it, being convicted by their own conscience, went out one by one, beginning at the eldest, even unto the last: and Jesus was left <u>alone, and the woman standing in the midst</u>.** [10]**When Jesus had lifted up himself, and saw none but the woman, he said unto her, Woman, where are those thine accusers? hath no man condemned thee?** [11]**She said, No man, <u>Lord</u>. And Jesus said unto her, Neither do I condemn thee: go, and sin no more.**

Jesus does not ignore her sin because He told her to **sin no more**. While it is true that Jesus has power on earth to forgive sins (Matthew 9:6, Mark 2:10, Luke 5:24) and would be justified in doing so with this woman. The truth about why he does not condemn her also lies in the law and a New

Testament principle. Deuteronomy 19:15, Matthew 18:16, and 2 Corinthians 13:1 state: **In the mouth of two or three witnesses shall every word be established**. The witnesses are no longer present at the scene; therefore, Christ cannot condemn this woman.

Also, if we examine this story within the context of the entire Bible, there is a scriptural truth illustrated.

- The law condemns and once condemned the penalty is death (Romans 3:19, Romans 6:23a) – just like this woman.
- As a result of being condemned by the law, the law brings you to Jesus Christ (Galatians 3:22-24) – just like this woman.
- Once alone with Christ, salvation is freely available to whosoever believes and calls on the name of the Lord Jesus Christ (Romans 10:9-13) – just like this woman called Jesus Lord.

[12]**Then spake Jesus again unto <u>them</u>, saying, I am the light of the world: he that followeth me shall not walk in darkness, but shall have the light of life.** [13]**The Pharisees therefore said unto him, Thou bearest record of thyself; thy record is not true.**

Jesus addresses those Pharisees in the temple again (v.1). They seem to be listening for they understand that Jesus is the light and that following Him is not walking in darkness. However, because they don't want Him, they reject Jesus and His words.

The Light (John 1) is right in front of them, and they miss it. Did they not just see how Jesus wittingly dodged the trap set before Him? How can they say His record is not true? It is because they reject Him. Thus, they are in darkness and cannot see what is clearly in front of them (see chapter 1).

[14]**Jesus answered and said unto them, Though I bear record of myself, yet my record is true: for I know whence I came, and whither I go; but ye cannot tell whence I come, and whither I go.** [15]**Ye judge after the flesh; I judge no man.** [16]**And yet if I judge, my judgment is true: for I am not alone, but I and the Father that sent me.** [17]**It is also written in your law, that the <u>testimony of two men is true</u>.** [18]**I am one that bear witness of myself, and the Father that sent me beareth witness of me.**

Once again Jesus just claimed that He and the Father are one (v. 16). Secondly, His record is true because **in the mouth of two or three witnesses shall every word be established**. Since He and the Father bear the same witness, their testimony and judgments are true.

Please note that v. 14 is not a contradiction of John 5:31: **If I bear witness of myself, my witness is not true.** The context of John 5 dealt with ignoring Jesus' own testimony while taking the testimony of four other witnesses: John the Baptist, His works, the Father, and the scriptures.

[19]Then said they unto him, Where is thy Father? Jesus answered, Ye neither know me, nor my Father: if ye had known me, ye should have known my Father also.

It is a quite simple truth we all need to understand – knowing Jesus Christ is the same as knowing the Father. Jesus will bring out this truth again in chapters 14 and 17.

[20]These words spake Jesus in the treasury, as he taught in the temple: and no man laid hands on him; for his hour was not yet come.

I will ask it again ... Do you see that Jesus is not going to the cross until the time and hour is right? This is a prevailing truth throughout this Gospel.

[21]Then said Jesus again unto them, I go my way, and ye shall seek me, and shall die in your sins: whither I go, ye cannot come. [22]Then said the Jews, Will he kill himself? because he saith, Whither I go, ye cannot come. [23]And he said unto them, Ye are from beneath; I am from above: ye are of this world; I am not of this world. [24]I said therefore unto you, that ye shall die in your sins: for if ye believe not that I am he, ye shall die in your sins.

They still do not get it. Jesus Christ came down from heaven, from the Father who sent Him (supported by every chapter up to this point). He will return unto the Father when the time and hour is right, and if you do not believe that He is Christ the Messiah you will die condemned and lost in your sins (John 3:18).

[25]Then said they unto him, Who art thou? And Jesus saith unto them, Even the same that I said unto you from the beginning.

His answer has not changed. He keeps telling these Pharisees the same truths, but they simply refuse to listen.

See John 5:17-18. There He made Himself equal with the Father and that is what began their hatred for Him.

26I have many things to say and to judge of you: but he that sent me is true; and I speak to the world those things which I have heard of him. **27**They <u>understood not</u> that he spake to them of the Father.

They do not understand because they do not have light, and they do not have light because they do not want it. They do not want the light because they do not want Him (the Light).

28Then said Jesus unto them, When ye have lifted up the Son of man, <u>then</u> shall ye know that I am he, and that I do nothing of myself; but as my Father hath taught me, I speak these things.

When Christ was lifted up on the cross the earth shook, rocks were rent, the sun was darkened, and the vail in the temple was rent from the top to the bottom (Matthew 27:50-51). Three days later He resurrected where many of the dead saints came out of the graves and walked into the city and appeared unto many (Matthew 27:52-53), and before long He was seen of over 500 brethren (1 Corinthians 15:3-6). These Pharisees may not believe now, but after the crucifixion and resurrection events come to pass, <u>then</u> they shall know Christ is equal with the Father. In the end, they truly did know Jesus was the Son of God and were **without excuse** (Romans 1:20). They just chose to ignore these **infallible proofs** (Acts 1:3).

29And he that sent me is with me: the Father hath not left me alone; for <u>I do always those things that please him</u>. **30**As he spake these words, many believed on him.

If Jesus is just a man, He's lying. No sinful man could make such a statement and be telling the truth. He would have to be **holy, harmless, undefiled, separate from sinners, and made higher than the heavens** (Hebrews 7:26), and He is!

People think of pleasing themselves more than pleasing God. One example is God said to **love the LORD thy God with all thine heart, and with all thy soul, and with all thy might** (Deuteronomy 6:5), and not a single person has ever done that except Jesus. If you are unsure whether that is true, reexamine your thoughts once we visit chapter 17.

31Then said Jesus to those Jews which believed on him, If ye continue in my word, then are ye my disciples indeed; **32**And ye shall know the truth, and the truth shall make you free. **33**They answered him, We be Abraham's seed, and <u>were never in bondage to any man</u>: how sayest thou, Ye shall be made free?

WOW, what a ridiculous statement! The entire Old Testament is full of promises stating if Israel were to love God, obey Him, keep His commandments, and follow His law then because of their obedience they could live peacefully among each other without outside oppression from the surrounding heathen nations. Yet their entire history is nothing but a long record of disobedience that resulted in captivity after captivity after captivity. First it was Egyptian captivity, then oppression by the Philistines, the Midianites, the Chaldeans, the Babylonians, the Medes, Persians, the Greeks, and are currently under Roman bondage. They are living in a complete state of denial!

[34]Jesus answered them, Verily, verily, I say unto you, Whosoever committeth sin is the servant of sin. [35]And the servant abideth not in the house for ever: but the Son abideth ever. [36]If the Son therefore shall make you free, ye shall be free indeed. [37]I know that ye are Abraham's seed; but ye seek to kill me, because my word hath no place in you. [38]I speak that which I have seen with my Father: and ye do that which ye have seen with your father.

Jesus is sinless and does exactly what His Father does. These people are sinful and sin exactly as their fathers did. If you want freedom - freedom from sin, God's wrath, Gentile bondage, etc. … it only comes from Jesus.

[39]They answered and said unto him, Abraham is our father. Jesus saith unto them, If ye were Abraham's children, ye would do the works of Abraham. [40]But now ye seek to kill me, a man that hath told you the truth, which I have heard of God: this did not Abraham. [41]Ye do the deeds of your father.

Abraham's work involved believing God when he heard the truth. These people have the opportunity to do the same but refuse. They might be the physical children of Abraham, but not his spiritual children (c.f. Romans 4, Galatians 3, and Hebrews 11).

Then said they to him, <u>We be not born of fornication</u>; we have one Father, even God.

That is as low an insult as could be given. Fornication during this time was not viewed as it is today – live as you want to live and do what you want to do as long as you practice *safe sex*. During this age, and even back sixty or seventy years ago, you were shunned if you committed fornication. I

94

feel quite sure that people consistently brought this up regarding Jesus' miraculous birth.

You are probably well aware that fornication is a sin against God, **For this is the will of God, even your sanctification, that ye should abstain from fornication: that every one of you should know how to possess his vessel in sanctification and honour; not in the lust of concupiscence** (1 Thessalonians 4:3-5). If you need further verses to reference – see Romans 1:29, 1 Corinthians chapters 5 – 7, Ephesians 5:3, Colossians 3:5. These are just a few passages on the subject.

[42]Jesus said unto them, If God were your Father, ye would love me: for I proceeded forth and came from God; neither came I of myself, but he sent me. [43]Why do ye not understand my speech? even because ye cannot hear my word. [44]Ye are of your father the devil, and the lusts of your father ye will do. He was a murderer from the beginning, and abode not in the truth, because there is no truth in him. When he speaketh a lie, he speaketh of his own: for he is a liar, and the father of it.

We have seen much of this truth presented before, but now we have more information given: children of the devil. Not everyone is a child of God as some modern preachers like to proclaim. They usually say, **for ye are all the children of God...**" quoting Galatians 3:26, but they are not quoting the entire sentence. The verse continues to say **for ye are all the children of God by faith in Christ Jesus**. It takes faith in Jesus Christ to become God's child. See also John 1:12.

Look at Ephesians 2:2-3 for more support. **Wherein in time past ye walked** (past tense) **according to the course of this world, according to the prince of the power of the air, the spirit that now worketh in the children of disobedience: Among whom also we all had** (past tense) **our conversation in times past in the lusts of our flesh, fulfilling the desires of the flesh and of the mind; and were** (past tense) **by nature the children of wrath, even as others**. So, what brought you from that state? **For by grace are ye saved through faith** (Ephesians 2:8). God brought you from being dead in trespasses and sins and quickened you (Ephesians 2:1) all by His grace through faith.

[45]And because I tell you the truth, ye believe me not.

This is the same struggle everyone faces when trying to present the truth of the Bible: people simply refuse to believe.

⁴⁶Which of you convinceth me of sin? And if I say the truth, why do ye not believe me?

I am convinced that the more people you talk to about Jesus, the more and you will ask yourself, "Why do people not believe?" You will present undeniable truth and evidence showing Jesus is God, just as Jesus has before these Pharisees, but they will still refuse to believe.

⁴⁷He that is of God heareth God's words: ye therefore hear them not, because <u>ye are not of God</u>.

These Pharisees think they are of God and therein is the root of the problem. They are a part of the nation of Israel: God's chosen people. Within that nation, there are two basic religious groups: Pharisees and Sadducees. The Pharisees are the ones who take the scriptures literal, which is the correct thing to do. So, naturally they think they are right with God because they are of the right religion sect inside God's chosen nation. A similar comparison would be you telling someone they are not of God even though they attend a God-fearing church. Being religious does not make you God's child. It takes faith.

⁴⁸Then answered the Jews, and said unto him, Say we not well that thou art a Samaritan, and hast a devil? ⁴⁹Jesus answered, I have not a devil; but I honour my Father, and ye do dishonor me. ⁵⁰And I seek not mine own glory: there is one that seeketh and judgeth. ⁵¹Verily, verily, I say unto you, If a man keep my saying, <u>he shall never see death</u>.

Once again, Jesus is talking spiritually and not physically.

⁵²Then said the Jews unto him, Now we know that thou hast a devil. Abraham is dead, and the prophets; and thou sayest, If a man keep my saying, he shall never taste of death. ⁵³Art thou greater than our father Abraham, which is dead? and the prophets are dead: whom makest thou thyself? ⁵⁴Jesus answered, If I honour myself, my honour is nothing: it is my Father that honoureth me; of whom ye say, that he is your God: ⁵⁵Yet ye have not known him; but I know him: and if I should say, I know him not, I shall be a liar like unto you: but I know him, and keep his saying. ⁵⁶<u>Your father Abraham rejoiced to see my day: and he saw it, and was glad</u>.

Jesus had to be alive for Abraham to see His day. Of course, He was because He is God manifest in the flesh, the creator of the universe. He was alive when Abraham walked this earth, but these Jews are not going to take

96

this truth very well because there is only one way for that to be possible: they would have to believe that Jesus is God.

57Then said the Jews unto him, Thou art not yet fifty years old, and hast thou seen Abraham? 58Jesus said unto them, Verily, verily, I say unto you, Before Abraham was, I am.

Any Jew alive would know exactly what Jesus meant by using those two words. When Moses went into Egypt to deliver Israel out of bondage, he told them, **I AM hath sent me unto you** (Exodus 3:14), and when Jesus said He was **I am,** He meant that He was the very God that sent Moses into Egypt. What a declaration!

59Then took they up stones to cast at him: but Jesus hid himself, and went out of the temple, going through the midst of them, and so passed by.

Interesting! The chapter began with a stoning attempt and ends with yet another attempt.

It is no mystery as to why these Jews responded the way they did. Nonetheless, when Jesus professed to be the very God who brought their fathers out of the land of Egypt, He was telling the truth. The only thing that is required now is to believe Him.

John 9

And he said, Lord, I believe. And he worshipped him — John 9:39:
Jesus is worshipped as God

[1]**And as Jesus passed by, he saw a man which was blind from his birth.**
[2]**And his disciples asked him, saying, Master, who did sin, this man, or his parents, that he was born blind?**

      For the disciples to ask this question, they must have been taught this idea by the religious leaders. Even today, people have preconceived notions that when someone is born with a physical handicap it is as if God is punishing the person for some sort of sin. If that were true, when would the child have had a chance to sin? In the womb? The only references to actions by children in the womb are below, and I do not see how any support for sin prior to birth could be established.[22]

    1) Jacob grabbing his brother Esau's heal in the womb (Genesis 25: 22-26, Hosea 12:2-3).
    2) The birth of the twins Zarah and Pharez of Tamar where Zarah stuck his hand out of the womb first but was born second (Genesis 38:27-30).
    3) John the Baptist leaping in his mother's womb (Luke 1:41).

[3]**Jesus answered, Neither hath this man sinned, nor his parents: but <u>that the works of God should be made manifest in him</u>. **[4]**I must work the works of him that sent me, while it is day: the night cometh, when no man can work. **[5]**As long as I am in the world, I am the light of the world.**

      Our question above has been answered. When people are born with a physical handicap it is **that the works of God should be made manifest in him**. When people see someone with a physical handicap glorifying God despite their physical problems, those people usually wonder how such a person could praise God and not curse Him given their physical condition. The person does not blame God and as a result those people see clearly that the God of this universe is not the reason for their problems but the comforter in their problems.

      My brother and sister-in-law's eldest son, Chandler, was born with SMA (Spinal Muscular Atrophy). He died at just 6 months of age. At the funeral, his father and grandfather stood up in front of the congregation and

---

[22] Psalm 51: 5 states **Behold, I was shapen in iniquity; and in sin did my mother conceive me,** but that doesn't support the unborn child committing sin before birth. That simply supports what we discuss in the Appendix – *Why ye must be born again.*

praised God for how good He is, how thankful they were that Chandler would not have to go through this life constantly battling his handicap, and spoke of how they could not wait to see the day where they too would **be absent from the body, and to be present with the Lord** (2 Corinthians 5:8). I do not know what it is like to experience the death of a child, but what I do know is that because of their glorifying God, people would later testify to the truth that God must have been with them in their circumstances comforting them. The works of God were indeed made manifest.

⁶When he had thus spoken, he spat on the ground, and made clay of the spittle, and he anointed the eyes of the blind man with the clay, ⁷And said unto him, Go, wash in the pool of Siloam, (which is by interpretation, Sent.)

One might say that even the spit of Jesus is holy, and I would not disagree. The point I want to draw your attention to is how this relates to God creating the first man Adam. **And the LORD God formed man of the <u>dust of the ground</u>, and breathed into his nostrils the breath of life; and man became a living soul** (Genesis 2:7). God used dirt to generate a body for the first man, and He is again using dirt to restore this man's blindness.

He went his way therefore, and washed, and came seeing. ⁸The neighbours therefore, and they which before had seen him that he was blind, said, Is not this he that sat and begged? ⁹Some said, This is he: others said, He is like him: but he said, I am he. ¹⁰Therefore said they unto him, How were thine eyes opened? ¹¹He answered and said, <u>A man</u> that is called Jesus made clay, and anointed mine eyes, and said unto me, Go to the pool of Siloam, and wash: and I went and washed, and I received sight.

Make sure you take note of the descriptions this man provides on behalf of Jesus. He starts by describing Him as a man, and by the time the dialogue is finished the description will escalate to Jesus being God.

¹²Then said they unto him, Where is he? He said, I know not. ¹³They brought to the Pharisees him that aforetime was blind. ¹⁴And it was the sabbath day when Jesus made the clay, and opened his eyes.

Oh no, here we go again. Jesus performs another miracle on the Sabbath day and the Pharisees are not going to approve yet again.

¹⁵Then again the Pharisees also asked him how he had received his sight. He said unto them, He put clay upon mine eyes, and I washed, and do see. ¹⁶Therefore said some of the Pharisees, This man is not of God, because he keepeth not the sabbath day.

Yes, He does. As we discussed in chapter 5, Jesus is equal with the Father and works on that day just as the Father does.

Others said, How can a man that is a sinner do such miracles? And there was a division among them. ¹⁷They say unto the blind man again, What sayest thou of him, that he hath opened thine eyes? He said, He is <u>a prophet</u>.

The description has now escalated from a man (v. 11) to a prophet. My question is: How does he know Jesus is a prophet?

One clue to an answer is the fact that throughout the Bible you will read of prophets being described as wearing rough clothing (2 Kings 1:8, Zechariah 13:4). However, this raises another question. How would he know what Jesus wore[23] considering he is blind? The best answer I can provide is to say that the Holy Ghost is getting involved with leading this man into what to say.

¹⁸But the Jews <u>did not believe</u> concerning him, that he had been blind, and received his sight, until they called the parents of him that had received his sight. ¹⁹And they asked them, saying, Is this your son, who ye say was born blind? how then doth he now see?

The Pharisees are not listening. The blind man just told them how he received his sight, but they refuse to believe Jesus could do this.

²⁰His parents answered them and said, We know that this is our son, and that he was born blind: ²¹But by what means he now seeth, we know not; or who hath opened his eyes, we know not: he is of age; ask him: he shall speak for himself. ²²These words spake his parents, because they feared the Jews: for the Jews had agreed already, that if any man did confess that he was Christ, he should be put out of the synagogue. ²³Therefore said his parents, He is of age; ask him.

---

[23] The idea that Jesus wore rough clothing could very well be supported by Isaiah 53:2: **he hath no form nor comeliness; and when we shall see him, there is no beauty that we should desire him.**

His parents fear these Jews who operate the synagogue, and because of their fear they do not want to say anything that might cause them to be thrown out.

Some people in churches today (whether you label them under a certain denomination, faction, or ilk is of little relevance) care more for the building of worship than for who they are there to worship. And the decisions they make as a basis for their actions are in sole thought to men rather than God. The question we all need to answer is, are my actions performed so that I might please men, or God? **For do I now persuade men, or God? or do I seek to please men? for if I yet pleased men, I should not be the servant of Christ** (Galatians 1:10).

[24]Then again called they the man that was blind, and said unto him, Give God the praise: we know that this man is a sinner.

If you are so sure of that fact, on what are you basing your conclusion? In other words, where is your proof that He is a sinner? They do not have any proof, nor can they know that He is a sinner. These people just hate Jesus.

[25]He answered and said, Whether he be a sinner or no, I know not: one thing I know, that, whereas I was blind, now I see. [26]Then said they to him again, What did he to thee? how opened he thine eyes? [27]He answered them, I have told you already, and ye did not hear: wherefore would ye hear it again? will ye <u>also</u> be his disciples? [28]Then they reviled him, and said, <u>Thou art his disciple</u>; but we are Moses' disciples.

Unlike his parents, He is taking a stand for Jesus rather than trying to remain neutral to please men. These few verses (v.25-28) are a perfect illustration of how simple it is to witness to others:

1. Answer their questions honestly as he has.
   "I know not."
   "I know that whereas I was blind, now I see."
   You do not have to possess all the answers, just be truthful with whom you are speaking.
2. Make your position clear that you are a disciple of Jesus Christ.

[29]We know that God spake unto Moses: as for this fellow, we know not from whence he is. [30]The man answered and said unto them, <u>Why herein is a marvelous thing</u>, that ye know not from whence he is, and yet he hath opened mine eyes. [31]Now we know that God heareth not sinners: but if

any man be a worshipper of God, and doeth his will, him he heareth. **[32]Since the world began was it not heard that any man opened the eyes of one that was born blind. [33]If this man were not of God, he could do nothing.**

OUCH! His words to these Pharisees stir me up inside because this reminds me of a court scene. The Pharisees have presented their arguments, and here this young man stands up and refutes everything they have proclaimed.

The Pharisees two arguments:
1. Jesus is a sinner
2. They do not know where He is from or how He is able to do the things He does.

Then, this young man plainly states, "This is a marvelous thing. If Jesus were not of God, He would not be able to do these things. Therefore, I know exactly who He is, where He is from, and how He gave me sight. HE'S OF GOD!"

Not only that, but he also points these Pharisees right to the scriptures that they are supposed to know and understand as proof for his argument. **The LORD openeth the eyes of the blind: the LORD raiseth them that are bowed down: the LORD loveth the righteous: the LORD preserveth the strangers; he relieveth the fatherless and widow: but the way of the wicked he turneth upside down** (Psalm 146: 8-9).

Back in v.17 I mentioned that the Holy Ghost must be getting involved by leading this man into what to say, and this is why I made that statement. What this young man just said has completely turned these wicked Pharisees' arguments upside down.

[34]They answered and said unto him, Thou wast altogether born in sins, and dost thou teach us? And they cast him out.

Once again, truth has been presented and they refuse to hear and receive it.

Recall what we discussed regarding the parents' decision to remain neutral. This young man decided to stand with Jesus and as a result was cast out of the synagogue by men. I'd like to think that if I were ever in a similar situation, I too would choose to stand with Jesus and be cast out by man because of my actions than to receive the approval of man and for Jesus to cast me out. **I** [Jesus] **know thy works, that thou art neither cold nor hot** [neutral]**: I would thou wert cold or hot** [take a stand]**. So then because thou art lukewarm, and neither cold nor hot, I will spue thee out of my**

mouth (Revelation 3:15-16). Those words were written to the church of the Laodiceans, and accurately describe the church of our day and age. Christians today are expected to be politically correct and not to offend anyone. Thus, they conform to the expectations of men, and as a result are neutral, not taking a stand for Jesus!

I am not condoning Christians being angry to the point of wrath, nor am I saying that Christians should be violent. I am simply saying exactly what we discussed in v. 28 – stand with the Bible proclaiming what you know and what you do not know and make it noticeably clear that you are Jesus' disciple. **Wherefore take unto you the whole armour of God, that ye may be able to withstand in the evil day, and having done all to stand. Stand therefore, having your loins girt about with truth, and having on the breastplate of righteousness; And your feet shod with the preparation of the gospel of peace; Above all, taking the shield of faith, wherewith ye shall be able to quench all the fiery darts of the wicked. And take the helmet of salvation, and the sword of the Spirit, which is the word of God: Praying always with all prayer and supplication in the Spirit, and watching thereunto with all perseverance and supplication for all saints; And for me, that utterance may be given unto me, <u>that I may open my mouth boldly, to make known the mystery of the gospel, For which I am an ambassador in bonds: that therein I may speak boldly, as I ought to speak</u>** (Ephesians 6:13-20). Take a stand!

[35]**Jesus heard that they had cast him out; and when he had found him, he said unto him, Dost thou believe on the Son of God?** [36]**He answered and said, Who is he, <u>Lord</u>, that I might believe on him?** [37]**And Jesus said unto him, Thou hast both seen him, and it is he that talketh with thee.** [38]**And he said, Lord, I believe. And he worshipped him.**

Salvation is that simple: believe on the Lord Jesus Christ, and thou shalt be saved (Acts 16:31, Romans 10:9).

[39]**And Jesus said, For judgment I am come into this world, that they which see not might see; and that they which see might be made blind.** [40]**And some of the Pharisees which were with him heard these words, and said unto him, Are we blind also?** [41]**Jesus said unto them, If ye were blind, ye should have no sin: but now ye say, We see; therefore your sin remaineth.**

They are blind because they claim to know all about God, yet when they are presented with the truth of Jesus Christ they do not believe.

103

Therefore, this is further proof of what we discussed in v. 2: physical handicaps are not proof of sin.

When someone refuses to believe on Jesus Christ, the Lamb of God which taketh away the sin of the world (chapter 1), their sin remains on them along with the wrath of God that abides on them (chapter 6). You must believe or your sin remains!

John 10

¹**Verily, verily, I say unto you, He that entereth not by the door into the sheepfold, but climbeth up some other way, the same is a thief and a robber. ²But he that entereth in by the door is the shepherd of the sheep. ³To him the porter openeth; and the sheep hear his voice: and he calleth his own sheep by name, and leadeth them out. ⁴And when he putteth forth his own sheep, he goeth before them, and the sheep follow him: for they know his voice. ⁵And a stranger will they not follow, but will flee from him: for they know not the voice of strangers. ⁶This parable spake Jesus unto them: but they understood not what things they were which he spake unto them.**

Jesus is still speaking to the Pharisees from John 9:40, by presenting them with this parable. In the following verses He will give a complete explanation, but for clarity let's dissect the information and characters presented thus far:

1. Sheep – only sheep enter a sheepfold and for a sheep to become part of the fold they must enter by the door. There is no other acceptable way (v.1). They know the shepherd's voice and follow him (v.4) while fleeing from strangers whose voices they do not know (v.5).
2. Shepherd of the sheep – the sheep belong to him (v.3), he leads the sheep (v.3 & 4), and he calls the sheep by name (v.3)
3. The Porter – the one who opens the door for the shepherd (v.3).
4. Stranger(s) – apparently those that would try to steal or lead the sheep away from the shepherd.
5. Door – the only entrance way into the sheepfold (v.1)

⁷**Then said Jesus unto them again, Verily, verily, I say unto you, I am the door of the sheep. ⁸All that ever came before me are thieves and robbers: but the sheep did not hear them. ⁹I am the door: by me if any man enter in, he shall be saved, and shall go in and out, and find pasture.**

A few things have been explained to us.

- The door is Jesus (v.7)
- The stranger(s) are those thieves and robbers who came before Jesus trying to take Jesus' sheep away from Him, but the sheep did not follow (v.8).

105

- The sheep are men who came to Jesus (the door) for salvation (v.9)

[10]**The thief cometh not, but for to steal, and to kill, and to destroy: I am come that they might <u>have life</u>, and that they might have it more abundantly.**

All the stranger wants to do is to steal men away from Jesus, kill them, and destroy them. Jesus wants to give them life and once they have it, He wants to enable them to have it more abundantly. What an amazing truth that is so often misconstrued in this modernistic preaching age that we live in.

I would dare say that in most pulpits across America, and on the Christian television/radio broadcasts you will hear something like the following, *"Invite Jesus into your life because He wants to make it better."* Then, the preacher will probably follow with a sermon involving God's promises to give health, wealth, and prosperity;[24] however, the truths of John 10:10 have been completely missed.

You will hear little to no preaching on sin. You will hear little to no preaching on repentance. You will hear little to no preaching on your true standing before an almighty God: you are DEAD in trespasses and sins! You do NOT have life to invite Jesus into because YOU ARE DEAD! Jesus came to give life (salvation), and that you might have it more abundantly (outworking of salvation).

Ephesians 2:1-3 describes perfectly who a saved person was before Jesus saved them. **And you hath he quickened** (made alive)**, who <u>were dead in trespasses and sins</u>: Wherein in time past ye walked according to the course of this world, according to the prince of the power of the air, the spirit that now worketh in the children of disobedience: Among whom also we all had our conversation in times past in the lusts of our flesh, fulfilling the desires of the flesh and of the mind; and were by nature the children of wrath, even as others**. Do you see? You were dead, but now Jesus has given you life the moment He saved you.

---

[24] The verses from the Old Testament involving God's promises to "heal their land," to "heal all diseases," and to keep the words of the covenant "that ye may prosper" are all written to God's chosen people, the nation of Israel, regarding their lives in the promised land. We must be careful to rightly divide the word of truth (2 Timothy 2:15) and understand that the church has not replaced the Jewish nation. Yes, the church is a people that were not a people before salvation (1 Peter 2:10) but the word of God is clear that the Jew, the Gentile, and the church of God are separate entities (1 Corinthians 10:32).

[11]**I am the good shepherd: the good shepherd giveth his life for the sheep.** [12]**But he that is an hireling, and not the shepherd, whose own the sheep are not, seeth the wolf coming, and leaveth the sheep, and fleeth: and the wolf catcheth them, and scattereth the sheep.** [13]**The hireling fleeth, because he is an hireling, and careth not for the sheep.**

I wish that all preachers across this country, and even the world, would understand and take to heart these verses. It is a very unfortunate truth, but I would dare say that many of them preach only to receive money[25] (hireling), and they hold the opinion that they are the shepherd of their congregation. This MUST be avoided.

History proves men are unsuccessful in the eyes of God when they try to function as shepherds of God's flock. In Jeremiah 23:1-4, we read **Woe be unto the pastors that destroy and scatter the sheep of my pasture! saith the LORD. Therefore thus saith the LORD God of Israel against the pastors that feed my people; Ye have scattered my flock, and driven them away, and have not visited them: behold, I will visit upon you the evil of your doings, saith the LORD. And I will gather the remnant of my flock out of all countries whither I have driven them, and will bring them again to their folds; and they shall be fruitful and increase. And I will set up shepherds over them which shall feed them: and they shall fear no more, nor be dismayed, neither shall they be lacking, saith the LORD.** God decided to set up shepherds over His flock to feed them, but they did not do as instructed. **My people hath been lost sheep: their shepherds have caused them to go astray, they have turned them away on the mountains: they have gone from mountain to hill, they have forgotten their restingplace** (Jeremiah 50:6).

Centuries later, the Bible tells us that Christ beholds the multitudes being **moved with compassion on them, because they fainted, and were scattered abroad, as sheep having no shepherd** (Matthew 9:36, Mark 6:34). The Pharisees, Sadducees, and scribes of Israel were not feeding God's people the words of the LORD. There is only one true shepherd (John 10:16), who is the great shepherd (Hebrews 13:20), the good shepherd (John 10:11), the chief shepherd (1 Peter 5:4), and the shepherd and Bishop of our souls (1 Peter 2:25). That shepherd is Jesus Christ. Therefore, preachers should do all they can to draw the attention of God's people off them and towards Jesus Christ.

---

[25] 1 Timothy 3:3, Titus 1:7, and 1 Peter 5:2 admonish the elder, bishop, and preacher not to perform his duties for filthy lucre. Money is not a justifiable reason for preaching the gospel! Those in it solely for money will leave as soon as trouble arises because they only care for money, not the people – John 10:13

His commandments, truths, teachings, and doctrine are what matter. He is the head of the church (Ephesians 1:22), not the preacher. He is the shepherd of His body, not the preacher.

Notice the wording of 1 Peter 5:1-4. **The elders which are <u>among</u> you I exhort, who am also an elder, and a witness of the sufferings of Christ, and also a partaker of the glory that shall be revealed**. The elders are <u>among</u> the church, not over it as we read in Jeremiah 23:4. **Feed the flock of God which is <u>among</u> you, taking the oversight thereof, not by constraint, but willingly; not for filthy lucre, but of a ready mind: <u>Neither as being lords over God's heritage, but being ensamples to the flock</u>**. The word of God is so clear! The preachers are sheep just like every other saved member of Christ. Thus, they must take the oversight among God's people by being ensamples[26] to the flock.

[14]I am the good shepherd, and know my sheep, and am known of mine.

Obviously, a relationship must exist for Jesus to know His sheep, and for the sheep to know Him. You can read all the commentaries that become available, attend Bible schools, and learn all the facts about Jesus that are possible to learn in a lifetime, but that does not mean anything if you do not have a personal relationship with Him. There is a big difference between knowing about Jesus and knowing Him.

[15]As the Father knoweth me, even so know I the Father: and <u>I lay down my life</u> for the sheep.

When His hour comes (John 7:30, 8:20, 12:23, 12:27, 13:1, and 17:1) He will lay down His own life: the final sacrifice to pay the wages of sin for the entire world.

[16]And other sheep I have, which are not of this fold: them also I must bring, and they shall hear my voice; and there shall be one fold, and one shepherd.

Hallelujah! This calls for rejoicing among the Gentiles. **Wherefore remember, that ye being in time past Gentiles in the flesh, who are called Uncircumcision by that which is called the Circumcision (Jew) in the flesh made by hands; That all that time <u>ye were without Christ, being aliens from the commonwealth of Israel, and strangers from the covenants of promise, having no hope, and without God in the world</u>: But now** (Praise

---

[26] Ensample is the plural form of example.

God!) **in Christ Jesus ye who sometimes were far off** (Gentile) **are made nigh by the blood of Christ. For he is our peace, who hath** made both one**, and hath broken down the middle wall of partition between us; Having abolished in his flesh the enmity, even the law of commandments contained in ordinances; for to make in himself of twain one new man, so making peace; And that he might reconcile both** (Jew and Gentile) **unto God in one body by the cross, having slain the enmity thereby: And came and preached peace to you which were afar off** (Gentile)**, and to them that were nigh** (Jew) - Ephesians 2:11-13.

Gentiles were once without God in the world, and not part of His sheep fold. BUT NOW, through the blood of Jesus Christ shed on Calvary, He has made both Jew and Gentile one in Christ!

[17]**Therefore doth my Father love me, because I lay down my life, that I might take it again.** [18]**No man taketh it from me, but I lay it down of myself.** **I have power to lay it down, and I have power to take it again. This commandment have I received of my Father.**

As mentioned in the summary of this commentary, this statement is only found in the Gospel John. Each gospel has a theme. Matthew portrays Jesus as King of the Jesus, Mark as the servant, Luke as the Son of man, and John as God. No person (King, servant, or man) possesses the power to lay down their own life and in return take it up again. **There is no man that hath power over the spirit to retain the spirit; neither hath he power in the day of death: and there is no discharge in that war; neither shall wickedness deliver those that are given to it** (Ecclesiastes 8:8). However, Jesus will dismiss His spirit on the cross (John 19) proving He is God. Ecclesiastes 8:8 just told us no man has that ability. Considering John's theme showing Jesus as God, it is fitting that this statement is only found here in John.

[19]**There was a division therefore again among the Jews for these sayings.** [20]**And many of them said, He hath a devil, and is mad; why hear ye him?** [21]**Other said, These are not the words of him that hath a devil. Can a devil open the eyes of the blind?**

The people are divided, and we have seen this several times already throughout John. Truly **the word of God is quick, and powerful, and sharper than any twoedged sword, piercing even to the dividing asunder of soul and spirit, and of the joints and marrow, and is a discerner of the thoughts and intents of the heart** (Hebrews 4:12). God's word discerns our every thought and intents of our hearts. The Bible reads us, and that is why most people do not want to read it.

[22]And it was at Jerusalem the feast of the dedication, and it was winter.

Exodus 23 and Leviticus 23 tell us of the feasts God ordained for His people Israel. However, this *feast of dedication* is not one of them.

This does not appear to be the feast for the dedication of the altar (Numbers 7:84-88, 2 Chronicles 1:10, 1 Kings 8:2) for this happened on the twenty-third day of the seventh month, Tishri. This would not be in winter.[27]

This could be a feast in remembrance of the house of God being completed on the third day of the month Adar under the reign of king Darius (Ezra 6:15-17). The month of Adar is at the close of winter occurring around the middle of February until the middle of March.

This also very well could be the celebration of Hanukkah (or Chanukkah) which occurs in December. Hanukkah is an eight-day celebration where each day a candle is lit on an eight candle stand menorah. The word means "dedication" and is observed in remembrance of the Jewish revolt in the second century B.C. against their Greek-Syrian oppressors. This is known as the Maccabean Revolt according to history.

Nonetheless, this feast (whatever it was in dedication of) does not appear to be directly ordained by God. The Jews decided to add this to their religion, like Christians today add Easter, Christmas, Halloween, etc. to their religion even though God never instituted such observances.

Considering we are touching on the topic of religious activities God never instituted, let's consider Galatians 4:9-10. **Howbeit then, when ye knew not God, ye did service unto them which by nature are no gods. But now, after that ye have known God, or rather are known of God, how turn ye again to the <u>weak and beggarly elements</u>, whereunto ye desire again to be in bondage? Ye <u>observe days, and months, and times, and years</u>.** These verses refer to the church of Galatia returning to the law to observe days, months, times, and years that were never intended for the church to observe, because the church is not under the law (see also Acts 15).

Notice that God called the elements of the law (what God Himself ordained) weak and beggarly. If God considers something He instituted weak and beggarly, then what do you reckon God thinks about the manmade religious traditions of Easter, Christmas, etc. that He never instituted for the church to observe?

---

[27] See Appendix – *Biblical Calendar*

²³And Jesus walked in the temple in Solomon's porch. ²⁴Then came the Jews round about him, and said unto him, How long dost thou make us to doubt? If thou be the Christ, tell us plainly.

How can Jesus be any plainer? Nonetheless, if He has not been clear enough up to this point, He is about to state without any doubt that He is the Christ.

²⁵Jesus answered them, I told you, and ye believed not: the works that I do in my Father's name, they bear witness of me. ²⁶But ye believe not, because ye are not of my sheep, as I said unto you. ²⁷My sheep hear my voice, and I know them, and they follow me:

They do not hear what Jesus has said because they are not His sheep. His sheep hear His voice and follow Him, but they refuse to follow all because of their unbelief. One's relationship with God always hinges on one factor: BELIEF.

²⁸And I give unto them eternal life; and they shall never perish, neither shall any man pluck them out of my hand. ²⁹My Father, which gave them me, is greater than all; and no man is able to pluck them out of my Father's hand.

In John 3:33 and 6:39 we briefly discussed the idea of *eternal security*, but this is one of the greatest verses (if not the greatest) on that topic. When you get saved, you have eternal life and shall NEVER perish because no man (not even yourself) can pluck (i.e., detach) you out of the Father's hand. If no man can pluck you out of His hand, that means you are not just sitting in His hand, but this verse adequately states that you are attached to His hand.

Someone might try a rebuttal by saying, "Well I just think…" It does not matter what you think because the Father is greater than your thoughts (1 John 3:20). "Well, I could sin badly enough to where…" God is greater than your sin. He is greater than ALL.

If He says you have eternal life and shall never perish, He means what He says regardless of what happens after salvation. NO MAN can pluck them (those that believe Jesus, thus being counted as sheep of His fold) out of the Father's hand. What a wonderful truth! **I know whom I have believed, and am persuaded that he is able to keep that which I have committed unto him against that day** (2 Timothy 1:12). **The LORD shall preserve thee from all evil: he shall preserve thy soul. The LORD shall preserve thy** going out and thy coming in from this time forth, and even for evermore (Psalm 121:7-8).

³⁰I and my Father are one.

Jesus cannot speak any plainer than this. He tried to tell them this truth back in John 5:18, but they refused to believe it then and they still refuse it now.

³¹Then the Jews took up stones again to stone him. ³²Jesus answered them, Many good works have I shewed you from my Father; for which of those works do ye stone me? ³³The Jews answered him, saying, For a good work we stone thee not; but for blasphemy; and because that thou, being a man, makest thyself God.

They fully understand that Jesus just claimed to be God, however their problem has not changed. They refuse to believe Him.

³⁴Jesus answered them, Is it not written in your law, I said, Ye are gods?

WOW! Jesus claims to be God, and the Pharisees want to stone Him for it. Then, without hesitation, Jesus proclaims next that He said and spoke into existence the law. Oh, how I love this book that proves Jesus is indeed God!

The statement Jesus is referencing is Psalm 82:6. **I have said, Ye are gods; and all of you are children of the most High.**

³⁵If he called them gods, unto whom the word of God came, and the scripture <u>cannot</u>[28] be broken; ³⁶Say ye of him, whom the Father hath sanctified, and sent into the world, Thou blasphemest; because I said, I am the Son of God? ³⁷If I do not the works of my Father, believe me not. ³⁸But if I do, though ye believe not me, believe the works: that ye may know, and believe, that the Father is in me, and I in him.

When Jesus references Psalm 82:6, He uses it to show that His claim to being the Son of God is very similar to what Jehovah God confessed of the children of Israel: **all of you are children of the most High**. It is the same

---

[28] Seven contexts where "cannot" is used in John. 1. The natural man cannot enter the kingdom of God (3:3-5), 2. The lost cannot go where Christ is (7:34, 8:21-23), 3. The unsaved cannot hear the word of the Lord (8:43), 4. The scripture cannot be broken (10:35), 5. The world cannot receive the Holy Spirit (14:17), 6. A believer cannot bear fruit of himself (15:4), 7. The Lord cannot teach us more rapidly than we can learn (16:12).

idea we discussed back in Chapter 1. He is the Son of God, and we (through our faith in the Lord Jesus Christ) are sons of God. These children of Israel might be gods (little g), but Jesus is God (big G). The proof is in the works of the Father that Jesus performs.

In the Old Testament only the LORD Jehovah God opened the eyes of the blind (Psalm 146:8), controlled the stormy winds (Psalm 107:25), cleansed the lepers (2 Kings 5), raised the dead (John 5:21), etc. Thus, there is only one conclusion these Jews can draw: Jesus is indeed sanctified by the Father, the LORD God Jehovah, and they should believe He is in the Father and the Father is in Him based on the works He performs.

Recall the theme verses of John 20:30-31. **And many other signs truly did Jesus in the presence of his disciples, which are not written in this book: But these are written, that ye might believe that Jesus is the Christ, the Son of God; and that believing ye might have life through his name**. I have said it repeatedly, and I will say it once more … They simply refuse to believe.

[39]Therefore they sought again to take him: but he escaped out of their hand, [40]And went away again beyond Jordan into the place where John at first baptized; and there he abode. [41]And many resorted unto him, and said, John did no miracle: but all things that John spake of this man were true. [42]And many believed on him there.

Despite those that refused to believe on Him, thankfully there were many that did.

From chapter 1 through chapter 10 we have seen many that refuse to believe on Him, and as we saw in John 6:66, there are many that have decided to stop following Him. As we progress forward through this Gospel, Jesus' popularity will continue to decrease leading to the hour He came into world for: to die on the cross at Calvary.

John 11

She saith unto him, Yea, Lord: I believe that thou art the Christ, the Son of God, which should come into the world – John 11:27: Martha professes Jesus to be the Son of God

¹Now a certain man was sick, named Lazarus, of Bethany, the town of Mary and her sister Martha. ²(It was that Mary which anointed the Lord with ointment, and wiped his feet with her hair, whose brother Lazarus was sick.)

I have always found verse two to be rather interesting. We will not read of Mary anointing Jesus' feet with oil to wipe them with her hair until the next chapter. So, either God is just giving us this parenthetical addition of information just as a *heads up*, or God is trying to bring to our remembrance something that we should have previously read. When reading the Bible from front to back, we read of that story in Matthew 26 and Mark 14. To me, this is just further evidence of the undeniable truth that God had his hand, not only in writing the scriptures, but in placing them in their proper order as well.

Secondly, did you notice that more emphasis and attention is given to Mary's actions rather than to Lazarus – the one who will shortly be raised from the dead? The natural and carnal man would look at these two individuals, and when given the choice on what story they would rather tell, (Mary worshipping the Lord or Lazarus being raised from the dead) Lazarus being resurrected would take precedence every time. However, God and His word puts more emphasis on individuals worshipping Him than on the miraculous events He performs.

³Therefore his sisters sent unto him, saying, Lord, behold, he whom thou lovest is sick. ⁴When Jesus heard that, he said, This sickness is not unto death, but for the glory of God, that the Son of God might be glorified thereby.

Jesus is going to raise Lazarus from the dead after being dead for four days and thereby be glorified.

⁵Now Jesus loved Martha, and her sister, and Lazarus. ⁶When he had heard therefore that he was sick, he abode two days still in the same place where he was.

Wait a minute. If Jesus loved Lazarus, why wait two days before going to Bethany? We will see in just a minute that whether He immediately left or delayed made little difference. Lazarus was already dead.

On another note, so often in our churches today (I feel safe in making this general assumption about all churches) we receive prayer requests from individuals asking others, that are willing, to pray for them regarding sickness, disease, bad health, illness, physical problems, etc. We should pray for these requests because James 5:16 tells us to **pray one for another, that ye may be healed. The effectual fervent prayer of a righteous man availeth much**. However, those prayers are answered in different ways. Sometimes God immediately responds. Sometimes God responds slower than we might would like or expect, just as Mary and Martha will react to Jesus' delayed arrival. Sometimes God will not take our infirmities away as was the case for Paul (2 Corinthians 12:7-9). Nonetheless, when, and how God responds is dictated by one simple truth: **that the Son of God might be glorified thereby** (v.4).

⁷Then after that saith he to his disciples, Let us go into Judaea again. ⁸His disciples say unto him, Master, the Jews of late sought to stone thee; and goest thou thither again?

Recall John 5:18 and 10:31. The Jews sought to kill Jesus because He claimed to be equal with God.

My immediate thought to their comment is, "He's always gotten away before, so why such concern for His safety now?" I do believe they feared for Jesus' life, but after reading v.16 it appears the disciples feared equally as much for their own safety. Maybe that is the reason for their comment.

⁹Jesus answered, Are there not twelve hours in the day? if any man walk in the day, he stumbleth not, because he seeth the light of this world. ¹⁰But if a man walk in the night, he stumbleth, because there is no light in him.

Yet again, Jesus is using a physical example to explain the spiritual. How do we know that? Jesus said there is no light in him. Light does not exist inside a person when speaking of the physical realm, so this must have a spiritual application.

Physically speaking, when light is present (the sun) any man can see where they are going to avoid the obstacles ahead. When it is dark those obstacles cannot be seen, thus they are prone to stumble. To put this simply, Jesus is the **light of the world which lighteth every man that cometh into the world**, and **he that followeth** Him **shall not walk in darkness** (John 1:3-13, John 8:12).

You might be wondering, as I often have, why does Jesus tell them this? The best answer I know to give is two-fold. He is either reminding them of the truth that He must eventually go to Jerusalem to die (John 2:19-21, 3:14), or He is preparing them for His following statement regarding death as sleep. Either way, the disciples need to get their minds off the physical and on the spiritual.

[11]These things said he: and after that he saith unto them, Our friend Lazarus sleepeth; but I go, that I may awake him out of sleep. [12]Then said his disciples. Lord, if he sleep, he shall do well. [13]Howbeit Jesus spake of his death: but they thought that he had spoken of taking of rest in sleep.

This is the statement I referred to above. When we read the word sleep, we think of what people do at night but scripturally speaking, death is often pictured and described as sleep. The disciples don't recognize this truth because they are thinking only of the physical.

[14]Then said Jesus unto them plainly, Lazarus is dead. [15]And I am glad for your sakes that I was not there, to the intent ye may believe; nevertheless let us go unto him.

What is Jesus intending for them to believe? **My sheep hear my voice, and I know them, and they follow me: and I give unto them eternal life; and they shall never perish, neither shall any man pluck them out of my hand** (John 10:27-28). Jesus is going to prove to them, by raising Lazarus from the grave, that He truly can give individuals eternal life, and they shall never perish. Truly the Son of God is going to be glorified thereby (v.3). Hallelujah!

[16]Then said Thomas, which is called Didymus,[29] unto his fellowdisciples, Let us also go, that we may die with him.

Again, this very well could be the reason the disciples addressed Jesus' safety (v.8).

[17]Then when Jesus came, he found that he had lain in the grave four days already.

Recall the commentary from verses 5 and 6. If Lazarus had been in the grave for four days, and Jesus only waited two days before going to

---

[29] Didymus means twin.

Bethany, then by the time Jesus received the news of Lazarus' sickness he had already been dead two days.

[18]Now Bethany was nigh unto Jerusalem, about fifteen furlongs off:

We learned in John 6:19 that one furlong is roughly one-eighth of a mile; thus, fifteen furlongs is approximately 2 miles.

[19]And many of the Jews came to Martha and Mary, to comfort them concerning their brother.

It is an absolute blessing for people to show concern for an individual's well-being at the loss of a loved one. I know I appreciate it when people come around to comfort me during such circumstances.

One question people tend to ask themselves when trying to comfort someone like this is, "What do I say to them?" 1 Thessalonians 4:13-18 is the best answer I know to provide. **But I would not have you to be ignorant, brethren, concerning them which are asleep, that ye sorrow not, even as other which have no hope.**

Jesus wants us to know something regarding those who have died that we sorrow not! We have a glorious hope the lost people of this world do not have. What is that hope? **For if we believe that Jesus died and rose again** (that is why the lost do not have this hope), **even so them also which sleep in Jesus will God bring with him. For this we say unto you <u>by the word of the Lord</u>, that we which are alive and remain unto the coming of the Lord shall not prevent them which are asleep. For the Lord himself <u>shall descend</u>** (this is guaranteed to happen according to the truth of God's word) **from heaven with a shout, with the voice of the archangel, and with the trump of God: and the dead in Christ shall rise first: Then we which are alive and remain <u>shall be caught up together with them in the clouds</u>, to meet the Lord in the air: and so shall we ever be with the Lord.** If our loved ones have believed on Jesus Christ, we shall be with them again! This will happen either by us entering God's presence through the door of death, or by Jesus coming again to catch us up in the air to be with Him. Either way, I find it a great comfort to know that not only will I be with Jesus Christ for all eternity but will also see those that have gone on before me in faith. That is why 1 Thessalonians 4:13-18 finishes with v.18 by stating: **Wherefore comfort one another with these words.** This information, that God does not want us to be ignorant of, is all the comfort a believer in Jesus Christ should need.

²⁰Then Martha, as soon as she heard that Jesus was coming, went and met him: but Mary sat still in the house.

Martha and Mary are a perfect example of how different people handle death. Some, like Martha, have no trouble talking and interacting with those that have arrived to comfort them. Others, like Mary, tend to want to be left alone. No matter how different people cope with death, the one thing that should always be constant is people being there to provide comfort. Just being present is a comfort.

²¹Then said Martha unto Jesus, Lord, if thou hadst been here, my brother had not died.

Here is yet another truth about people regarding death: they tend to blame God. That is exactly what Martha is doing. She just stated that if He would have come Lazarus would still be alive, thus she is blaming Him for their current situation.

The real blame does not belong to God for He came that we might have life (John 10:10). What is really to blame is sin. Sin has an end result. It has a consequence. It has a wage that will be paid, and that payment is death (Romans 6:23). Sin is the reason we all die **for all have sinned, and come short of the glory of God**, so if we are to blame anyone or anything for death, blame what is really the cause, not God.

²²But I know, that even now, whatsoever thou wilt ask of God, God will give it thee. ²³Jesus saith unto her, Thy brother shall rise again. ²⁴Martha saith unto him, I know that he shall rise again <u>in the resurrection at the last day</u>.

Martha proclaims two great truths regarding Jesus Christ, but these truths contradict her claim. She said that she believed whatever Jesus asked of the Father, the Father would give it to Him. BUT, upon hearing that Lazarus would rise again, she did not acknowledge that it could happen now. She did not think Jesus could resurrect Lazarus, only that the resurrection would occur at the last day.

²⁵Jesus said unto her, I am the resurrection, and the life: he that believeth in me, though he were dead, yet shall he live: ²⁶And whosoever liveth and believeth in me shall never die. Believest thou this?

What great spiritual truths! Let's deal with Jesus' statement before addressing His question to Martha.

First, Jesus states that someone can believe in Him while being dead. He cannot possibly be talking about physical death, so we must look at this statement spiritually. Ephesians 2:1-7 says **And you hath he quickened, who were dead in trespasses and sins;** (This is the death Jesus is talking about. Though he were dead *in trespasses and sins,* yet shall he have life upon believing in Jesus Christ) **Wherein in time past** (following is the proof we are all dead in trespasses and sins) **ye walked according to the course of this world, according to the prince of the power of the air, the spirit that now worketh in the children of disobedience: Among whom also we all had our conversation in times past in the lusts of our flesh, fulfilling the desires of the flesh and of the mind; and were by nature the children of wrath, even as others.** That accurately describes every single person on the face of the earth before they believe on Jesus Christ. We were all dead in trespasses and sins and our thoughts, actions, desires of our flesh, and our lifestyle proved it.

How does God act on our behalf? He gives us the gift of His Son and saves us by His marvelous grace through our faith in His word. Simply put – when we believe in Him, we have eternal life and shall never die (v.26).

Now, let me be just as clear as the word of God is. We all have a physical birth in Adam that is conceived in sin (Psalm 51:5) and as a result our physical bodies will die. However, if we have believed on the Lord Jesus Christ, we shall be made alive (quickened), and our soul shall never die. **For as in Adam all die, even so in Christ shall all be made alive** (1 Corinthians 15:22).

I do not think Martha believed that.

²⁷She saith unto him, Yea, Lord: I believe that thou art the Christ, the Son of God, which should come into the world.

That is not an answer to His question. What Martha believes is a wonderful truth that all should believe, but not an appropriate answer to the question.

²⁸And when she had so said, she went her way, and called Mary her sister secretly, saying, The Master is come, and calleth for thee. ²⁹As soon as she heard that, she arose quickly, and came unto him.

People came to comfort her (v.19), yet she desires the solitude of her own home until the Master arrives. I will reiterate what we discussed previously by saying again that the best way to comfort those who are grieving over the death of a loved one is to give them Jesus. That is who Mary desired to see, and He is the best comfort anyone can offer.

³⁰Now Jesus was not yet come into the town, but was in that place where Martha met him. ³¹The Jews then which were with her in the house, and comforted her, when they saw Mary, that she rose up hastily and went out, followed her, saying, She goeth unto the grave to weep there.

Wrong. Not a bad thought by these Jews, but she is going to see Jesus.

³²Then when Mary was come where Jesus was, and saw him, she fell down at his feet, saying unto him, Lord, if thou hadst been here, my brother had not died.

So, she reacts to her brother's death the same way Martha did. She blames Jesus for not coming in time to heal him of his sickness.

³³When Jesus therefore saw her weeping, and the Jews also weeping which came with her, he groaned in the spirit, and was troubled. ³⁴And said, Where have ye laid him? They said unto him, Lord, come and see. ³⁵Jesus wept. ³⁶Then said the Jews, Behold how he loved him!

Yes, Jesus loved Lazarus along with Mary and Martha, but His love does not end there! He loved the whole world enough to die for every single person (John 3:16), even while we were yet sinners (Romans 5:8), and takes no pleasure in the death of the wicked (Ezekiel 33:11).

³⁷And some of them said, Could not this man, which opened the eyes of the blind, have caused that even this man should not have died?

Not only did Mary and Martha blame Jesus for Lazarus' death, but even those that may or may not believe on Him are blaming Him. If that doesn't describe the way of the world, I don't know what does. Lost people in the time of sorrow say things like:
"If God is so loving, why did He allow this to happen?"
"If there truly is a God, why did He do this?"
Again, I say God is not to blame. Sin is the problem.

³⁸Jesus therefore again groaning in himself cometh to the grave. It was a cave, and a stone lay upon it. ³⁹Jesus said, Take ye away the stone. Martha, the sister of him that was dead, saith unto him, Lord, by this time he stinketh: for he hath been dead four days.

I feel confident in saying Jesus knows that. We, just like Martha, tend to let God know how we think things ought to be done as if He really needs our input. Jesus says to roll the stone away and Martha responds by practically saying, "Are you sure about that? You know the body is going to stink." Martha just needs to get out of God's way and let Him work, as do we all. We are so often our own worst enemy hindering the work of God because we think something should be done a certain way, or we feel that this way or that way is the right course of action. **There is a way that seemeth right unto a man, but the end thereof are the ways of death** (Psalm 16:25). So, we just need to trust God on His spoken word and allow His word to take precedence over our thoughts and feelings.

[40] Jesus saith unto her, Said I not unto thee, that, <u>if thou wouldest believe, thou shouldest see the glory of God?</u>

Therein lies the problem: unbelief. Our unbelief is the reason we do not see God's glory manifested in our lives.

[41] Then they took away the stone from the place where the dead was laid. And Jesus lifted up his eyes, and said, Father, I thank thee that thou hast heard me. [42] And I knew that thou hearest me always: <u>but because of the people which stand by I said it, that they may believe that thou hast sent me.</u>

The words that Jesus is speaking did not need to be said aloud. For Lazarus to be resurrected, Jesus only had to will it to happen, and it would have been done. However, He speaks aloud to God the Father so that those listening can hear, see, and believe.

[43] And when he thus had spoken, he cried with a loud voice, Lazarus, come forth.

I'm sure many of you reading this commentary have heard the common teaching that Jesus had to be very specific in naming Lazarus to come forth. Had he only said, "Come forth," all the graves might have emptied. Well, I'm sure Lazarus was not the only Lazarus to have died in the world (Luke 16:19-31) so I'm not in one-hundred percent agreement with this common teaching. However, one thing I am sure that we can all agree on, according to the context of the passage, is that Jesus wanted everyone to know He was resurrecting Lazarus, the brother of Mary and Martha, who had been dead for four days. This proves John 10:27-28: **My sheep hear my voice, and I know them, and they follow me: And I give unto them eternal life;**

and they shall never perish, neither shall any man pluck them out of my Father's hand.

[44]And he that was dead came forth, <u>bound hand and foot</u> with grave clothes: and <u>his face was bound about with a napkin</u>. Jesus saith unto them, Loose him, and let him go.

I just want to point out to you, while we are here, that Lazarus did not walk out of the tomb. He was bound from head to toe and unable to walk. I do not know how to accurately describe this scene (hopefully God has a home-made recording for us to watch in heaven), but Lazarus was called forth, and came out either by floating, hopping, or just appearing from the tomb. I would say the latter considering we have encountered a similar event previously in John 6:21 where the ship immediately arrived at its destination. All I can say with certainty is Lazarus was called by name, then he was out of the tomb.

[45]Then many of the Jews which came to Mary, and had seen the things which Jesus did, <u>believed on him</u>.

This is the appropriate response. What other evidence do you need to believe God?

[46]But some of them went their ways to the Pharisees, and told them what things Jesus had done.

This is the inappropriate response. When Jesus resurrects a man from the grave that should eliminate all doubt someone might have about Jesus. Although, some of these people's first response was, "Oh no, the Pharisees need to know about this."

Really?!

Some verses I read in the Bible leave me dumbfounded with little to no words to comment with. This verse is one of them. I am absolutely baffled as to why someone would not believe on Him after witnessing this event.

[47]Then gathered the chief priests and the Pharisees a council, and said, What do we? for this man doeth many miracles.

I want to place myself in this scene and raise my hand while saying, "Pick me, pick me, I've got an idea." Then after being called on, I'd say, "YOU SHOULD BELIEVE ON HIM!" I'm sure it would have little impact on changing their minds, but come on, what else could possibly be done to convince these people that Jesus is God?

⁴⁸If we let him thus alone, all men will believe on him: and the Romans shall come and take away both <u>our</u> place and nation.

This verse helps me understand their unbelief from verse 46. They do not want to lose what they profess belongs to them. They want the power. They want the control, and they will do anything to keep it. Believing on Jesus Christ requires too much self-denial for these Pharisees.

Also notice the order: "our" place (#1) and nation (#2). They are putting themselves and their position ahead of the benefit of those they are supposed to be serving. That is not a group of leaders I want looking after my best interests.

⁴⁹And one of them, named Caiaphas, being the high priest that same year, said unto them, Ye know nothing at all, ⁵⁰Nor consider that it is expedient for us, that one man <u>should die for the people</u>, and that the whole nation perish not. ⁵¹And this spake he not of himself: but being high priest that year, he prophesied that Jesus should die for the nation; ⁵²And not for that nation only, but that also he should gather together in one the children of God that were scattered abroad.

Caiaphas knows nothing at all either. He does not realize his prophecy is exactly what scripture states would happen to the Messiah in accordance with the will of God (Daniel 9:26).

He thinks his plan will kill two birds with one stone. They hate Jesus and since the Romans have taken over the rule of the world through blood shed, he puts the two together by thinking the Romans will be happy if they get to continue killing people. Killing Jesus would satisfy both parties interests. Nice guy, wouldn't you say?

⁵³Then from that day forth they took counsel together for to put him to death.

Naturally the rest of the Pharisees think the plan is perfectly fitting for their given situation. I would say Jesus agrees considering He came into this world to lay down His life for us.

⁵⁴Jesus therefore walked <u>no more openly among the Jews</u>; but went thence unto a country near to the wilderness, into a city called Ephraim, and there continued with his disciples.

Every detail of God's plan is falling right into place and Jesus will only go to the cross to be put to death exactly when He's supposed to. Not a moment before or after. He is making sure of that.

⁵⁵And the Jews' passover was night at hand: and many went out of the country up to Jerusalem before the passover, to purify themselves.

The Levitical law under various circumstances would pronounce individuals unclean. For example, someone that touches a dead animal was considered unclean (Leviticus 5:2). Even a woman was considered unclean after giving birth to a child (Leviticus 12:2-5). Their type of uncleanness determined how and when they could be pronounced clean, which generally meant offering a sacrifice.

As for the Passover, everyone was required to partake of the feast regardless of their cleanliness state (Number 9:10-13). So, those who went to purify themselves were probably due for their cleansing sacrifice according to the law. They were just being obedient to avoid partaking of the Passover feast while unclean.

⁵⁶Then sought they for Jesus, and spake among themselves, as they stood in the temple, What think ye, that he will not come to the feast? ⁵⁷Now both the chief priests and the Pharisees had given a commandment, that, if any man knew where he were, he should shew it, that they might take him.

Passover will be a perfect opportunity to take Him considering its strict observance under the law. Given Jesus' reputation for obeying the law, they know He will be somewhere in town eating the meal that night. All they need now is someone to report back to the Pharisees as to His location. Thus, Judas Iscariot's role as a betrayer will soon come into play.

John 12

And I, if I be lifted up from the earth, will draw all men unto me –
John 12:32: Jesus declares He can draw all men unto Him

[1]**Then Jesus six days before the passover came to Bethany, where Lazarus was, which had been dead, whom he raised from the dead. [2]There they made him a supper; and Martha served: but Lazarus was one of them that sat at the table with him.**

I am not certain whether this holds any real significance, but we find Lazarus eating in the chapter immediately following his resurrection from death unto life. I mention this because similar occurrences are found elsewhere in your Bible. See Mark 5:43 (the daughter of a ruler of the synagogue is resurrected) and Luke 15:23-24 (the prodigal son returning home) for two examples.

[3]**Then took Mary a pound of ointment of spikenard, very costly, and anointed the feet of Jesus, and wiped his feet with her hair: and the house was filled with the odour of the ointment.**

Prior to men of God pointing out certain truths of God's word to me surrounding the details of what we just read, I would often read this event and wonder, "Why is she doing this? Would another woman be willing to do that? What were the other disciples thinking besides Judas?" With those questions in mind, let's consider the matter.

1.   She sacrifices her money to glorify God.

This spikenard is very costly: worth 300 pence (pennies) according to v.5. Exactly how much is that worth? Matthew 20:1-9 explains that a day's wage was worth one single penny. To put this into further perspective, the Bible explains, in other places as well as Matthew 20:1-9, that a single day's workload is 12 hours. You work that amount of time 6 days a week (Exodus 20:8-11), which comes to 50 weeks' worth of labor a year. That is essentially an entire year's income Mary decides to take and dump out onto Jesus' feet. Incredible!

I would be willing to concede that most Christians give more money to their cable, phone, and internet provider than to God. We give more money to entertainment than to God. Now, what you give is all a matter of the heart (2 Corinthians 9:7), but when was the last time we offered money that was truly a sacrifice and not a carefully planned and calculated contribution?

Please do not misunderstand what I am saying. We are supposed to be good stewards of what God's given us (1 Peter 4:10). I am just simply asking, when was the last time you decided not to buy the newest piece of technology so that you might give that money to God. Or when was the last time we sacrificed something esteemed at high value so that we might give to God in its place? It is not how much we give, but what we give out of the abundance of our heart (Mark 12:42-44). We should all be more like Mary in this area of our lives.

2. She sacrifices her glory for the glorification of God.

Earlier I posed the question, "What other woman would be willing to do that?" and for good reason. Here in America, women spend *loads of time* (I'm trying to be discreet) in front of the mirror trying to get their hair to look perfect. Each of them has an image in their mind that they are trying to mimic, and with the billion-dollar industry of hair products at their side they will surely succeed. Come on ... We have all seen the commercials for hair products that claim to forever remove the problem of split ends and guarantee to make your hair feel so buttery soft that any woman not using such a product would look from afar thinking, "Oh, I wish my hair would do that." Having great hair makes them look good!

The Bible also supports women putting such emphasis on their hair in 1 Corinthians 11:15 by stating **it is a glory to her**. So, the idea of a woman using a non-approved hair product such as spikenard on her hair is unthinkable.

The point is that Mary placed no care or concern for the very thing that is a glory to her. Without questioning her actions or the results of such actions she sacrificed her glory to glorify Jesus Christ. We should all be more like Mary in this area of our lives.

3. She sacrifices the opinions of others to glorify God.

Beyond question, those watching her perform her act must have had a negative opinion of her. Surely the average woman would look on in bewilderment as to why she would be doing that to herself, and the average man would just simply ask, "What is she thinking?" Nonetheless, Mary did not let the opinions of others stop her from glorifying God.

I wonder how often we have opportunities to glorify God with our actions, but we choose not too because of who is watching and what they might think? We should all be more like Mary is this area of our lives.

⁴Then saith one of his disciples, Judas Iscariot, Simon's son, which should betray him, ⁵Why was not this ointment sold for three hundred pence, and given to the poor? ⁶This he said, not that he cared for the poor; but because he was a thief, and had the bag, and bare what was put therein.

Judas does not care about the poor. He just wants more money to stuff into his own pocket. Sounds to me like Judas is a perfect modern-day candidate for political office. Why? Most politicians will say and act like they care for the poor. They will claim to push for political action to benefit the poor, yet it is primarily a means to increase votes. They say what the people want to hear and if the political nominee can gain enough favor among the populous, they have successfully lined their own pockets by claiming to help the less fortunate. If you want proof, consider this. Upon entering office their net worth begins at less than six figures and quickly increases to more than seven figures. Once they leave office, they and their family will continue to receive such amounts of money until the day of the politician's death. Maybe some of them do really care about the poor, but I would dare say their own pockets being filled with money takes precedence to that of others.

⁷Then said Jesus, Let her alone: against the day of my burying hath she kept this. ⁸For the poor <u>always</u> ye have with you; but me ye have not always.

Ok, this is the last thing I will say regarding the political realm, and then we can move on to a greater truth. Many modern-day politicians are moving and pushing for a Socialist government where everyone is *equal*. The idea is to take money from the wealthy and distribute it to the poor, placing everyone on the same level.

If we imagine America did that and every single person starts out with an equal amount of money…say $100,000. Do you know what kind of economy you would have in three years or less? The exact same situation you have now where some are extremely wealthy, some are poor waiting around for another handout, while most people fall into what we call the middle class.

I am not being mean. I am just speaking in terms of reality. Some people can take that money and turn it into millions. Thus, they are among the rich and rightfully so. Others will take that money and slowly spend it until it is completely gone. The rest will take the money and turn it into thousands of dollars in the negative because all they know to do with money is to go deeper and deeper into debt. The point is, Jesus is right. **The poor <u>always</u> ye have with you**. Some people in this world are poor and they cannot

127

help it. Others are poor because of extremely bad decision making. Either way Jesus is right. Socialism will not work the way it has been glorified.

When Jesus uses the word always, He means always. We tend to use this word in place of the phrase: "most of the time." That is not the case for Jesus.

Consider the following fact. Jesus, according to Revelation and prophesy regarding the millennial kingdom, will rule and reign from a throne at Jerusalem for 1,000 glorious years. Surely, He will not allow anyone in His kingdom to be poor. Buckle your seat belts and hang on tight because the truth is…**the poor <u>always</u> ye have with you**.

Zephaniah 3:11-15 is a passage dealing with Jesus' reign and this is what we read: **In that day shalt thou not be ashamed for all thy doings, wherein thou hast transgressed against me: for then I will take away out of the midst of thee them that rejoice in thy pride, and thou shalt no more be haughty because of my holy mountain. <u>I will also leave in the midst of thee an afflicted and poor people</u>, and they shall trust in the name of the LORD. The remnant of Israel shall not do iniquity, nor speak lies; neither shall a deceitful tongue be found in their mouth: for they shall feed and lie down, and none shall make them afraid. Sin, O daughter of Zion; shout, O Israel; be glad and rejoice with all the heart, O daughter of Jerusalem. The LORD hath taken away thy judgments, he hath cast out thine enemy: <u>the king of Israel, even the LORD, is in the mist of thee</u>: thou shalt not see evil any more**. Even under the Lord's reign there will be poor people.

[9]**Much people of the Jews therefore knew that he was there: and they came not for Jesus' sake only, but that they might see Lazarus also, whom he had raised from the dead.**

Well of course they want to see Lazarus. Who wouldn't? I'm sure in this town the news of Lazarus' resurrection reached every ear in a matter of hours if not minutes.

Modern day headlines would probably even read, "Scientist baffled, man back to life after 4 days of death." I bet this whole town wanted to see Lazarus up walking with their own eyes.

[10]**But the chief priests consulted that they might put Lazarus <u>also</u> to death;** [11]**Because that by reason of him many of the Jews went away, and believed on Jesus.**

So, not only do they want to kill Jesus, but they want to kill Lazarus as well. Wow! They are contemplating a double homicide.

I wonder if it ever crossed their minds that just maybe Jesus would perform the same miracle again after they had Lazarus killed. They are so desperate to hold onto their **place and nation** (John 11:48) that they will do anything they deem a necessity to keep it.

[12]On the next day much people that were come to the feast, when they heard that Jesus was coming to Jerusalem, [13]Took branches of palm trees, and went forth to meet him, and cried, Hosanna: Blessed is the King of Israel that cometh in the name of the Lord.

They are essentially crying out Psalm 118:25-26. **Save now, I beseech thee, O LORD: O LORD, I beseech thee, send now prosperity. Blessed be he that cometh in the name of the LORD: we have blessed you out of the house of the LORD**. What they want is for Jesus to save them from Roman bondage NOW. They want prosperity NOW. These same people, a few days from now, will see the Jewish leaders turn Jesus over to Pilate for crucifixion, and their chants will change to CRUCIFY HIM.

They do not want Him. They only want what He has to offer and that is national salvation. Read the entire context of Psalm 118 for further support of this truth.

This accurately describes this new-age Christianity of health, wealth, and prosperity NOW. People hear that this man named Jesus can provide you with everything you desire and more, even though that is not why Jesus came. He came to save you from your sins! Nonetheless, they buy into that preaching and when they do not receive their desires in a timely manner, they turn away from God. It is why the new mega church on the street corner downtown will be full in a matter of weeks, but the majority of those that attended at the beginning will not be the same attendees two or three years later. They like Jesus as long as He is giving them stuff, but they want the stuff more than they want Him. Nothing has changed over the last 2,000 years and it will never change. My question for you is, "Do you want Jesus or the monetary values He can possibly provide you?" The correct answer is Jesus.

[14]And Jesus, when he had found a young ass, sat thereon; as it is written, [15]Fear not, daughter of Sion: behold, thy King cometh, sitting on an ass's colt.

That reference comes from Zechariah 9:9. Rejoice **greatly, O daughter of Zion; shout, O daughter of Jerusalem: behold, thy King cometh unto thee: he is just, and** <u>**having salvation**</u>**; lowly, and riding upon an ass, and upon a colt the foal of an ass. And I will cut off the chariot from Ephraim, and the horse from Jerusalem, and the battle bow shall be cut off: and he shall speak peace unto the heathen: and** <u>**his dominion shall be from sea even to sea, and from the river even to the ends of the earth**</u>**. As for thee also, by the blood of thy covenant I have sent forth thy prisoners out of the pit wherein is no water. Turn you to the strong hold, ye prisoners of hope: even to day do I declare that I will render double unto thee; When I have bent Judah for me, filled the bow with Ephraim, and raised up thy sons, O Zion, against thy sons, O Greece, and made thee as the sword of a mighty man. And the LORD shall be seen over them, and his arrow shall go forth as the lightning: and the Lord GOD shall blow the trumpet, and shall go with whirwinds of the south.** <u>**The LORD of hosts shall defend them; and they shall devour, and subdue with sling stones**</u>**; and they shall drink, and make a noise as through wine; and they shall be filled like bowls, and as the corners of the altar. And** <u>**the LORD their God shall save them in that day as the flock of his people**</u> (Zechariah 9:9-16a).

Do you see how this is a reference to national salvation from their enemies, not spiritual salvation from their sins?

Luke 24:18-21a should be the conclusive proof we need. Two men are walking on a road to Emmaus after Jesus had resurrected from the grave, and Jesus appears unto them have the following dialogue. **And he** [Jesus] **said unto them, What manner of communications are these that ye have one to another, as ye walk, and are sad? And the one of them, whose name was Cleopas, answering said unto him, Art thou only a stranger in Jerusalem, and hast not known the things which are come to pass there in these days? And he said unto them, What things? And they said unto him, Concerning Jesus of Nazareth, which was a prophet mighty in deed and word before God and all the people: And how the chief priests and our rulers delivered him to be condemned to death, and have crucified him.** <u>**But we trusted that it had been he which should have redeemed Israel**</u>. Every person that "believed" (John 11:45) on Jesus before His death, burial, and resurrection had the belief that Jesus would deliver them from their enemies.

¹⁶**These things understood not his disciples at the first: but when Jesus was glorified, then remembered they that these things were written of him, and that they had done these things unto him.** ¹⁷**The people therefore that was with him when he called Lazarus out of his grave, and raised him from the dead, bare record.** ¹⁸**For this cause the people also met him, for that they heard that he had done this miracle.** ¹⁹**The Pharisees therefore said among themselves, Perceive ye how ye prevail nothing? behold the world is gone after him.**

Why would they make such a claim: **behold <u>the world</u> is gone after him**? Exodus 23:14-19 describes three annual feasts where every man within the nation of Israel was to appear before the Lord (review John 5:1 commentary). This is the time of the year where those three feasts would occur, and in Acts 2:5 we read: **And there were dwelling at Jerusalem Jews, devout men, <u>out of every nation under heaven</u>**. Devout men had gathered in Jerusalem during this time of the year from all over the world and the Pharisees naturally perceived the worst-case scenario that they would believe on Jesus Christ. Thus, a worldwide assimilation among the Jews would result.

Can you see how quickly these events are unfolding to necessitate criminal action by the Pharisees?

²⁰**And there were certain Greeks among them that came up to worship at the feast:** ²¹**The same came therefore to Philip, which was of Bethsaida of Galilee, and desired him, saying, Sir, we would see Jesus.** ²²**Philip cometh and telleth Andrew: and again Andrew and Philip tell Jesus.**

This marks the end of Jesus' public ministry in John.

²³**And Jesus answered them, saying, The hour is come, that the Son of man should be glorified.**

Jesus' hour for why He came into the world has finally arrived (John 2:4, 7:30, 8:20).

²⁴**Verily, verily, I say unto you, Except a corn of wheat fall into the ground and die, it abideth alone: but if it die, it bringeth forth much fruit.**

This is yet again a physical truth told to teach a spiritual truth. When a farmer drops corn into the ground, that thing will first die, then sprout roots to eventually produce a plant, and then finally bear fruit. Jesus is simply saying that He must go and die, or He will abide alone. He is life eternal. He is the way unto the Father. He is the truth. Without His finished work on

Calvary nobody could receive justification from their sins for justification, redemption, and forgiveness of sins only comes through faith in Christ's death, burial, and resurrection.

²⁵He that loveth his life shall lose it; and he that hateth his life in this world shall keep it unto life eternal.

We must keep this verse in its context. Every verse leading up to this one has shown support of the nation of Israel desiring peace, hope, prosperity, and freedom from their enemies. They desired a better life. So, Jesus counters their desires with a very simple but great truth: anybody that loves their life here on this earth is just eventually going to lose it. Everybody dies.

What benefit is there to someone having everything they could possibly imagine in this life only to die in their sins and go to hell? There is no benefit to that at all. Jesus must die for all the world, and every person must put the life that exists in Him before their own lives.

²⁶If any man serve me, let him follow me; and where I am, there shall also my servant be: if any man serve me, him will my Father honour. ²⁷Now is my soul troubled; and what shall I say? Father, save me from this hour: but for <u>this cause</u> came I unto this hour.

He did not come to deliver Israel nationally. He did not come to set up an earthly kingdom. He came to die on the cross for all the sins of the entire world! Thank you, Lord Jesus!

²⁸Father, glorify thy name. Then came there a voice from heaven, saying, I have both glorified it, and will glorify it again.

The Father glorifying His name through His Son is vitally important doctrinally. He had to be glorified in Christ's life and again in His death. When we discuss chapter 17, we will cover the importance of this truth. The fact is that salvation would not be possible if Christ was not glorified.

²⁹The people therefore, that stood by, and heard it, said that it thundered: other said, An angel spake to him. ³⁰Jesus answered and said, This voice came not because of me, <u>but for your sakes</u>.

God the Father speaking audibly to the Son is simply for the benefit of man.

[31]**Now is the judgment of this world: now shall the prince of this world be cast out. [32]And I, if I be lifted up from the earth, will draw all men unto me. [33]This he said, signifying what death he should die.**

If Jesus had come to set up a kingdom and to deliver Israel from Roman oppression, Satan would not have received the judgement that was due him and he would still have the dominion of this world he stole from Adam back in the Garden of Eden. But, because Jesus died on the cross at Calvary, He bruised the serpent's head with His heal (Genesis 3:15), judged him with the judgement he was due, and cast him out! That is why you do not read of the church being devil possessed in the Bible after Jesus' death. Jesus has all power now that Satan has been judged (Colossians 2:14-15).

[34]**The people answered him, We have heard out of the law that Christ abideth for ever: and how sayest thou, The Son of man must be lifted up? who is this Son of man?**

Do you understand what these Israelites are thinking now? They have no recollection of the scriptures indicating that the Messiah would die (Isaiah 53 for one example). All they have on their mind is that the Messiah will set up an eternal kingdom and deliver them from their enemies (Isaiah 9:6-7). He came to die, and they do not understand that.

Since we are on this topic, I might as well address some preaching that I have heard quite often over the years, as I am sure you have. Many preachers have said that people before Calvary *looked forward to the cross*, and the people after Calvary *look backward to the cross*. This idea is nowhere supported in scripture. The people here in John 12, and in other similar places of the Gospel accounts only looked forward to national salvation. Even the disciples did not understand the truth that Christ would die and rise again three days.

A more accurate statement would be "SCRIPTURE before Christ looks forward to the cross, and SCRIPTURE after Christ looks backward to the cross." The simple point I am trying to make is that these Israelites simply wanted Christ to set up a kingdom and to overthrow their enemies, and that is not what He came to do.

[35]**Then Jesus said unto them, Yet a little while is the light with you. Walk while ye have the light, lest darkness come upon you: for he that walketh in darkness knoweth not whither he goeth. [36]While ye have light, believe in the light, that ye may be the children of light. These things spake Jesus,**

and departed, and did hide himself from them. **[37]But though he had done so many miracles before them, yet they believed not <u>on him</u>:**

I am going to say it again, and again, and again. They believed Jesus would deliver them nationally. They believed He would set up a kingdom. They believed He would give them prosperity, but they did not believe ON HIM. You must believe on Him, not what He can or cannot provide.

[38]That the saying of Esaias the prophet might be fulfilled, which he spake, Lord, who hath believed <u>our report</u>? and to whom hath the arm of the Lord been revealed? [39]<u>Therefore they could not believe</u>, because that Esaias said again, [40]He hath blinded their eyes, and hardened their heart; that they should not see with their eyes, nor understand with their heart, and be converted, and I should heal them. [41]These things said Esaias, when he saw his glory, and spake of him.

We need to be extremely careful with this portion of scripture because some people like to run with this from a *Calvinistic* view of "some were predetermined to go to heaven and others were predetermined to go to hell," claiming their predestination was why they could not believe. That is not true contextually, nor is that idea supported anywhere else in the Bible.

God's report is found in Isaiah 52:13-53:1: **Behold, my servant shall deal prudently, he shall be exalted and extolled, and be very high. As many were astonied at thee; <u>his visage was so marred more than any man, and his form more than the sons of men</u>** (He was beaten and whipped beyond human recognition the day He died): **So shall he sprinkle many nations; the kings shall shut their mouths at him: for that which had not been told them shall they see; and that which they had not heard shall they consider. Who hath believed our report? and to whom is the arm of the LORD revealed?**

So, here is the context of the verses: they did not believe on Jesus Christ because of their belief that He would deliver their nation from Rome. Thus, their false belief kept them from believing the truth of God's report. Their eyes were blinded, and their hearts hardened by God's report simply because they refused to abandon their false belief to receive God's truth.

[42]Nevertheless among the chief rulers also many believed on him; but because of the Pharisees they did not confess him, lest they should be put out of the synagogue: [43]For they loved the praise of men more than the praise of God.

I understand that there are places on this earth that if governing authorities were to find out you are a believer on Jesus Christ, your life would be in danger. Under those circumstances I understand keeping your belief a secret. However, keeping your belief a secret so you can keep your popularity at the Moose Lodge, or at the local community center, or on the job here in America is a real problem.

Jesus Christ died for our sins under the pains of crucifixion. He completely took our sins and iniquities away never to remember them again (Hebrews 8:12, 10:17), and His body was beaten and whipped beyond recognition. God forbid that we should desire the praise of men over the praise of God! We only think in terms of the here and now, and never even think about laying up treasures for us in heaven because we are so busy getting our treasures here where moth and rust doth corrupt (Matthew 6:19).

Recall v.26b: **if any man serve me, him will my Father honour**. Confessing the Jesus of the Bible could very well get us put out of places in this life, but oh, if we could just grab hold of the truth above and forget about the praise of men. If we serve Him now, then once we step out of this life into eternity, we shall receive honor from the Father. That is so much better than any man's praise.

[44]**Jesus cried and said, He that believeth on me, believeth not on me, but on him that sent me. [45]And he that seeth me seeth him that sent me. [46]I am come a light into the world, that whosoever believeth on me should not abide in darkness. [47]And if any man hear my words, and believe not, I judge him not: for I came not to judge the world, but to save the world. [48]He that rejecteth me, and receiveth not my words, hath one that judgeth him: the word that I have spoken, the same shall judge him in the last day.**

The equivalent statement to what Jesus just made is this, "If you believe in God but you do not believe on Jesus Christ, then you don't believe in God." That pronounces every single religion under God's heaven to be a false religion if it renounces Jesus Christ as God. That may not be politically correct, but that is the truth of the Bible.

Secondly, while you are here on this earth, God is not judging you. He just simply wants you to believe on Him because He did everything necessary to save every single person in all the world. However, the moment you step out into eternity, judgement is coming, and it is God's word that will judge you. His word is fixed, constant, forever settled (Psalm 118:89, Mark

13:31), and His word says that if you deny Him, He will deny you. If you reject Him, you will go to hell (Luke 16:19-31, Revelation 20:12-15). Period.

[49]For I have not spoken of myself; but the Father which sent me, he gave me a commandment, what I should say, and what I should speak. [50]And I know that his commandment is life everlasting: whatsoever I speak therefore, even as the Father said unto me, so I speak.

If you want to know Jesus Christ which is the same as knowing the Father, then you are going to have to listen to the words Jesus spoke. The only place you will find those words are in the Bible.

John 13

Ye call me Master and Lord: and ye say well; for so I am – *John 13:13: Jesus claims to be the Lord*

¹Now before the feast of the passover, when Jesus knew that his hour was come that he should depart out of this world unto the Father, having loved his own which were in the world, he loved them unto the end.

Pay close attention to the words: he loved them unto the end. They will be vitally important while going through this portion of scripture.

²And supper being ended, the devil having now put into the heart of Judas Iscariot, Simon's son, to betray him;

We know from the previous chapters that Judas Iscariot is going to betray Jesus. John 6:64, 6:71, 12:4 have already told us this information, and God will continue to bring out this truth again in 13:11, 13:21, 18:2, and 18:5. Even in John 6:70 Jesus Himself made mention that one of the 12 disciples He had chosen was a devil.

The thing that is striking to me about all this information, as these events unfold, is that the moment Jesus tells His disciples one of them would betray him, nobody knew who it would be. I just want to bring this truth to your attention now, but we will revisit it again shortly.

³Jesus knowing that the Father had given all things into his hands, and that he was come from God, and went to God; ⁴He riseth from supper, and laid aside his garments; and took a towel, and girded himself. ⁵After that he poureth water into a bason, and began to wash the disciples' feet, and to wipe them with the towel wherewith he was girded.

I do not know the number of times I had to read these verses, nor the amount of preaching I had to listen to surrounding these verses before the truth of this passage became clear to me.

1. Jesus knows that His hour was come to depart out of this world.
2. Jesus knows that the Father had given ALL things into His hands.

What Jesus decides to do with all this power, in his last hours of life on this earth, is to humble Himself to the point where He decides to pick up a towel and wash a group of men's dirty, nasty, disgusting feet. I say disgusting because I do not know many people who are comfortable enough to touch someone else's feet. Sure, they might do this for a family member, or close friend, but a man doing this for another man is unheard of. Such an action requires the man doing the washing to humble himself.

⁶Then cometh he to Simon Peter: and Peter saith unto him, Lord, dost thou wash my feet?

This is the first verse so far in the passage that makes natural sense, and I understand where Peter's initial thoughts are coming from. If anyone should be doing this, it should be one of the disciples washing Jesus' feet. I mean come on. He's God manifest in the flesh. However, there is much more going on here in this passage than what may initially meet the eye.

⁷Jesus answered and said unto him, <u>What I do thou knowest not now</u>; but thou shalt know hereafter.

Jesus is wanting to emphasis something other than feet washing. He is using the action of washing their feet to present something else … a far greater truth. What is He doing? We need to keep reading.

⁸Peter saith unto him, Thou shalt never wash my feet. Jesus answered him, If I wash thee not, thou hast no part with me.

Again, I appreciate where Peter is coming from, but He is missing the truth Jesus is presenting.

The first piece of vital information we need to gather is that unless Jesus "washes you," you have no part with Him. What does He mean by that? **Christ also loved the church, and gave himself for it; That he might sanctify and cleanse it with the <u>washing of water by the word</u>, That he might present it to himself a glorious church, not having spot, or wrinkle, or any such thing; but that it should be holy and without blemish** (Ephesians 5:25b-27). When someone believes on the Lord Jesus Christ, Jesus considers them to be washed and cleansed.

⁹Simon Peter saith unto him, Lord, not my feet only, but also my hands and my head.

And here Peter jerks the proverbial car to the other side of the road.
"You shall never wash my feet."
"If I wash thee not, thou hast no part with me."
"Oh, in that case, wash me all over."
Don't you just love Peter?

¹⁰Jesus saith to him, He that is washed needeth not save to wash his feet, but is clean every whit: and ye are clean, but not all. ¹¹For he knew who should betray him; therefore said he, Ye are not all clean.

Peter does not need to be washed all over. He is already clean by his belief in Jesus. He just needs to have his feet washed.

Now, let's revisit Judas Iscariot. They are all clean except for him. He does not believe on the Lord Jesus Christ so of course he is unclean. You only become clean by believing God's word. For those of you that think people are saved by works, I have a simple question for you. With all that Judas has done (miracles, casting out devils, healings, etc.[30]), if someone is saved by works would that not be enough to save him? I mean, that is more than we will ever do. The answer is obvious. You do not get saved by keeping the law. You do not get saved by performing good works (not even by performing miraculous works). You do not get saved because of having your good deeds outnumber your bad deeds. You are saved strictly through faith in the Lord Jesus Christ and nothing else.

[12]So after he had washed their feet, and had taken his garments, and was set down again, he said unto them, <u>Know ye what I have done to you</u>?

Ok, key point that must be noted. Jesus is obviously doing something more than just washing their feet. If washing their feet was truly what Jesus was trying to teach these men to do, He would not have asked such an obvious question. What has He just done? Keep reading.

[13]Ye call me Master and Lord: and ye say well; for so I am. [14]If I then, your Lord and Master, have washed your feet; ye also ought to wash one another's feet. [15]For <u>I have given you an example,</u> <u>that ye should do as I have done to you</u>.

I am sure there are churches across the globe that conduct services where the members wash one another's feet, but that is not the point. Jesus just gave them an example to follow, and the example is this...

Jesus, who is Master and Lord, and has been given all things into His hands by the Father, HUMBLES HIMSELF far below who He is that He might be of service, and a blessing to those He loves by washing their nasty, dirty, smelly feet. His example of humility is the truth to this event we should all heed.

Come on, this is Jesus! **The blessed and only Potentate, the King of kings, and Lord of lords** (1 Timothy 6:15), **the Saviour of the world** (1

---

[30] Matthew 10:1: **And when he had called unto him his <u>twelve disciples</u>, he gave them power against unclean spirits, to cast them out, and to heal all manner of sickness and all manner of disease**. That includes Judas.

John 4:14) who is **far above all principality, and power, and might, and dominion, and every name that is named, not only in this world, but also in that which is to come** (Ephesians 1:21)! These men should be washing His feet, but NO. Jesus wants us to humble ourselves, in like manner as He did, to serve others.

Something else to consider is that He washed Judas' feet as well, even though He knew he would betray Him. Not only that, but He loved every one of these men unto the end (v.1) even though He knew they would all be offended because of Him that very night (Matthew 26:31) and would scatter the moment of His arrest. Oh, what unconditional love and humility Jesus has for every person in the world. If only we could live up to such an example. We tend to only love those who love us, and to do good unto those that have been good to us. Not Jesus!

Just as God put all things into Jesus' hands, He **hath blessed us with all spiritual blessings in heavenly places in Christ** (Ephesians 1:3). We should, by the grace of God, be willing to humble ourselves with the blessings God has given us, just like Jesus did, and serve others no matter who they are or what they may have done unto us. That is the example Christ left for us in this passage.

[16]**Verily, verily I say unto you, <u>The servant is not greater than his lord</u>; neither he that is sent greater than he that sent him.** [17]**If ye know these things, <u>happy are ye if ye do them</u>.**

Oh, if only every saved person in this world would live according to these verses. It is the key to true happiness.

I have met some miserable Christians in my lifetime and have even been miserable at various times in my Christian walk. Why? It is because people are prideful (me included), and we tend to rank ourselves greater than others around us, and misery is guaranteed to follow. You do not need to take my word for it, for God's word says **<u>only</u> by pride cometh contention** (Proverbs 13:10).

What I must learn and be reminded of, as well as everyone else that is saved by the grace of our Lord Jesus Christ, is that **the servant is not greater than his lord**. Nobody is greater than another. Nobody is less than another. We are all blessed with the same blessings from God. We are all saved by the same grace. We are all the same when it comes to our standing before God. If we can simply learn to view our relationship with others like that, we can do well unto them no matter what they have done to us. We can humble ourselves just like Jesus did with His disciples. Then, guess what?

140

Happy are ye if ye do them. You can truly live a happy Christian life. It just simply requires you to dismiss your pride, your ego, and your imagined status among the brethren.

[18]**I speak not of you all: I know whom I have chosen: but that the scripture may be fulfilled, He that eateth bread with me hath lifted up his heel against me.**

  The scripture being referenced is Psalm 41:9, and it speaks of Judas. **Yea, mine own familiar <u>friend</u>, in whom I trusted, which did eat of my bread, hath lifted up his heel against me**. What an amazing thing for Christ to call Judas, the traitor, a friend.

[19]**Now I tell you before it come, that, when it is come to pass, ye may believe that I am he.** [20]**Verily, verily, I say unto you, He that receiveth whomsoever I send receiveth me; and he that receiveth me receiveth him that sent me.**

  Verse 20 is the truth surrounding anyone willing to tell others of Jesus Christ. Those listening must first receive the messenger, and once they have received the messenger's message of Jesus Christ, they have received both Jesus and the Father.

[21]**When Jesus had thus said, he was troubled in spirit, and testified, and said, Verily, verily, I say unto you, that one of you shall betray me.** [22]**Then the disciples looked one on another, doubting of whom he spake.**

  This reiterates what we previously discussed in verse 2. Nobody suspected Judas. He played his role perfectly by doing everything the other eleven did as well as going everywhere they went. **And no marvel; for Satan himself is transformed into an angel of light** (1 Corinthians 11:14).

[23]**Now there was leaning on Jesus' bosom one of his disciples, whom Jesus loved.** [24]**Simon Peter therefore beckoned to him, that he should ask who it should be of whom he spake.** [25]**He then lying on Jesus' breast saith unto him, Lord, who is it?** [26]**Jesus answered, He it is, to whom I shall give a sop, when I have dipped it. And when he had dipped the sop, he gave it to Judas Iscariot, the son of Simon.**

  My first instinct, every time I read this, is to think they must know Judas is the betrayer. But verses 28 and 29 show they still had no idea.

[27]**And after the sop Satan entered into him.**

Prior to Jesus going to the cross, we read in scripture of many people being possessed with devils or evil spirits. This is the only place we read of Satan himself possessing a person.

Then said Jesus unto him, That thou doest, do quickly. [28]**Now no man at the table** <u>**knew for what intent he spake this unto him**</u>**.**

Just as we mentioned above: they still do not know Judas is the betrayer.

[29]**For some of them thought, because Judas had the bag, that Jesus had said unto him, Buy those things that we have need of against the feast; or, that he should give something to the poor.** [30]**He then having received the sop went immediately out:** <u>**and it was night**</u>**.**

I truly believe that God placed every word in the Bible for a reason. If you study the scriptures regarding these events, you can successfully determine that it was nighttime (a truth presented in Appendix: The last days of Jesus' ministry. This should be read after completing chapter 19 commentary.). So, why did God deem it necessary to tell us **it was night**? Jesus said in John 12:46, as well as in other places, **I am come a light into the world, that whosoever believeth on me should not abide in darkness**. Judas did not believe on Him; thus, he has turned himself aside unto Satan to abide in darkness.

[31]**Therefore, when he was gone out, Jesus said, Now is the Son of man glorified, and God is glorified in him.** [32]**If God be glorified in him, God shall also glorify him in himself, and shall straightway glorify him.** [33]**Little children**[31]**, yet a little while I am with you. Ye shall seek me: and as I said unto the Jews, Whither I go, ye cannot come; so now I say to you.** [34]**A new commandment I give unto you, That ye love one another;** <u>**as I have loved you**</u>**, that ye also love one another.**

Again, we tend to love people who reciprocate love for us. Or we love people that have not wronged us in any way. That is exactly what Jesus wants us to avoid.

Take this chapter of the Bible for example. The first verse tells us that Jesus loved them unto the end. In just a few short hours from this moment, every disciple will scatter to go their own way once Jesus is arrested, and Peter will deny Him three times. For many of us, if someone were to

---

[31] It is interesting to note that Jesus only called them children after Judas left the room, not before. Fitting considering Judas was not a child of God.

abandon us like they did or deny us like Peter did, that would be a breaking point in our love for them.

Husbands abandon their spouses, or wives do something to wrong their husbands and the love they have one for another ends. Children do something to wrong their parents or parents do something to wrong their children and their love for each other is severed. The proof is when such a circumstance happens to an individual and they do not stop loving the person that has wronged them, everyone looks on in amazement thinking, "I just don't think I could continue loving that person after they did that to me."

Is not that, right?

Jesus never stopped loving His disciples no matter what they did. He even loved all the world enough **in that, while we were yet sinners, Christ died for us** (Romans 5:8). Everybody has been done wrong by someone else. Christ wants us to humble ourselves and to love them unconditionally unto the end. **If ye know these things, happy are ye if ye do them** (v.17).

[35] **By this shall all men know that ye are my disciples, if ye have love one to another.**

You could graduate from Bible college with more biblical knowledge than anyone else in the world. You could be the best teacher of the Bible at your church or be the most actively involved member of the congregation, but still not be known as Christ's disciple according to his definition of discipleship. What makes a Christian a true disciple, is when they have love one for another.

[36]**Simon Peter said unto him, Lord, whither goest thou? Jesus answered him, Whither I go, thou canst not follow me <u>now</u>; but thou shalt follow me afterwards.**

There are two truths about this verse. Peter cannot follow Christ now because ...

1. Christ is going to die and go back to the Father. Now is not the time for Peter to die.
2. When Peter does enter through the door of death to be absent from the body and present with the Lord, history tells us that Peter was crucified on a cross just like Christ, but with one minor difference. Peter asked to be hung upside down because he did not feel worthy enough to die in the same manner as hi savior, Jesus Christ. This will be mentioned again in the John 21:18-19 commentary.

37Peter said unto him, Lord, why cannot I follow thee now? I will lay down my life for thy sake. 38Jesus answered him, Wilt thou lay down thy life for my sake? Verily, verily, I say unto thee, The cock shall not crow, till thou hast denied me thrice.

This is a perfect example of why we need our feet washed from time to time (spiritually speaking). Even though we have believed on Jesus Christ and cleansed with the washing of water by the word (Ephesians 5:26), we, just like Peter, *mess up* or pick up things of this world from time to time. As a result, we need a little spiritual cleaning by those that love us unconditionally as Christ does.

John 14

He that hath seen me hath seen the Father – John 14:9: Jesus claims to have equality with the Father

[1]**Let not your heart be troubled: ye believe in God, believe also in me.**

If you (a saved and born-again believer in Christ) have a troubled heart, it is because you let your heart get that way. There is no other way to interpret this verse because God just commanded us to not let our hearts be troubled. Then, He explains how to do that: **ye believe in God, believe also in me**.

This takes us all the way back to the truth we discussed in chapter 1 while referencing Romans 1. Every single person born into this world has a knowledge manifested in them that there is a God to whom they are accountable (Romans 1:18-21). Jesus states this fact with an added piece of information: **believe also in me**. These disciples, as well as everyone else, should believe in Jesus just as much as they believe in God. This will be further discussed in verse 27.

[2]**In my Father's house <u>are</u> many mansions: if it were not so, I would have told you. I go <u>to prepare</u> a place for you.**

I am speculating here a little, but it appears to me there must have been a common teaching among the Jews that God's house did not have mansions. Jesus could be simply refuting such false teaching, because why else would He have said, **if it were not so, I would have told you**?

Also, notice the wording Jesus uses. **In my Father's house are** (present tense) **many mansions. I go to prepare** (future tense) **a place for you**. The mansions were not yet prepared. They are there, just not yet ready. My question for the Calvinist, who believes there are a *predetermined number* of people to be saved, is, "If God truly did choose only a select group of people to be saved, whom you call the elect, why did He not already have His house prepared for them?"

Biblically speaking, no person is predestined until the moment they are saved (Ephesians 1, Romans 8). Someone must first put their faith and trust in Christ, THEN their destination is predetermined. That destination is to be with Christ.

[3]**And If I go and prepare a place for you, I will come again, and receive you unto myself; that where I am, there ye may be also.**

The soon coming of our Lord and Savior Jesus Christ is a saved person's blessed hope (Acts 23:6, 1 Thessalonians 2:19, 4:13-18, Titus 2:13). The only two ways we will leave this present world is by way of the grave (2 Corinthians 5:8), or by Christ catching away His church at the start of the seven-year period of tribulation (1 Thessalonians 4:13, 1 Corinthians 15:51-52). That is a hope this world does not have (Ephesians 2:12).

Without a doubt, Christ will come again. The proof of this fact is a logical one indeed. Everything else Jesus said would happen has happened; therefore, simple logic dictates that Christ will come again. Even Titus 1:2 tells us He cannot lie!

I also want to draw to your attention to Jesus' wording: **that <u>where</u> I am, <u>there</u> ye may be also**. Jesus just brought out the truth of His Father's house is being prepared for the disciples, and us as well. Contextually, Jesus could have said, "There in those mansions, ye may be also with me," and it would be true but not true enough. If you think about it, that is how we read the verse, but it is not the truth of the statement.

The average Christian boasts how they will one day be absent from the body to walk on streets of gold in a city with pearl gates for ALL ETERNITY. But that is not quite the truth. The Bible accurately states in 2 Corinthians 5:8 **we are confident, I say, and willing rather to be absent from the body, and to be <u>present with the Lord</u>**. The truth is not that we will be in heaven for all eternity, but that we will be with Christ for all eternity. A very subtle difference but it must be addressed because our problem is that we place more emphasis on the place Jesus has prepared rather than placing that emphasis on Him.

After the great tribulation has run its course, and Jesus sets up His rule and reign of the Kingdom of Heaven here on this earth for 1,000 glorious years, every saved member of the church will be WITH HIM, in that kingdom ruling and reigning WITH HIM. Do you see my point? **Where I am** (that is in heaven or on earth), **there ye may be also**.

⁴And whither I go ye know, and the way ye know. ⁵Thomas saith unto him, Lord, we know not whither thou goest; and how can we know the way?

I have read Thomas' words over the years, and for the longest time they bothered me more than they were a blessing. I do appreciate his honesty, but I cannot help but wonder and be bothered by why he does not know what Jesus is talking about after spending three years with Christ. Why does he not know? Was he not listening? We have several recorded instances in the

146

Bible where Jesus told His disciples He would die, rise again after three days, and return unto the Father, so why does Thomas not get it?

The blessing comes in when I realize that, like Thomas, I may have to spend years reading a passage of the Bible repeatedly before the truth of God's word is finally understood. So, this verse may be a little bit of a disappointment, but it is a blessing to know that if Thomas did not understand a few things after spending daily time with Christ, I surely will not understand everything in the Bible the first time through. That is why we must **study to shew thyself approved unto God, a workman that <u>needeth not to be ashamed</u>, rightly dividing the word of truth** (2 Timothy 2:15). When we come across those passages that are hard to be understood (2 Peter 3:16), we simply have to ask Christ for wisdom (James 1:5) and He'll give it as He sees fit.

⁶**Jesus saith unto him, I am the way, the truth, and the life: no man cometh unto the Father, but by me.**

All religions do not eventually get you to the same place. There are not many different roads that eventually lead to heaven. **No man cometh unto the Father, but by me**! Judaism does not believe in Jesus so it will not get you unto the Father. Islam does not believe in Jesus so it will not get you unto the Father. Hinduism, Mormonism, Catholicism, and every other "-ism" that does not believe in the finished work of Jesus Christ at Calvary as the ONLY means of coming unto the Father will not get you there. **Enter ye in at the strait gate: for wide is the gate, and broad is the way, that leadeth to destruction, and many there be which go in thereat: Because strait is the gate, and narrow is the way, which leadeth unto life, and few there be that find it** (Matthew 7:13-14).

This American society we live in today does not like to hear verses like John 14:6. Political correctness, and an open mind are what Bible believing Christians are expected to adopt, but why is it that Christian's are expected to change instead of everyone else adopting the truth of the Bible? Jesus is the only way! Every other religion must go. **Neither is there salvation in any other: for there is none other name under heaven given among men, whereby we must be saved** (Acts 4:12).

They also claim we need to "coexist," but according to John 14:6 that is not possible. Bible Christianity has nothing in common with any other religion or belief. Just look at the *coexist* stickers on the back of people's car representing Islam, Pacifism, Gay Rights, Judaism, Paganism, Taoism, and Christianity and think for even a brief second about what they believe.

"Islam wants to kill Gay Rights, Judaism, Christianity, and Pacifism. If Islam got its way, Taoism and Paganism would convert or die. Pacifism can only offer non-violent resistance to Islam. The problem is Islam has no trouble suppressing dissent with violence, so Pacifism would be wiped out. Gay Rights has been suppressed by all religions, which makes it intolerant of Islam, Judaism, and Christianity. Judaism is threatened by annihilation not only by Islam but also by Pacifism who supports Islam over Judaism. Paganism and Taoism are statistically insignificant but needed to help the sticker make sense. The sticker is directed against Christianity, but Christianity poses no threat to the others."[32]

After considering all that, please tell me how those groups can coexist.

EXTRA NOTES

- Jesus is the way of truth. **But there were false prophets also among the people, even as there shall be false teachers among you, who privily shall bring in damnable heresies, even denying the Lord that bought them, and bring upon themselves swift destruction. And many shall follow their pernicious ways; by reason of whom the way of truth shall be evil spoken of** (2 Peter 2:1-2).

- Jesus is the way into the Holiest of all[33] by a new and living way. **The Holy Ghost this signifying, that the way into the holiest of all was not yet made manifest, while as the first tabernacle was yet standing...Having therefore, brethren, boldness to enter into the holiest by the blood of Jesus, By a new and living way, which he hath consecrated for us, through the veil, that is to say, his flesh** (Hebrews 9:8 and 10:19-20).

- Jesus is the way of escape. **There hath no temptation taken you but such as is common to man: but God is faithful, who will not suffer you to be tempted above that ye are able; but will with the**

---

[32] Quotation comes from a tract sold and distributed by TractPlanet.com.
[33] The Holiest of all (Hebrews 9:3) is the inner most room of the Tabernacle/Temple where God resided on the mercy seat atop the Ark of the Covenant. It is also necessary to note that this room is often referred to as the Holy of Holies, however that name never appears in scripture.

temptation also make a way to escape, that ye may be able to bear it (1 Corinthians 10:13).

- Jesus is the way of righteousness. **For if after they have escaped the pollutions of the world through the knowledge of the Lord and Saviour Jesus Christ, they are again entangled therein, and overcome, the latter end is worse with them than the beginning. For it had been better for them not to have known the way of righteousness, than, after they have known it, to turn from the holy commandment delivered unto them** (2 Peter 2:20-21).

[7]**If ye had known me, ye should have known my Father also: and from henceforth ye know him, and have seen him.** [8]**Philip saith unto him, Lord, shew us the Father, and it sufficeth us.**

Philip, are you like Thomas and have not been listening? Jesus just said that you have seen the Father and know Him. Oh, how these disciples are so much like us (well, me at least): not noticing the simple truths right in front of them.

[9]**Jesus saith unto him, Have I been so long time with you, and yet hast thou not known me, Philip? he that hath seen me hath seen the Father; and how sayest thou then, Shew us the Father?**

Seeing Jesus Christ is the same as seeing the Father. They are one. I have lost count on how many times I may have mentioned this throughout this commentary, but I am going to say it repeatedly if necessary. Jesus is either all truth, or the biggest liar that has ever lived. The correct statement is that He is THE TRUTH.

Please also recall the commentary from John 1:18 where we addressed the supposed contradiction in the Bible around this idea of seeing God. If you would like two more examples of men who beheld God in the Old Testament, reference Exodus 24:10 and Isaiah 6:1. Based on this verse, and what we discussed in John 1:18, men saw Jesus while looking at God.

[10]**Believest thou not that I am in the Father, and the Father in me? the words that I speak unto you I speak not of myself: but the Father that dwelleth in me, he doeth the works.** [11]**Believe me that I am in the Father, and the Father in me: or else <u>believe me for the very works' sake</u>.**

In John 5:36, we discussed how the works Jesus performed were works God the Father gave Him to finish, and they testified that the Father sent Jesus into the world. Now, Jesus is asking us to look at those works and understand that they testify unto us to believe that Jesus is in the Father and the Father is in Jesus.

Reference Isaiah 35:4-6 for further proof. **Say to them that are of a fearful heart, Be strong, fear not: behold, your God will come with vengeance, even God with a recompence; he will come and save you.** So, God is coming. What will He do? **Then the eyes of the blind shall be opened, and the ears of the deaf shall be unstopped. Then shall the lame man leap as an hart, and the tongue of the dumb sing: for in the wilderness shall waters break out, and streams in the desert.** Jesus did exactly what scripture said God would do. Jesus must be God!

[12]Verily, verily, I say unto you, He that believeth on me, the works that I do shall he do also; and greater works than these shall he do; because I go unto my Father.

You must keep verses like this in its context, or you will easily make the mistake of believing people who claim they have the power to heal, receive poisonous snake bites without being hurt, restore the sight of the blind, and all this other stuff that only applied to the Apostles (Acts 4:33, 5:12).

Verse 10 just told us that Jesus speaks WORDS (those words are not of Himself, but of the Father), and after the words are spoken, the Father performs WORKS. Therefore, after believing on Jesus Christ, we will be able to speak the words of God found in the Holy Bible, and if people will hear and believe, God will perform His work of saving their soul. The reason we have the capability of performing greater works than what Christ was able to do is because Christ was limited to one body in one region of the earth. God the Holy Spirit now dwells within the bodies of every single believer all over the earth, so naturally God will be able to perform greater works through us because the Holy Spirit is not limited to one body.

If the verse did refer to miracles as works (which we now know it doesn't), who do you know that claims to be a faith healer has ever raised a man from the grave after being dead for four days? Which of those fakers has successfully healed every single person they attempted to heal like Christ did? None! When those fakers are not able to con someone into believing in their *mystical powers,* they claim the person they are trying to heal does not have sufficient faith. My response to that is, when did Christ or the apostles ever put forth faith as a requirement for someone to receive healing? Not one!

[13]**And whatsoever ye shall ask in my name, that will I do, that the Father may be glorified in the Son.** [14]**If ye shall ask any thing in my name, I will do it.**

Here we go again. Another verse we must keep in its context, or we will be tempted to use it incorrectly.

The common teaching today associated with this verse is that if you want something to be given to you from God, just name it and claim it. In other words, demand God to give you what you want, but just make sure you use the magic words: "in Jesus' name." I am sure someone will criticize me for oversimplifying, but that is exactly what is preached.

If that were true, then please give me one example in the Bible of someone who demanded something from God. The only example I know of is Satan demanding God to turn stones into bread in Matthew 4:3. I sure do not want to follow Satan's example.

The truth of this verse, contextually, is that God will only do that which produces one common result: **that the Father may be glorified in the Son**. If your request of God does not glorify the Son, God is not required to answer your request.

God wants us to have the spiritual walk and relationship with Him as Christ had with the Father. Christ wanted the Father's will to be accomplished and not His own for He said in Luke 22:42, **not my will, but thine, be done**. If we desire God's will to be accomplished in our life, we will more than likely only ask of God to accomplish that which directly correlates with His desires instead of asking amiss that we may consume it upon our own lusts (James 4:3).

[15]**If ye love me, keep my commandments.**

Jesus is not asking much of us **for this is the love of God, that we keep his commandments: and his commandments are not grievous** (1 John 5:3). If we love Him, we should desire to keep His commandments.

People say they cannot handle or do not like all these rules associated with Christianity, but what else can you do in this life without rules? There are rules, guidelines, boundaries, etc. in everything we do. Nobody has a problem with those rules. They only have a problem with God's commandments. Thus, the conclusion is simple. Such people truly have a problem with God. That is why they do not like His commandments.

16And I will pray the Father, and he shall give you another Comforter, that he may abide with you for ever;

Clearly there is a trinity.

The New Testament epistles teach that when a person is saved, they receive the Holy Spirit. Some churches believe that someone can commit a certain sin that causes them to *fall from grace* and lose their salvation; therefore, if they die without becoming *re-saved,* they will die in their sin and go to hell. If that were true, this verse says the Holy Spirit will go to hell with those individuals considering He abides with them FOREVER. Obviously, that is not going to happen so such teaching is false.

17Even the Spirit of truth; whom the world cannot receive, because it seeth him not, neither knoweth him: but ye know him; for he dwelleth with you, and shall be in you. 18I will not leave you comfortless: I will come to you.

We have already discussed that seeing Jesus is the same as seeing the Father, and knowing Jesus is the same as knowing the Father. Since the Father, Jesus, and the Spirit are one (1 John 5:7 with John 1:1), this same truth must apply to the Spirit. When you see Jesus, you see the Spirit. Only believing can allow you to see (vs. 7-10).

Why can the world not receive the Spirit? The answer is John 1:11-12. **He [Jesus] came unto his own, and his own received him not. But as many as received him, to them gave he power to become the sons of God, even to them that believe on his name**. Those that do not believe on Jesus cannot receive Him, thus they cannot receive the Spirit.

The last part of the verse: **he dwelleth** (present progressive tense) **with you, and shall be** (future tense) **in you**, is a dispensational matter. The Holy Spirit did not dwell inside an individual prior to Calvary. There were only a few exceptions to this throughout the Old Testament (Isaiah 63:11 for example). The Spirit was most often described as being upon an individual, in front of or before an individual, behind, beneath, and beside individuals. That's why Jesus states "with you" in the present tense. However, these disciples are about to receive the Spirit to dwell within them, and every believer after Calvary shall receive the Spirit in them at the precise moment of belief.[34]

---

[34] See the author's work: Acts for additional insight and commentary involving this truth.

¹⁹Yet a little while, and the world seeth me no more; but ye see me: because I live, ye shall live also. ²⁰At that day ye shall know that I am in my Father, and ye in me, and I in you.

Jesus is going to go to the cross, die, resurrect three days later, and return unto the Father for a *little while* (more on that in just a moment). Since **light is come into the world, and men loved darkness rather than light, because their deeds are evil** (John 3:19), they will not receive Jesus and cannot receive the Spirit, so the world cannot see Him anymore. As for believers, we see Him daily working in our lives as well as in the lives of others, and because He lives, **we shall live also**. I say Praise God!

It is evident that these disciples do not understand exactly what Jesus is talking about. At least, not until His resurrection. We on the other hand, reading these words with the Holy Spirit living within us, see clearly what Jesus is saying. So, comparing us in this present moment to them during these events, we can see much clearer than they can. Why is that? It is because of the Holy Spirit living within us. **Howbeit when he, the Spirit of truth, is come, he will guide you into all truth: for he shall not speak of himself; but whatsoever he shall hear, that shall he speak: and he will shew you things to come** (John 16:13).

What about this saying, *yet a little while*? It has been 2,000 years since Jesus resurrected so how can that be a little while? The truth of Daniel 9 and Acts 1:7 is that God determined 490 years from Israel's return to the Promised Land out of Babylonian captivity until the end of the world. After 483 years, the Bible says that the Messiah was to be cut off (Daniel 9:26). This happened when Christ was taken to be crucified. So, according to God's timetable there are only 7 years remaining until He wraps up His work with mankind. Those last 7 years are the Great Tribulation period.[35]

To keep this simple, God has essentially turned off the clock. According to His time keeping, there are only 7 years until Christ returns to this earth for the second time. That is truly a *little while* in the grand scheme of things.

²¹He that hath my commandments, and keepeth them, he it is that loveth me: and he that loveth me shall be loved of my Father, and I will love him, and will manifest myself to him. ²²Judas saith unto him, not

---

[35] See the author's work: <u>Matthew</u> for additional insight and commentary involving this truth.

Iscariot[36], Lord, how is it that thou wilt manifest thyself unto us, and not unto the world? **[23]Jesus answered and said unto him, If a man love me, he will keep my words: and my Father will love him, and we will come unto him, and make our abode with him. [24]He that loveth me not keepeth not my sayings: and the word which ye hear is not mine, but the Father's which sent me.**

Have you ever met someone in your Christian walk that God just seems so real to them? You talk with them about God and their face, along with their demeanor, radiates to you the love they have for Him. Why is that? It is because those individuals love God enough to keep His commandments and God responds by …

1. Loving them
2. Coming unto them, and
3. Abiding with them.

Someone might say, "God loves everyone equally." I agree with you, but don't miss the two mentions of the word AND in v. 23.

Read the verses again. The verses above say that when someone truly loves God, they will keep His commandments. As a result of keeping His commandments, God will love them AND manifest Himself to them.

The undeniable truth about vs. 21-24 is this: If you want God to manifest Himself to you – I mean to experience Him in such a way that it seems He is physically standing right next to you, or you experience Him in such a way that you are completely convinced He is with you everywhere you go (Hebrews 13:5), then love Him enough to keep His commandments. He (the Father, the Son, and the Holy Ghost) will as a result manifest Himself to you like you have never experienced Him before. That is a fact.

[25]These things have I spoken unto you, being yet present with you. [26]But the Comforter, which is the Holy Ghost, whom the Father will send in my name, he shall <u>teach you all things</u>, and bring all things to your remembrance, whatsoever I have said unto you.

First, v. 26 is my favorite verse to lean on in support of the Bible being one hundred percent correct and without error. Many Bible colleges,

---

[36] God is very careful to separate Judas Iscariot from the other people named Judas in the Bible. In fact, there are 6 total: 1. A disciple – the brother of James (Luke 6:16) who is also called Thaddaeus/Lebbaeus (Matthew 10:2-4, Luke 6:14-16), 2. A disciple – Judas Iscariot, 3. The Lord's brother (Matthew 13:55), 4. Judas of Galilee (Acts 5:37), 5. Judas of Damascus (Acts 9:11), and 6. Judas Barsabas (Acts 15:22).

based on what I have heard and been told, teach that the writers of the Gospels did the best they could to remember every detail of what Jesus said and did during His ministry, but surely, they could not have recalled everything correctly. This verse refutes such thinking because the Holy Ghost brought everything to their remembrance of what Jesus said and did. I say Hallelujah. You truly can rest assured the Bible is right and without error.[37]

Secondly, please be careful with how you use the word "all" when handling verses containing that word. If we do not limit the word strictly to the context of the passage in which it's found, we might try to teach things incorrectly. So, let's reexamine the context.

God can teach you to know and understand the way unto the Father (v.5). He can teach you to know and understand that seeing Jesus is the same as seeing the Father (v.9). He can teach you His commandments (v.21). He can teach you how not to let your heart be troubled (v.1 and v.27). He can even teach you the meaning of being born again (John 3). Ultimately, He will teach us the meaning and understanding of whatsoever He has said unto us through His word (v.26).

[27]Peace I leave with you, <u>my peace</u> I give unto you: not as the world giveth, give I unto you. Let not your heart be troubled, neither let it be afraid.

God has given us a peace that is not of this world and passes all understanding (Philippians 4:7). The reason for that is because He has given us HIS peace. What a remarkable thing!

In just a few short hours Christ will be betrayed by His friend (Psalm 41:9), arrested, tortured beyond anyone's imagination, and lead away to be crucified on a cross. John 18:4 tells us He knew all this was going to happen, and He does not try to avoid it! He is calm. He is unafraid. He is not even worried about what He will face. That very same peace has been given to us and is precisely why we can avoid letting our hearts be troubled and afraid.

[28]Ye have heard how I said unto you, I go away, and come again unto you. If ye loved me, ye would rejoice, because I said, I go unto the Father: for my Father is greater than I. [29]And now I have told you before it come to pass, that, when it is come to pass, ye might believe.

Christ is going to go to the Father, and surely that would be cause for sorrow among His disciples who have spent so much time with Him over the

---

[37] See the author's work: <u>Mark,</u> for information regarding the translation of the King James Bible into the English language.

past few years. This is very similar to how we feel when a family member or close friend passes away. However, that should be a time of rejoicing. Not only because those friends and loved ones have moved on to spend eternity with our Lord, because they believed on Him, but we have a promise: Christ will come again. Just as these men will see Christ again, we shall see our loved ones again as well that have died in faith.

[30]**Hereafter I will not talk much with you: for the prince of this world cometh, and hath nothing in me.** [31]**But that the world may know that I love the Father; and as the Father gave me commandment, even so I do. Arise, let us go hence.**

The next 3 chapters record 1,935 direct words of Christ. That is 23.7% of the entire Gospel. Therefore, if those words are considered *not much* talk, there must be loads that God did not allow John to record. That is why the last verse of John says **And there are also many other things which Jesus did, the which, if they should be written every one, I suppose that even the world itself could not contain the books that should be written. Amen**.

What we do have recorded here in John is exactly what we need from God to believe that Jesus is God, that He came to finish the work the Father gave Him to do, and that He loves the Father. **These are written, that ye might believe that Jesus is the Christ, the Son of God; and that believing ye might have life through his name** (John 20:31).

John 15

¹**I am the <u>true</u> vine, and my Father is the husbandman.**

If Jesus is the vine that is true, who or what is the vine that is false? It is a necessary question we must ask. If Jesus simply wanted to compare Himself to a vine, He would not have included the word true. Thus, there must be a vine these disciples are aware of that is false for Jesus to be the vine that is true.

Our search needs to begin in the Old Testament. **Now will I sing to my wellbeloved a song of my beloved touching his vineyard. My wellbeloved hath a vineyard in a very fruitful hill: And he fenced it, and gathered out the stones thereof, and planted it with the choicest vine, and built a tower in the midst of it, and also made a winepress therein: and he looked that it should bring forth grapes, and it brought forth wild grapes. And now, O inhabitants of Jerusalem, and men of Judah, judge, I pray you, betwixt me and my vineyard. What could have been done more to my vineyard, that I have not done in it? wherefore, when I looked that it should bring forth grapes, brought it forth wild grapes? And now go to; I will tell you what I will do to my vineyard: I will take away the hedge thereof, and it shall be eaten up; and break down the wall thereof, and it shall be trodden down: And I will lay it waste: it shall not be pruned, nor digged; but there shall come up briers and thorns: I will also command the clouds that they rain no rain upon it. For <u>the vineyard of the LORD of hosts is the house of Israel</u>, and the men of Judah his pleasant plant; and he looked for judgment, but behold oppression; for righteousness, but behold a cry** (Isaiah 5:1-7). Israel is the only other vine mentioned in scripture and must be the false vine Jesus is comparing Himself to.

God just told us in Isaiah that He planted the **choicest vine** which He personally chose Himself. It is the nation of Israel chosen to be a peculiar people and God placed them **in a very fruitful hill**. A land flowing with milk and honey that God delivered them unto out of Egyptian bondage (Psalm 80:8). What does God do next? He promised to protect them from their enemies if they did not turn aside to other gods and would obey Him that delivered them. Israel did not listen. They were supposed to bring forth the best fruit, but instead brought forth **wild grapes**. **What more could have been done** by God on behalf of Israel? Nothing.

As a result of Israel's disobedience, God turns them over to the hands of their enemies. He took **away the hedge thereof** and refused to do anything more on Israel's behalf. They were to **lay in waste** and be **trodden down** by their enemies.

All the reasons as to why this happened can be summarized by Hosea 10:1. Israel **is an empty vine, <u>he</u> bringeth forth fruit unto <u>himself</u>: according to the multitude of <u>his</u> fruit <u>he</u> hath increased the altars; according to the goodness of <u>his</u> land they have made goodly images.** Look at the use of the personal pronouns: he, himself, and his. Israel completely refused to follow God and instead did things according to their own desires, thoughts, inclinations, and intentions to satisfy their own lusts. God was in no way, shape, or form acknowledged despite all He had done on their behalf. Because of this, Israel is the false fine.[38]

[2]Every branch in me that beareth not fruit he taketh away: and every branch that beareth fruit, he purgeth it, that it may bring forth more fruit.

We must stay in the context here. Isaiah 5:1-7 told us how God did all He could to make Israel produce good grapes instead of wild ones. The same idea applies to Christians in the New Testament age. Every born-again believer in Christ does indeed bear fruit (v.5) and God will do everything necessary for us to bear more fruit.

Therefore, we will get a little ahead of ourselves as far as these verses are considered and address the belief of Christians being cast out and burned (v.6) because of not bearing fruit. Consider the facts…

- Israel, the false vine, produced fruit but it was bad.
- Christ, the true vine, produces fruit that is good.
- The husbandman, God the father, of the false vine Israel, did not prune or dig the vine Israel because it produced bad fruit.
- The husbandman, God the father, of the true vine Jesus Christ, purges the branches so they will produce more fruit.

Do you see how completely contrary these vines and the fruit they bear are one to another?

Considering that every person in Christ bears fruit, what happens when a branch stops bearing fruit? The husbandman will take it away. That is far different than what God the Father did unto Israel. For them, He let

---

[38] Reference Jeremiah 2:21, and Psalm 80:8-15 for additional support regarding Israel as a vine.

158

them lay in waste, without pruning, without protection, and without a means of defense. In another word: desolate. Therefore, given the fact that all Christians bear fruit as a direct result of believing on Christ, the only reason they would stop bearing fruit is by means of entering through the doorway of death. At that moment, God takes them away.

If you are still not convinced that is what God is talking about in these verses, then consider an example of the picture God just presented. Look at a tree. The trunk is essentially the vine, and the branches are obviously the branches. Every branch on that tree, if it is alive, will produce a bud in the springtime of the year because of the vine supplying the necessary nourishment to the branch. Then, the buds will bloom, and fruit will be produced. Once the branch dies, no fruit can nor will result. The branch is dead, and for that tree to produce more fruit on the living branches, the dead ones need to be taken away.

This verse cannot possibly support the false idea that *if* Christians do not bear fruit, God will take away their salvation. Verse five plainly states that every branch in Christ (i.e., those that have trusted Him as their Lord and savior) bears fruit. So, the idea that some Christians are unfruitful goes completely against scripture.

One more cross-reference just in case it is needed: Mark 4:3-20. This is the parable of the sower. **Hearken; Behold, there went out a sower to sow: … the sower soweth the word … And some fell on good ground, and did yield fruit that sprang up and increased, and brought forth, some thirty, and some sixty, and some an hundred … And these are they which are sown on good ground; such as hear the word, and receive it, and bring forth fruit, some thirtyfold, some sixty, and some an hundred**. Do you see? All that hear the word and receive it bear fruit. Some just simply bear more than others.

What fruit is it we bear? We need to keep reading before we can answer that question.

³Now ye are clean through the word which I have spoken unto you.

This is the truth we discussed in John 13:8. The only way we are clean is through the word of God. By believing on Jesus Christ based on what is written in God's word, we are considered washed and cleansed (Ephesians 5:25-27, Titus 3:5).

⁴Abide in me, and I in you. As the branch cannot bear fruit of itself, except it abide in the vine; no more can ye, except ye abide in me.

This is simple logic. A branch that is not attached to the vine cannot produce fruit. That pictures us in Christ, and no person can bear fruit unless they abide in Him.

⁵I am the vine, ye are the branches: He that abideth in me, and I in him, the same bringeth forth much fruit: for <u>without me ye can do nothing</u>.

Before we discuss the fruit that all Christians bear, another fact needs to be addressed: **without me ye can do nothing**. Christians can, and often do, fall into the prideful snare of the devil after they decide to do something for Jesus Christ to further the gospel. They want everyone to know what they have done and accomplished. They want everyone to praise them. They want the glory that belongs to Jesus Christ.

Some pastors want members and visitors in the congregation to be in awe of their sermon delivery. Teachers want the listeners to be impressed with their Bible knowledge and understanding of the scriptures. Those are just two examples. The ultimate truth is that everything they have learned, and the knowledge they possess was passed on to them from someone that also had the same knowledge and understanding passed on to them. **There is no new thing under the sun** (Ecclesiastes 1:9).

Let's look at this scenario within the context of what we have read in John. Imagine a branch comparing itself to another branch to boast or show off the fruit it bears by saying, "Look at me and what I've done." Now let's ask a simple question: "what has the branch done to bear that fruit?" God is the one who sent the nurturance of sunshine and rain to keep the vine healthy and alive. God is the one who created the soil the vine's roots take root in. God, the vine, is the one who takes the water from the roots, up the vine, to the branches to help the fruit bud that sprouts in the springtime to bloom. God is also the one who created the bees and insects who pollinate that fruit bud for that bud to become a piece of fruit. So, again I ask: "what has the branch done to bear that fruit?" The answer is nothing **for without me ye can do nothing**!

All the abilities we possess, and the talents we have, combined with our knowledge and understanding of God's word that was developed and shaped by other godly men and women only proves one thing: God has been very good to us!

Christian, please allow the Holy Ghost to work in you using the abilities and talents God has given you to bring forth an abundance of fruit. Not to bring you glory, but to bring glory to God.

In order to determine what fruit Christians bear as a result of abiding in Christ Jesus, we need to reference Galatians 5:22. **The fruit of the Spirit is love, joy, peace, longsuffering, gentleness, goodness, faith, Meekness, temperance: against such there is no law**. Just take an honest look at these nine fruits and ask yourself if you can perform them on your own ability. Someone might say yes. However, let's examine a few of them under a likely scenario.

Can you honestly be gentle, loving, longsuffering, and good to someone that has said bad things about you? Maybe that someone made false accusations about you to someone else. Will you be as loving, gentle, longsuffering, and good to them as you are to your spouse, parents, or children who have not wronged you in any way? That is the honest approach you need to examine these verses, and you then should see clearly that you cannot bear these fruits apart from God.

⁶**If <u>a man</u> abide not in me, he is cast forth as a branch, and is withered; and men gather them, and cast them into the fire, and they are burned.**

This verse is often used incorrectly by taking it out of its context to teach that men can lose their salvation and thus burn in the last day. However, the context is about Jews saving themselves from this untoward generation (Acts 2:40) by spiritually getting out of the nation of Israel and into Christ.

Notice the grammar of verses one through five and compare them to verse six. When Jesus is speaking to the disciples directly, He says **ye**. Now He changes the conversation to a broader scope that includes any man not abiding in Him. Thus, the accurate response to these verses is, "If you abide in Him, you will bear fruit and are clean through the word. BUT, if a man (a Jew based on the context and cross references) decides not to receive the word of God to abide in Jesus, he will eventually be gathered up and burned by men." God is not the one doing the burning. This is true nationally for the Jewish nation, and on the individual level which includes all Gentiles.

Just look through history for support that men burned Jews. While the Jews were in Babylonian captivity, they were cast into the fiery furnace. In Europe from the thirteenth to the eighteenth century, Jews were burned at the stake under the movement of the Roman Catholic Inquisition. In 1348 and 1349 Jews were blamed for the black plague and thus burned consequently. Hitler during World War II burned the bodies of the Jewish people. Time and time again men chose to burn Jews.

On the individual level, anyone that rejects Christ will be cast into the lake of fire: the second death (Revelation 20:11-15). In Matthew 13:24-30 and 37-43, we read a parable of the kingdom of heaven where a man sowed good seed in his field. While he, and the men that oversaw the field slept, his enemy came in and sowed tares among the wheat. It was decided to let them grow together until the harvest where they would be separated. The wheat would be gathered into the barn and the tares would be bound and burned. This is interpreted in verses 36-43. **He that soweth the good seed is the Son of man; The field is the world; the good seed are the children of the kingdom; but the tares are the children of the wicked one; The enemy that sowed them is the devil; the harvest is the end of the world; and the reapers are the angels. As therefore the tares are gathered and burned in the fire; so shall it be in the end of this world. The Son of man shall send forth his angels, and they shall gather out of his kingdom all things that offend, and them which do iniquity; and shall cast them into a furnace of fire: there shall be wailing and gnashing of teeth. Then shall the righteous shine forth as the sun in the kingdom of their Father. Who hath ears to hear, let him hear**. Matthew 13 describes angels doing the burning, while John 15:6 describes men doing the burning. This is not a contradiction because all angels, according to your Bible, are men.

[7]If ye abide in me, and my words abide in you, ye shall ask what ye will, and it shall be done unto you.

Jesus shifts the conversation back to the disciples and reiterates what we have previously discussed in John 14:13: If God's words abide in you, then when you ask something of the Father that is in accord with the Father's will and His word, He will indeed answer your request.

[8]Herein is my Father glorified, that ye bear much fruit; so shall ye be my disciples.

God will work on us by pruning and cutting when necessary that we bear much fruit. I so doing, He is glorified.

[9]As the Father hath loved me, so have I loved you: continue ye in my love. [10]If ye keep my commandments, ye shall abide in my love; even as I have kept my Father's commandments, and abide in his love. [11]These things have I spoken unto you, that my joy might remain in you, and that your joy might be full. [12]This is my commandment, That ye love one another, as I have loved you. [13]Greater love hath no man than this, that a man lay down his life for his friends. [14]Ye are my friends, if ye do whatsoever I command you.

The Father loved the Son, and nothing would or could change the Father's love for Him. This same expression of love was manifested from Jesus Christ toward His disciples, and nothing would or could change His love for them. Judas Iscariot was a devil and soon to be a betrayer, but Jesus loved him as a friend even during the betrayal (Matthew 26:50). Simon Peter would deny Jesus three times, but Jesus still loved him. The disciples on several occasions showed their self-centeredness by once reasoning among themselves as to who should be the greatest (Luke 9:46). James and John even desired to sit beside Jesus in glory (Mark 10:35-37). Many people would get discouraged, frustrated, and even angry at such a display of pride, but not Jesus. **He loved them unto the end** (John 13:1).

Jesus commanded us to **love one another, as I have loved you**. What a commandment! We must look beyond one another's faults, failures, and shortcomings and love them no matter what. How do we do that? By abiding in His love as He abided in the Father's love. Every time someone mistreated Jesus, He knew the Father loved Him. Every time someone did something to Him that would cause a carnal man to act out in the flesh, He knew the Father loved Him. So, every time someone does something to us that makes our skin crawl, we must remember that Jesus loves us. He put our lives ahead of His. He has given us His joy that our joy might be full. So, we can walk in the Spirit bearing fruit no matter what people do, or say, or how they treat us.

[15]Henceforth I call you not servants; for the servant knoweth not what his lord doeth: but I have called you friends; for all things that I have heard of my Father I have made known unto you.

Hallelujah! God does not consider us a servant but a friend! What other religion on this earth views their god in such a way? Not one.

Not only does He consider us a friend, but we are joint heirs with Christ (Galatians 4:7). We are kings and priests (Revelation 1:6). We were also given power to become the sons of God (John 1:12, 1 John 3:1-2). Oh, what life there is to be in Christ!

[16]Ye have not chosen me, but I have chosen you, and ordained you, that ye should go and bring forth fruit, and that your fruit should remain: that whatsoever ye shall ask of the Father in my name, he may give it you.

Do you see that you cannot bear fruit of yourself? It is all about Christ. He chose us and ordained us that we should bring forth fruit, and that the fruit should remain all because we abide in Him (v.5 & 16). He cleaned us through the word that He gave (v.3). He purges us that we may bring forth more fruit (v.2). Our joy is full all because He spoke unto us His word (v.11). Do you see? Truly, we can do nothing without Him!

To the pastor, preacher, evangelist, deacon, teacher, etc., I ask the same question. Do you see what these verses also say? Christ chose you. Christ ordained you. If you are boasting about you, and what you are doing, or what you have done, or what you are going to do, I say STOP. Christ is the one bringing forth fruit in your life, so stop making everything about you when everything should truly be about everyone else. Want proof?

- 1 Timothy 1:12: **And I thank Christ Jesus our Lord, <u>who hath enabled me</u>, for that he counted me faithful, putting me into the ministry.** Praise the Lord for faithful leaders in our churches, but it is Christ who enables them.
- Acts 20:28: **Take heed therefore unto yourselves, and to all the flock, over the which the Holy Ghost hath made you overseers, to feed the church of God, which he hath purchases with his own blood.** It is all about Christ and His flock. Not you. Feed them.
- Ephesians 4:11-12: **And he gave some, apostles; and some, prophets; and some, evangelists; and some, pastors and teachers; <u>For</u> the perfecting of the saints, <u>for</u> the work of the ministry, <u>for</u> the edifying of the body of Christ.** Christ gave you a part of His flock for serving them, not you. It is all about them.

[17]These things I command you, that ye love one another.

I would to God that every single person in a leadership role in churches across this country would understand and take heed to these verses. Christ comes first, and everyone else comes in behind Him in a close second. If only the church leaders would put other's lives ahead of their own (v.13), then perhaps all Christians would follow their example.

That is why Christ gave spiritual leadership. Recall Ephesians 4:11-12 with verses 13-16: **Til <u>we all</u> come in the unity of the faith, and of the knowledge of the Son of God, unto a perfect man, unto the measure of the stature of the fullness of Christ: That <u>we</u> henceforth be no more children, tossed to and fro, and carried about with every wind of doctrine, by the sleight of men, and cunning craftiness, whereby they lie in wait to deceive; But speaking the truth in love, <u>may grow up</u> into him in all things, which is the head, even Christ: From whom <u>the whole body</u> fitly joined together and compacted by that which every joint supplieth, according to the effectual working in the measure of every part, maketh increase of the body unto the edifying of itself in love.**

[18]**If the world hate you, ye know that it hated me before it hated you.** [19]**If ye were of the world, the world would love his own: but because ye are not of the world, but I have chosen you out of the world, therefore the world hateth you.**

The world first hated Christ (**without a cause** – v.25), and once you are in Him it is only natural that the world will hate you. What if you have done nothing wrong? Christ did nothing wrong, and they still hated Him. What if you do not deserve to be hated? Christ did not deserve to be hated, but He was hated regardless. We just simply need to know and understand that it is not us they hate, but Him in us.

Now, this truth only extends so far. If you are a Christian and you lie to your neighbor who hates you as a result, it is you they hate. Not Christ. If you are a Christian and you do someone wrong or do something to someone that Christ would never do, those people hate you because of what you did, not Christ.

[20]**Remember the word that I said unto you, The servant is not greater than his lord. If they have persecuted me, they will also persecute you; if they have kept my saying, they will keep yours also.** [21]**But all these things will they do unto you for my name's sake, because they know not him that sent me.**

That fact is Christians will be persecuted for Christ's sake. As we just mentioned, the world is persecuting Christ.

Reference Acts 8:1-3 with 9:3-5. **And at that time there was a great persecution against the church which was at Jerusalem; and they were all scattered abroad throughout the regions of Judaea and Samaria, except the apostles. And devout men carried Stephen to his burial, and made great lamentation over him. As for Saul, he made havock of the church, entering into every house, and haling men and women committed them to prison. And as he journeyed, he came near Damascus: and suddenly there shined round about him a light from heaven: And he fell to the earth, and heard a voice saying unto him, Saul, Saul, why persecutest thou me? And he said, Who art thou, Lord? And the Lord said, I am Jesus whom thou persecutest.** Men and women of the church may have been hauled into prison, but it was the Lord Jesus Christ being persecuted.

Further proof that Jesus is the one being persecuted in the believer is seen when you look at when the persecutions started. It was not until the church received the Holy Spirit after Christ ascended back to the Father. In Luke 10:17, seventy disciples were sent out to preach and they came back rejoicing. No persecutions. In Matthew 15:2, the scribes and Pharisees had a problem with the disciples not washing their hands, but they went to Jesus with the matter and not the disciples. We will soon see in John 18:8 that the twelve disciples were not even arrested with Jesus in the garden even though Peter attacked one of the soldiers. However, once you begin reading of the acts of the Holy Spirit inside the believer in the book of Acts, the persecutions start happening to the believers. It is Christ in the believer the persecutions are direct toward.

²²If I had not come and spoken unto them, they had not had sin: but now they have no cloke for their sin. ²³He that hateth me hateth my Father also. ²⁴If I had not done among them the works which none other man did, they had not had sin: but now have they both seen and hated both me and my Father. ²⁵But this cometh to pass, that the word might be fulfilled that is written in their law, They hated me without a cause.

Jesus came into this world and preached about their sin, and completely removed any "cloak" they might have been hiding behind to justify their own righteousness. They, like us, are sinners. Jesus, the Light, came into this world to reprove it, and you will either receive that light or you won't. It is that simple. **And this is the condemnation, that light is come into the world, and men loved darkness rather than light, because their deeds were evil** (John 3:19).

²⁶But when the Comforter is come, whom I will send unto you from the Father, even the Spirit of truth, which proceedeth from the Father, <u>he shall testify of me</u>: ²⁷And <u>ye also shall bear witness</u>, because ye have been with me from the beginning.

If the Comforter's responsibility is to testify of Jesus, and the disciples are also supposed to bear witness of Jesus, what do you think our responsibility is? We are supposed to do likewise.

There are 7 witnesses in John that testify to the deity of Jesus: the Father (John 5:32, 37; 8:18), the Son (John 8:14; 18:37), the Holy Spirit (John 15:26; 16:13-14), the written word (John 1:45; 5:39, 46), Jesus' works (John 5:17, 36; 10:25; 14:11; 15:24), the forerunner (John 1:7; 5:33-35), and the disciples (John 15:27; 19:35; 21:24).

John 16

If I go not away, the Comforter will not come unto you; but If I depart, I will send him unto you – John 16:7: Jesus directs the Holy Spirit

¹**These things have I spoken unto you, that ye should not be offended.**

In the previous chapter, Jesus commanded His disciples to love one another as He had loved them, and that they would be hated and persecuted by the world because the world hated Him.

Great peace have they which love thy law: and nothing shall offend them (Psalm 119:165). This soon coming persecution will not offend the disciples because they love Christ and His word. We too can keep from being offended if we would love Him, love His word, and love others as He does.

Jesus also speaks these words because He is about to bring up the ultimate persecution many of these disciples will face – death. Excluding Judas Iscariot, only one apostle's death is recorded in the Bible. The rest we must refer to historical accounts to learn which ones were killed. Simon Peter was crucified upside down. James the son of Zebedee was killed by Herod (Acts 12:1-2). It is believed that Andrew was crucified in Achaia and reported that Matthew was killed in Ethiopia. James the son of Alpheus was supposedly stoned by the scribes and Pharisees.

²**They shall put you out of the synagogues: yea, the time cometh, that whosoever killeth you will think that he doeth God service. ³And these things will they do unto you, because they have not known the Father, nor me.**

The persecution account that immediately comes to my mind involves Paul. The interesting part is his testimony of being blameless in committing those actions. **If any other man thinketh that he hath whereof he might trust in the flesh, I more: Circumcised the eighth day, of the stock of Israel, of the tribe of Benjamin, and Hebrew of the Hebrews, as touching the law, a Pharisee; Concerning zeal, persecuting the church; touching the righteousness which is in the law, <u>blameless</u>** (Philippians 3:4-6). He just claimed that he was blameless in every aspect of the Jewish religion including persecuting the church. How can he say that?

Deuteronomy 13:1-4. **If there arise among you a prophet, or a dreamer of dreams, and giveth thee a sign or a wonder, And the sign or the wonder come to pass, whereof he spake unto thee, saying, Let us go**

167

after other gods, which thou hast not known, and let us serve them; Thou shalt not hearken unto the words of that prophet, or that dreamer of dreams: for the LORD your God proveth you, to know whether ye love the LORD your God with all your heart and with all your soul. Ye shall walk after the LORD your God, and fear him, and keep his commandments, and obey his voice, and ye shall serve him, and cleave unto him. And that prophet, or that dreamer of dreams, shall be put to death; because he hath spoken to turn you away from the LORD your God, which brought you out of the land of Egypt, and redeemed you out of the house of bondage, to thrust thee out of the way which the LORD thy God commanded thee to walk in. So shalt thou put the evil away from the midst of thee**. In Paul's mind, according to that passage, Jesus and any of His followers needed to be put to death. He thought he was doing God service. His only error was not recognizing that Jesus Christ was God.

[4]But these things have I told you, that when the time shall come, ye may remember that I told you of them. And these things I said not unto you at the beginning, because I was with you.

Could you image how these disciples might have responded if Jesus had brought this truth up at the beginning, three years ago? Jesus could have said, "I'll make you fishers of men. Come, follow me and die at the hand of those who hate me and seek to persecute me." I do not want to read into what is not written in the Bible, but Jesus knew what He was doing by keeping this information until the end.

[5]But now I go my way to him that sent me; and none of you asketh me, Whither goest thou? [6]But because I have said these things unto you, sorrow hath filled your heart.

I would say sorrow filling their hearts is a natural response. These disciples have forsaken everything to follow Christ. They have been with Him daily for years only to now find out they will be persecuted to the point of death, and Jesus will soon be leaving them. However, something grand will soon be coming.

[7]Nevertheless I tell you the truth; It is expedient for you that I go away: for if I go not away, the Comforter will not come unto you; but if I depart, I will send him unto you. [8]And when he is come, he will reprove the world of sin, and of righteousness, and of judgment:

The Comforter will only come when Jesus leaves. This is expedient, in other words necessary. He is coming to reprove the world of three things, and the fastest way to reprove all the world is to send the Holy Spirit. He is not limited to a single body like Jesus but will indwell all believers (1 Corinthians 6:19). Once those believers begin preaching the gospel in Jerusalem, Judaea, Samaria, and into the utter most parts of the world (Acts 1:8), then every single person on earth will hear the good news of Jesus Christ.

Someone might say that is impossible, cannot be done, and has not been done, but they would be wrong. Colossians 1:3-6 and 23 tells us that all the world indeed did hear the gospel. **We give thanks to God and the Father of our Lord Jesus Christ, praying always for you, Since we heard of your faith in Christ Jesus, and the love which ye have to all the saints, For the hope which is laid up for you in heaven, whereof ye heard before in the word of the truth of the gospel; Which is come unto you, <u>as it is in all the world</u> ... and which was <u>preached to every creature which is under heaven</u>.** Therefore, if a place in the world exists today that has never heard the gospel, it is not God's fault because at one time every place had heard it. If someone today has not heard, it is because Christians stopped doing what they have been called to do: preach the gospel.

[9]Of sin because they believe not on me;

The first thing the Holy Spirit will reprove the world of is sin. The truth regarding every person on earth is that we are all sinners (Romans 3:23), and we all are going to die because of our sin (Romans 6:23). Once we die, we will either be absent from the body and present with the Lord (2 Corinthians 5:8) or we will open our eyes being in torments in hell (Luke 16:23). Drinking alcohol will not send you to hell. Committing fornication or adultery will not send you to hell. Cheating on your taxes or lying to your employer on your time sheet will not send you to hell. Committing murder or suicide will not send you to hell. The one sin that will cause you to wake up in hell is not believing on the Lord Jesus Christ. If you believe on Him, you will be in His presence for all eternity. If you do not believe you will spend all eternity in torments. It is that simple. It does not matter your opinion. It does not even matter if you think that to be unfair. Romans 1 says everybody knows they are accountable to God that created them, so they are without excuse. You must believe on the Lord Jesus Christ (Romans 10:9)

[10]Of righteousness, because I go to my Father, and ye see me no more;

Many people like to set their own standard of righteousness. Some compare themselves among themselves, which is not wise (2 Corinthians 10:12) thinking their standing with God is ok because of how they view themselves in relation to whom they have compared themselves. Others imagine that if their good outweighs their bad, they will go to heaven based on merit. None of these views are accurate for the true measure of righteousness is Jesus Christ who you cannot see anymore. You must be as holy as He is holy, as right as He is right, as pure as He is pure, as undefiled as He is undefiled. Nobody even comes close to measuring up to Jesus Christ. When God compares our own righteousness to His Son, our **righteousness are as filthy rags** (Isaiah 64:6).

It seems the most popular religious view of obtaining righteousness is to think that one can earn it through law keeping. They follow the law (well the parts they agree with and think they can follow habitually) the best they can while thinking that is sufficient grounds for righteousness. Let's see what Romans 10:1-4 has to say.

Brethren, my heart's desire and prayer to God for Israel is, that they might be saved. For I bear them record that they have a zeal of God, but not according to knowledge. Israel, along with many so-called Christians of our day, have a zeal for God, but that zeal is not in line with the truths of the Bible. Why? **For they being ignorant of God's righteousness, and going about to establish their own righteousness, have not submitted themselves unto the righteousness of God.** They ignore the truth that is right in front of them in God's word. **For Christ is the end of the law for righteousness to every one that believeth.** Righteousness cannot be obtained through law keeping for **by the deeds of the law there shall no flesh be justified in his sight** (Romans 3:20). If someone offends in one point, they are guilty of all the law (James 2:10).

Christ puts an end to falsely following the law to hopefully earn righteousness. **The righteousness of God which is by faith of Jesus Christ unto all and upon all them that believe: for there is no difference: For all have sinned, and come short of the glory of God; Being justified freely by his grace through the redemption that is in Christ Jesus: Whom God hath set forth to be a propitiation through faith in his blood, to declare his righteousness for the remission of sins that are past, through the forbearance of God; To declare, I say, at this time his righteousness: that he might be just, and the justifier of him which believeth in Jesus** (Romans 3:22-26). If you want a righteous standing with God, you must believe on

His Son, the Lord Jesus Christ, and God will freely give you His righteousness.

[11]Of judgment, because the prince of this world is judged.

If you think you will not be judged by God, you better take a closer look at the prince of this world: Lucifer, the devil.

Ezekiel 28:12-15: **Thus saith the Lord GOD; Thou sealest up the sum, full of wisdom, and perfect in beauty. Thou hast been in Eden the garden of God; every precious stone was thy covering, the sardius, topaz, and the diamond, the beryl, the onyx, and the jasper, the sapphire, the emerald, and the carbuncle, and gold:** His complexion is perfect with beauty unmatched to any other creature in God's creation. Even his covering is described with the most precious and valuable stones found on the earth. He has more wisdom and knowledge of the scripture than the most faithful of preachers and could lead just about anyone he chooses into transgression (that is why we must resist him – James 4:7) as he did to Eve in the Garden of Eden.

The workmanship of thy tabrets and of thy pipes was prepared in thee in the day that thou wast created. Imagine the most beautiful singing voice you have ever heard, and whomever it is you have in mind does not even come close to Lucifer's voice.

Thou art the anointed cherub that covereth; and I have set thee so: thou wast upon the holy mountain of God; thou hast walked up and down in the midst of the stones of fire. He was once in the very presence of God – something none of us can proclaim. Not only was he in God's presence, but he was the anointed cherub that covered God's throne.

Thou wast perfect in thy ways from the day that thou wast created, til iniquity was found in thee. He was perfect, until he did one thing wrong. He became prideful. Before we reference the portion of scripture describing his fall, I must ask you, "How do you compare to him? If Lucifer was described with such adoration from God and was judged, what makes you think you won't be judged?"

Isaiah 14:12-15 describes his act of pride. **How art thou fallen from heaven, O Lucifer, son of the morning! how art thou cut down to the ground, which didst weaken the nations!** Notice the punctuation. No question is being asked. It is an exclamatory statement as to say, "Lucifer, the anointed cherub, the one with such beauty, wisdom, and perfection has fallen!" **For thou hast said in thine heart, I will ascend into heaven, I will exalt my throne above the stars of God: I will sit also upon the mount of** the congregation, in the sides of the north: **I will** ascend above the heights of the clouds; **I will** be like the most High. **Yet thou shalt be brought down to hell, to the sides of the pit**. He wanted to be like God and was judged as a result.

All these religious people who make up their own measurements for righteousness, and their own standards for being right with God are just like Lucifer. They are putting themselves on the throne. They may not see it that way, but that is the truth of the matter, and every single person will indeed be judged unless they believe on the one person who has already received their judgment on the cross at Calvary – Jesus Christ.

[12]**I have yet many things to say unto you, but ye cannot bear them now.**

I would dare say the rest of what Christ wanted to say is found in the remainder of the New Testament.

[13]**Howbeit when he, the Spirit of truth, is come, he will guide you into all truth: for he shall not speak of himself; but whatsoever he shall hear, that shall he speak: and he will shew you things to come.** [14]**He shall glorify me: for he shall receive of mine, and shall shew it unto you.**[39]

The Holy Spirit makes a point to glorify the Son by making all things about Jesus Christ. We should do the same.

Plus, verse 13 gives another benefit to Christ leaving and the Holy Spirit coming: He will guide you into all truth by showing it unto you. He is not just going to give you the truth but will guide you into the truth in your **study to shew thyself approved unto God, a workman that needeth not to be ashamed, rightly dividing the word of truth** (2 Timothy 2:15). Thank you, Lord!

[15]**All things that the Father hath are mine: therefore said I, that he shall take of mine, and shall shew it unto you.**

Here is another verse to make note of that supports the trinity. The Holy Spirit will take what the Father has (of which things belong to the Son) and will show it unto the disciples, and us as well.

[16]**A little while, and ye shall not see me: and again, a little while, and ye shall see me, because I go to the Father.** [17]**Then said some of his disciples among themselves, What is this that he saith unto us, A little while, and**

---

[39] In these two verses there are 7 things the Holy Spirit does for saved people.

ye shall not see me: and again, <u>a little while</u>, and ye shall see me: and, Because I go to the Father? [18]They said therefore, What is this that he saith, <u>A little while</u>? we cannot tell what he saith. [19]Now Jesus knew that they were desirous to ask him, and said unto them, Do ye enquire among yourselves of that I said, <u>A little while</u>, and ye shall not see me: and again, <u>a little while</u>, and ye shall see me?

The three words, *a little while* is used seven times in those four verses. Considering the number seven means perfection or completion, Jesus must go away in a little while, and after a little while appear again to His disciples to complete something for them. What is it He will complete? Read the next few verses.

[20]**Verily, verily, I say unto you, That ye shall weep and lament, but the world shall rejoice: and ye shall be sorrowful, but your sorrow shall be turned into joy.** [21]**A woman when she is in travail hath sorrow, because her hour is come: but as soon as she is delivered of the child, she remembereth no more the anguish, for joy that a man is born into the world.** [22]**And ye now therefore have sorrow: but I will see you again, and your heart shall rejoice, and your joy no man taketh from you.**

Scripture often refers to the tribulation period as a woman in travail. However, the context of this woman in travail has nothing to do with the tribulation period. Jesus is going away in a little while (going to die on the cross) and these disciples will experience great sorrow because of losing Him. After a little while (three days and three nights later) He will rise from the dead, show Himself to these men, and their sorrow will be gone and not even remembered because of His return just like how a woman forgets the anguish of labor the moment her child is born.

So, let's answer the question we asked above. What will Jesus complete for His disciples? Verse 22 says that upon Jesus rising from the dead, the disciple's sorrowful hearts will be filled with joy and rejoicing, and this joy **no man taketh from you**.

This whole chapter, along with the latter part of chapter 15, has been … well, quite depressing. I mean come on. Put yourself in place of the disciples and imagine how you might feel hearing Jesus is leaving you, men will hate you (15:18), persecute you (15:20), put you out of places of worship (16:2), and even kill you (16:2). Not a single person would receive such words with gladness. However, the moment Jesus comes back from the grave, the disciple's sorrow will be gone and, in its place, will be such joy that no matter what the future holds for these men, nothing can take that joy away. What victory there is in Jesus Christ! What joy there is in Jesus Christ!

²³And in that day ye shall ask me nothing. Verily, verily, I say unto you, Whatsoever ye shall ask the Father in my name, he will give it you. ²⁴Hitherto have ye asked nothing in my name: ask, and ye shall receive, <u>that your joy may be full</u>.

Here is one more piece of truth to add to our previous discussions regarding the asking and receiving of the Father (John 14:13-14).

Our previous discussion yielded the truth that God will grant our requests, if …

1. The request is in accord with the Father's will, and
2. The request brings glory to the Father.

As a result of God answering our request(s), our joy may be full. Do you see the truth that our joy needs to be closely connected to Father's will to bring Him glory? The bottom line is that if we tie our joy to things, stuff, possessions, or even experiences we've fallen short of the mark. True joy is in Him, and Him alone.

²⁵These things have I spoken unto you in proverbs: but the time cometh, when I shall no more speak unto you in proverbs, but <u>I shall shew you plainly of the Father.</u> ²⁶At that day ye shall ask in my name: and I say not unto you, that I will pray the Father for you:

Jesus has *told* them quite plainly in times past that if you have seen Jesus, you have seen the Father (John 14:9), for He and the Father are one (John 10:30). But Jesus will *show* them of the Father the day these disciples see Him after His resurrection.

²⁷For the Father himself loveth you, because ye have loved me, and have believed that I came out from God.

The love of God is a broad topic indeed, but I will keep my comments narrowed and focused to a simple truth. First, revisit the discussion from John 14:21 about experiencing God's love.

God indeed loves the whole world enough to die for it (John 3:16). What an astonishing truth! He even calls us sons of God (John 1:12, 1 John 3:1) because of us believing on Him and calling upon Him. What an even grander truth! We are in the family of God. Abba, Father is the cry of our heart now (Galatians 4:6, Romans 8:15). Oh, what love the Father has for all men!

Do you see though that this love is wholly connected to Jesus Christ? Verse 27 proclaims that God the Father loves us simply because we love the Son. The remarkable thing to me about all this is that we only love the Son simply because the Son first loved us! **We love him, because he first loved us** (1 John 4:19).

He doesn't just ask for us to love Him. God is the one who initiated the love. Have you experienced God's love? Do you love Jesus Christ? Loving Jesus is the only way to experience the love of God.

[28]I came forth <u>from the Father</u>, and am come into the world: again, I leave the world, and go to the Father. [29]His disciples said unto him, Lo, now speakest thou plainly, and speakest no proverb. [30]Now are we sure that thou knowest all things, and needest not that any man should ask thee: by this we believe that thou camest forth <u>from God</u>.

Here are a couple of notes regarding the last statement of verse 30. Their belief that Jesus came from God has been brought up several times by different people throughout John.

- 3:2 – Nicodemus: **The same came to Jesus by night, and said unto him, Rabbi, we know that thou art a teacher come from God**
- 4:29 – Woman at the well: **Come, see a man, which told me all things that ever I did: is not this the Christ?** Christ comes from God.
- 6:14 – The multitude: **Then those men, when they had seen the miracle that Jesus did, said, This is of a truth that prophet that should come into the world**.
- 6:69 – The disciples: **And we believe and are sure that thou art that Christ, the Son of the living God**.
- 11:27 – Martha: **She saith unto him, Yea, Lord: I believe that thou art the Christ, the Son of God, which should come into the world**.

Also, compare what Jesus said in verse 28 to what the disciples said in verse 30. Jesus said He came from the Father, but the disciples said He came from God. Yes, they are one in the same, but, as far as the scripture suggests, nobody called God "the Father" until after they were indwelt with the Holy Ghost.

Why do believers call God their Father? Romans 8:14-17 gives us that answer. **For as many as are led by the Spirit of God, they are the sons of God. For ye have not received the spirit of bondage again to fear; but ye have received the Spirit of adoption, whereby we cry, Abba, Father. The Spirit itself beareth witness with our spirit, that <u>we are the children</u>**

of God: **And if children, then heirs; heirs of God, and joint-heirs with Christ; if so be that we suffer with him, that we may be also glorified together.**

[31]**Jesus answered them, Do ye now believe?** [32]**Behold, the hour cometh, yea, is now come, that ye shall be scattered, every man to his own, and shall leave me alone: and yet I am not alone, because the Father is with me.**

They do indeed believe that Jesus is come from God, but that will not keep them from fleeing when Jesus is taken into custody, in just a few short hours from now, to be put on trial for crucifixion.

[33]**These things I have spoken unto you, <u>that in me ye might have peace</u>. In the world ye shall have tribulation: but be of good cheer; I have overcome the world.**

This is a perfect verse to wrap up the chapter, and to conclude what the future holds for the disciples.   The chapter begins and ends with future trouble for these disciples, and Jesus basically tells them in both places not to be bothered or worried about the coming trouble brought on by the world. Why? He has overcome the world.

Jesus is leaving to go back to the Father, but He is not going to leave them comfortless. He will send the Holy Spirit to take up residence in their bodies to lead, guide, and direct them into all truth. He will also leave them with His peace (John 14:27), and His joy (John 15:11). Those are the reasons why the apostles were able to stare persecution, tribulation, trouble, and even death right in the face without being offended. Christ resides in them so they too can overcome the world. Oh, what peace, joy, and security there is to be in Christ!

John 17

And now, O Father, glorify thou me with thine own self with the
glory which I had with thee before the world was – John 17:5: Jesus
claims to have been with the Father before the world began

This chapter of John contains the longest conversation (prayer) between Jesus and God the Father in all the Bible and is so loaded with information and truth that I felt it necessary to provide commentary a little differently. An outline of the chapter is provided below, followed by commentary, and lastly finished with a few final notes.

The outline of the chapter is as followed:

- Jesus prays for Himself (v.1-5)
- Jesus prays for His disciples (v.6-19)
- Jesus prays for future believers (v.20-26)

¹These words spake Jesus, and lifted up his eyes to heaven, and said, Father, <u>the hour is come</u>; glorify thy Son, that thy Son also may glorify thee:

This is the seventh and final time Jesus will mention the hour of His death. He knows He will die in less than twenty-four hours (18:4), and this does not change His agenda even in the slightest. He came into this world full of grace and truth (1:12), lived as the express image of God (Hebrews 1:3) to glorify the Father in life (v. 4) without committing a single sin (Hebrews 4:5), and He wants to continue to do so in death. Amazing!

Oh, if only all the world would truly examine Jesus for who He is, and what He has done for them!

²As thou hast given him power over all flesh, that he should give eternal life to as many as thou hast given him.

Verses 1 and 2 are one sentence. The colon at the end of verse 1 means that what follows in verse 2 is going to explain why Christ needed the Father to glorify Him.

Christ just said that He must receive glory from the Father **that he should give eternal life** to those that would believe on Him. Without the Father giving Jesus that glorification, eternal life would not be available to mankind.

We must understand that Christ left the glory of heaven, where He was in the presence of the Father, to come down to this earth **to be <u>made sin</u>**

for us, who knew no sin; that we might be made the righteousness of God in him (2 Corinthians 5:21). He will indeed be made sin, but He does not want to be sinful upon being made sin for us. He has never sinned, nor had a desire to sin. Therefore, He pleads with the Father to receive glory from Him so that He can be made sin while at the same time have the glory He has always shared with the Father. The question is … How did all this come to pass? We will discuss that answer in verses 4 and 5.

[3]**And this is <u>life eternal</u>, that <u>they might know thee the only true God, and Jesus Christ, whom thou hast sent</u>.**

When sinners get asked, "Do you have eternal life," their answers are so often as far away from the truth of this verse as one can get.

"I've lived a pretty good life,"

"I've never killed anybody,"

"My good outweighs my bad,"

"I'd like to think so" … are all answers they use to try and justify that they deserve eternal life. This verse should settle the dispute once and for all.

Eternal life is knowing the ONLY true God, and Jesus Christ. If you believe in Allah, you do not have eternal life. If you believe in Voodoo, you do not have eternal life. If you believe in Buddha, you do not have eternal life. If you believe in the millions of gods within Hinduism, you do not have eternal life. There is only one true God and His Son Jesus Christ. Once someone is willing to receive that truth, they are on the right path. The next step is knowing Him.

What does it mean to know Him? Let me give you a simple scenario to explain. I could write down a list of all the attributes of my wife: hair color, weight, height, favorite foods, and activities, etc. Then, hand that list to someone who does not know her to read and study. Afterward I would ask, "Do you know my wife?" The answer is NO. They might know as much about her as I do because of reading that list, but they do not know her simply because they have never met her.

The same principle applies to knowing Jesus. Reading and studying His word to learn about Him and believing what you have read is essential to getting to know Him. However, knowing about Him is not the same as knowing Him. Knowing someone means the two individuals have met to form a relationship.

Have you ever met Jesus Christ? Do you have a relationship with Him, or do you just know about Him?

^{4}I have glorified thee on the earth: I have finished the work which thou gavest me to do. ^{5}And now, O Father, <u>glorify thou me with thine own self with the glory which I had with thee before the world was</u>.

He deserves to be glorified (Revelation 4:11). He has never known anything but a perfect relationship with the Father, and in the act of being made sin for us (2 Corinthians 5:21) He wants to have the glory He has always shared with the Father. What an amazing thing!

Before the world was, God the Father and God the Son were in a one hundred percent state of glory. They knew man would sin thus breaking the relationship between God and man, and there would only be one way to repair what had been broken. Since man severed the relationship through sin, a man would have to fix it without sin (Romans 5). Christ chose to sacrifice Himself before the foundation of the world (Ephesians 1:4, 1 Peter 1:20, Revelation 13:8), and when the fullness of the time was come, He left the glory of heaven to take on the form of a man (Philippians 2). He indeed lived without sin (Hebrews 4:15, 1 Peter 2:22), but now He is about to go to the cross to bear all the world's sin and iniquity in and on His body (1 Peter 2:4, Isaiah 53:6) and become a curse for us (Galatians 3:13).

It is vitally important that He receives glory from the Father when He goes to the cross. Without it He could not have died for us, nor would our salvation through Jesus Christ be available.

Go to Hebrews 2:7-9. **Thou madest him** [Adam] **a little lower than the angels; thou <u>crownedst him with glory</u> and honour, and didst set him over the works of thy hands: Thou hast put all things in subjection under his feet. For in that he put all in subjection under him, he left nothing that is not put under him. But now we see not yet all things put under him. But we see Jesus, who was made a little lower than the angels for the suffering of death, <u>crowned with glory</u> and honour.** Why must he receive this glory? **<u>That</u> he by the grace of God should taste death for every man.** Christ had to receive glory from the Father so that He could die for every man. Hallelujah!

Go to 1 Peter 1:18-21. **Forasmuch as ye know that ye were not redeemed with corruptible things, as silver and gold, from your vain conversation received by tradition from your fathers; But with the precious blood of Christ, as of a lamb without blemish and without spot: Who verily was foreordained before the foundation of the world, but was manifest in these last times for you, Who by him do believe in God, that raised him up from the dead, <u>and gave him glory</u>.** Why did the Father give Him this glory? **<u>That</u> your faith and hope might be in God.** God the Father glorifying God the Son upon the cross was vitally important for several reasons:

- It allowed all Old Testament scripture that foreshadowed and prophesied of Jesus Christ to be fulfilled.
- It allowed Christ to be made sin without being sinful.
- It allowed the man Christ Jesus (the last Adam) to finish a life without sin to pay the sin debt man owed, and restore the relationship severed by the first Adam's fall.
- It allowed Him to officially die for all men.
- It forever settled that man's only hope of being accepted by a holy and righteous God was to put their faith and trust in Jesus Christ.

[6]I have manifested thy name unto the men which thou gavest me out of the world: thine they were, and thou gavest them me; and they have kept thy word. [7]Now they have known that all things whatsoever thou hast given me are of thee. [8]For I have given unto them the words which thou gavest me; and they have received them, and have known surely that I came out from thee, and they have believed that thou didst send me.

God the Father sent John the Baptist to bear witness of Jesus Christ that all men through him might believe (John 1:6-7). The disciples received God's word through John that Christ is the Son of God (John 1:34), and the Lamb of God who would take away the sin of the world (John 1:29). As a result, they followed Jesus (John 1:37) and received the preaching of God's word through Him.

These verses show the vital importance of God's word. By hearing and receiving the word, you and I can **surely know** Christ came from the Father, He was sent by the Father, and His words came from the Father. To have such surety, God's words (the Bible) must be completely accurate and without error. We have that in the Authorized King James Bible.[40]

[9]I pray for them: I pray not for the world, but for them which thou hast given me; for they are thine.

Upon first hearing this, one might think this to be an unusual thing for Jesus to say. If Christ so loved the world that He gave himself for it (John 3:16), why would He not pray for it?

---

[40] See the author's work: Mark for additional commentary regarding the inerrancy of scripture.

The world in scripture refers to the people, kingdoms, nations, and their system that exists upon the earth (1 Samuel 2:8). It **is stablished, that it cannot be moved** (Psalm 93:1) fully consisting of **the lust of the flesh, and the lust of the eyes, and the pride of life,** which **is not of the Father** (1 John 2:16). Honestly, when considering those truths what in this world is worth praying for? Christ's prayers, as well as ours, are better directed at praying on behalf of the church. Not the world.

The only time prayer and the world come together in scripture is on behalf of the believer. Thus, the believer is still being prayed for.

I exhort therefore, that, first of all, supplications, <u>prayers</u>, intercessions, and giving of thanks, <u>be made for all men; For kings, and for all that are in authority</u>. Keep reading to understand why we pray for these people. **That we may lead a quiet and peaceable life in all godliness and honesty** (1 Timothy 2:1-2). These prayers for the world are on behalf of the believer.

Now, does this mean we should not pray for the lost to get saved? Should we refrain from praying for unsaved individuals with sickness and disease simply because they do not belong to God? No, I am not saying that at all. Jesus indeed loves all the world and every individual that has ever lived and will ever live. We should pray for them. I am simply pointing out broad based truths that directly relate to Christ's statements about not praying for the world.

[10]**And all mine are thine, and thine are mine; and I am glorified in them.** [11]**And now I am no more in the world, but these are in the world, and I come to thee. Holy Father, keep through thine own name those whom thou hast given me, that they may be one, as we are.**

Jesus prayed for two things.

1. The believers would be kept through God's own name – the security of the believer.

   Ephesians 1:13-14 tells us this request was answered. **In whom [Jesus] ye also trusted, after that ye heard the word of truth, the gospel of your salvation: in whom also after that ye believed, <u>ye were sealed</u> with that holy Spirit of promise, Which is the earnest of our inheritance until the redemption of the purchased possession, unto the praise of his glory.** See also Ephesians 4:30 and 1 Corinthians 1:21.

2. The believers would be one just as Jesus and the Father are one.

   1 Corinthians 12, Colossians 3:15, Romans 12:4-5 along with other verses tells us this request was answered. **For as we have many members**

in one body, and all members have not the same office: So we, being many, are one body in Christ, and every one members one of another (Romans 12:4-5).

¹²While I was with them in the world, I kept them in thy name: those that thou gavest me I kept, and none of them is lost, but the son of perdition; that the scripture might be fulfilled.

Judas Iscariot never believed on Jesus. He was the devil's minister transformed as a minister of righteousness (2 Corinthians 11:14-15) deceiving everyone including the disciples, fulfilling Psalm 41:9. **Yes, mine own familiar friend, in whom I trusted, which did eat of my bread, hath lifted up his heel against me**.

¹³And now come I to thee; and these things I speak in the world, that they might have my joy fulfilled in themselves.

Jesus just prayed that His joy would be in them to the full. This even applies to us today considering He is about to pray for future believers (us) in the following verses. To even try and begin to understand the level of joy He has, you must analyze the current situation.

Jesus knows exactly what is about to happen to Him (John 18:4), yet His joy is not affected in the slightest. **Wherefore seeing we also are compassed about with so great a cloud of witnesses, let us lay aside every weight, and the sin which doth so easily beset us, and let us run with patience the race that is set before us, Looking unto Jesus the author and finisher of our faith; <u>who for the joy that was set before him</u> endured the cross, despising the shame, and is set down at the right hand of the throne of God** (Hebrews 12:1-2).

He is going to be arrested, beaten, whipped, ridiculed beyond measure, and nailed to a cross to pay the sin debt of the entire human race. How is it possible He could enter such abuse while being joyous? That level of joy is exactly what He desires for all believers. Keep reading to find out how to get it.

¹⁴<u>I have given them thy word</u>; and the world hath hated them, because they are not of the world, even as I am not of the world.

The same measure of joy that Jesus had upon going to the cross can only be found through God's word. We look for joy in a new car, in a new house, in a new boyfriend or girlfriend. We look for it in a job, or a career, or in social media. We look everywhere for joy except for where God told us to look. True joy will only be found in the word of God.

[15]I pray not that thou shouldest take them out of the world, but that thou shouldest keep them from evil. [16]They are not of the world, even as I am not of the world. [17]Sanctify them through thy truth: thy word is truth. [18]As thou hast sent me in to the world, even so have I also sent them into the world. [19]And for their sakes I sanctify myself, that they also might be sanctified through the truth.

This is why people are not raptured the moment they get saved. He wants us to stay in the world because we are the only way lost people can hear the word of God to be saved. He told us to go into the world and preach the gospel. That applies to every saved child of God, not just preachers. Many people, maybe even you, have their joy affected because witnessing and telling others about Jesus is something they refuse to do.

Revisit John 15:10-11.

Christ wants us here in the world, obeying His word and following His direction. If you want full joy, keeping His commandments is the only way to get it. Again, just look at the situation. Christ set out to do the will of the Father and to please Him. As a result, upon facing death He has fullness of joy. Our daily routines will never measure up to what Christ is facing here. He desires to please the Father and has joy despite imminent death. We desire to please ourselves and cannot even find joy while at the grocery store. Truly, joy can only be found in the word of God with a desire to obey every word.

In the meantime, Christ is praying that we be kept from the evil that is ever present everywhere we go. Praise His name for that!

[20]Neither pray I for these alone, but for them also which shall believe on me through their word; [21]That they all may be one; as thou, Father, art in me, and I in thee, that they also may be one in us: that the world may believe that thou hast sent me. [22]And the glory which thou gavest me I have given them; that they may be one, even as we are one: [23]I in them, and thou in me, that they may be made perfect in one; and that the world may know that thou hast sent me, and hast loved them, as thou hast loved me.

Notice how many times Jesus prays for the unity of future believers compared to the number of times he prayed for the disciples to be united. Four times he made that statement for us, and only once for the disciples. I would dare say Jesus knew exactly what would happen in the future.

The book of Acts tells us how the early church had all things in common (Acts 2:44 and 4:32). They truly were united. Yet slowly and surely, they began to be separated from the body they were called unto to the point that God had to give His inspired word to the churches urging them to **stand fast in one spirit** (Philippians 1:27), to not forsake **the assembling of ourselves together, as the manner of some is** (Hebrews 10:25), and to not be divided (Romans 16:17, 1 Corinthians 11:18).

Today the Southern Baptist Association cannot and will not agree on any common ground according to the scripture. The Independents cannot get along with each other. The Lutherans have their ways, and the Methodist have theirs. Those that want no association with any kind of denomination call themselves non-denominationalists. It is no wonder why Jesus prayed so fervently for the unity of future believers.

[24]**Father, I will that they also, whom thou hast given me, be with me where I am; that <u>they may behold my glory</u>, which thou hast given me: for thou lovedst me before the foundation of the world.** [25]**O righteous Father, the world hath not known thee: but I have known thee, and these have known that thou hast sent me.** [26]**And I have declared unto them thy name, and will declare it: that <u>the love wherewith thou hast loved me may be in them</u>, and I in them.**

According to these verses, the evidence that Christ and the Father are one is seen through the love they have one for another. The church will only be able to unite as one body once every individual member of that body has the same love one for another as they have for themselves. I do not see this happening anytime soon.

Go into any Christian bookstore and what you will see is shelf upon shelf, and aisle upon aisle of books promoting self.

"Your Best Life Now"

"Become a Better You"

"How to Think and Grow Rich"

"How to Win Friends and Influence People"

"Love Your Life"

We need a little less love for self, and a lot more love for others. Seeking God's glory should be our focus, not seeking self-glorification. May God help us to love the brethren just like God the Father and Jesus Christ love one other. May He help us to seek His will to be done to glorify Him, and not to glorify ourselves.

FINAL NOTES
- Jesus stated several things to God the Father that He had done:
  - v.4) **I have glorified thee on the earth**
  - v.4) **I have finished the work which thou gavest me to do**
  - v.6) **I have manifested thy name unto the men which thou gavest me out of the world**
  - v.8) **I have given unto them the word which thou gavest me**
  - v.12) **those that thou gavest me I have kept, and none of them is lost, but the son of perdition**
  - v.14) **I have given them thy word**
  - v.18) **I have sent them into the world**
  - v.22) **the glory which thou gavest me I have given them**
  - v.26) **I have declared unto them thy name**

- Jesus stated several things to God the Father that the disciples had done:
  - v.6) **they have kept thy word**
  - v.7) **they have known that all things whatsoever thou hast given me are of thee**
  - v.8) **they have received the words**
  - v.8) **they have known surely that I came out from thee**
  - v.8) **they have believed that thou didst send me**

- Jesus requests to be glorified according to 7 reasons: His Sonship (v.1), the appointed time had arrived (v.1), power over all flesh had been given to Him (v.2), power to give eternal life had been promised Him (v.2), that men might know the Father (v.3), He had glorified the Father on earth (v.4), He had finished the work (v.4)

- Jesus asks three things for His people based on seven reasons:
  - That the Father will keep them from evil (v.15)
  - And sanctify them through the truth (v.17)
  - That they may behold His glory (v.24)
- They were the Father's gift to the Son (v.9)
- The Father has a personal interest in them (v.9-10)
- The Son's glory is connected with them (v.10)
- He was leaving them (v.11)
- He was leaving them in the world (v.11 & 15)
- Because of the world's hatred for them (v.14)
- Because He was sanctified for them (v.19)

185

- This chapter contains seven things about the relation of believers to the world:
    - We are given to Christ out of the world (v.6)
    - We are left in the world (v.11)
    - We are not of the world (v.14)
    - We are hated by the world (v.14)
    - We are kept from the evil in the world (v.15)
    - We are sent into the world (v.18)
    - We will show the world His love (v.23)

- Jesus prayed for seven things He desires for believers to have in common with Him:
    - The words (v.8)
    - Joy (v.13)
    - Sanctification (v.19)
    - Sending (v.18)
    - Separation (v.16)
    - Glorification (v.22)
    - Love (v.26)

John 18

To this end was I born, and for this cause came I into the world, that I should bear witness unto the truth – John 18:37: *Jesus professes to have come into the world for a specific purpose*

[1]**When Jesus had spoken these words, he went forth with his disciples over the brook Cedron, where was a garden, into the which he entered, and his disciples.**

The brook Kidron (Old Testament spelling) is where many pagan idols and groves were destroyed – see 2 Kings 23, and 2 Chronicles chapters 15, 29, and 30.

The garden is the garden of Gethsemane – see Matthew 26:36-46 and Mark 14:32-42.

[2]**And Judas also, which betrayed him, knew the place: for Jesus ofttimes resorted thither with his disciples.** [3]**Judas then, having received a band of men and officers <u>from the chief priests and Pharisees</u>, cometh thither with lanterns and torches and weapons.** [4]**Jesus therefore, <u>knowing all things that should come upon him</u>, went forth, and said unto them, Whom seek ye?**

He knew Judas would betray Him. He knew Judas would know where to look for Him, and He still went to the garden. The transfiguration account of Jesus in the Gospel of Luke explains why Jesus walks into a trap.

And, behold, there talked with him two men, which were Moses and Elias: Who appeared in glory, and spake of his decease which he should <u>accomplish</u> at Jerusalem (Luke 9:30-31). Jesus had long made up His mind to die for the sins of the whole world well before this day came, and He will stop at nothing to fulfill it. **Forasmuch as ye know that ye were not redeemed with corruptible things, as silver and gold, from your vain conversation received by tradition from your fathers; But with the precious blood of Christ, as of a lamb without blemish and without spot: <u>Who verily was foreordained before the foundation of the world</u>, but was manifest in these last time for you** (1 Peter 1:18-20). **And all that dwell upon the earth shall worship him, whose names are not written in the book of life of <u>the Lamb slain from the foundation of the world</u>** (Revelation 13:8).

Also note where Judas got the band of men: **<u>from</u> the chief priests and Pharisees**. These people are putting into motion what they set out to do in John 11.

[5]They answered him, Jesus of Nazareth. Jesus saith unto them, I am he. And Judas also, which betrayed him, stood with them. [6]As soon then as he had said unto them, I am he, <u>they went backward</u>, and fell to the ground.

His spoken word has enough power to knock these men down flat on their backs. Even at the battle of Armageddon in Revelation 19 you see the power of Jesus' spoken word. **And out of his mouth goeth a sharp sword, that with it he should smite the nations…and the remnant were slain with the sword of him that sat upon the horse, which sword proceeded out of his mouth: and all the fowls were filled with their flesh** (Revelation 19:15a, 21). What amazes me is these soldiers continue to carry out their orders. It speaks volumes to their loyalty for duty, but they surely had to wonder what they were getting themselves into.

There is also an interesting truth about scripture illustrated here. Every time someone is worshipping God, if they fall to the ground, they always fall forward onto their face. Whenever someone is fighting against God, if they fall to the ground, they always fall backward. Today, there are *faith healers* or whatever title they might give themselves, who claim to be able to heal people by waiving their coat at the individuals or smacking them on the forehead. Interestingly, if the people fall, they fall backward. Now, these *faith healers* might consider what they are doing to be worship, but the Bible illustrates there is something going on during these events quite contrary to biblical worship.

[7]Then asked he them again, Whom seek ye? And they said, Jesus of Nazareth.

I often smile after reading this passage because I imagine these men still lying flat on their back with Jesus standing over them when He says for the second time, "Whom seek ye?"

[8]Jesus answered, I have told you that I am he: if therefore ye seek me, let these go <u>their</u> way: [9]That the saying might be fulfilled, which he spake, Of them which thou gavest me have I lost none.

The soldiers should be giving the orders, but it is just the opposite. Jesus is the one in charge, which makes sense considering how much power His spoken word has.

Also, notice the words **let these go <u>their</u> way**. Recall back in the upper room, Jesus mentioned that every one of the disciples would be offended by Him. **Then saith Jesus unto them, <u>All ye shall be offended because of me this night</u>: for it is written, I will smite the shepherd, and the sheep of the flock shall be scattered abroad. Peter said unto him, Though I should die with thee, yet will I not deny thee. <u>Likewise also said all the disciples</u>** (Matthew 26:31, 35). They did exactly as He said they would by going *their* way.

[10]**Then Simon Peter having a sword drew it, and smote the high priest's servant, and cut off his right ear. The servant's name was Malchus.**

The only way I can figure Peter to be able to do this without causing any other injuries to Malchus' body is for him to attack as the soldiers are getting up from off the ground. Luke 22:36-49 gives a possible explanation for why Peter had a sword in the first place, and that Jesus **touched his ear, and healed him**.

These soldiers must be in bewilderment. They show up to make an arrest and get knocked to the ground by the *prisoner's* spoken word. While they are on the ground, Jesus does not run away. Then, when one of the soldiers is attacked, the man they are arresting has compassion on him and heals him. In the next verse, Jesus even rebukes Peter for attacking the man. No soldier anywhere has ever experienced something like this before.

[11]**Then said Jesus unto Peter, Put up thy sword into the sheath: the cup <u>which my Father hath given me</u>, shall I not drink it?**

The bottom line is that Jesus is going to the cross. That is why He rebukes Peter. Jesus could have fled away if He wanted to, but scripture must be fulfilled. **Then said Jesus unto him, Put up again thy sword into his place: for all they that take the sword shall perish with the sword. Thinkest thou that I cannot now pray to my Father, and he shall presently give me more than twelve legions of angels? But how then shall the scriptures be fulfilled, that thus it must be?** (Matthew 26:52-54)

Secondly, it was the Father who gave Jesus this cup to drink. Some might say that the Jews are responsible for Jesus being crucified. Others might say the Romans are responsible. They all played their part, but it was God who orchestrated all the events.

[12]**Then the band and the captain and officers of the Jews took Jesus, and bound him,** [13]**And led him away to Annas first; for he was father in law to Caiaphas, which was the high priest that same year.**

Please take note that both Annas and Caiaphas were the high priests. **Annas and Caiaphas being the high priests, the word of God came unto John the son of Zacharias in the wilderness** (Luke 3:2). This is not a normal situation. According to the Old Testament, only one person was supposed to be the high priest as illustrated when Aaron was selected as the first one. However, there have been times in scripture where more than one person occupied the position at the same time. See 2 Samuel 8 for an example.

[14]**Now Caiaphas was he, which gave counsel to the Jews, that it was expedient that one man should die for the people.**

See John 11:47-53 to cite where Caiaphas made such statements. Also, it is my understanding that the Jews would turn over a prisoner to Rome once a year that was guilty of a death penalty offense. This in turn kept Rome happy because they got to kill someone, thus deterring them from killing all the Jews.

Think of what that says about the high priest. He is supposed to be the spiritual leader of the nation, and his best advice is to allow the Romans to kill a Jew every year. I do not care to have someone like that looking out for my spiritual wellbeing.

[15]**And Simon Peter followed Jesus, and so did another disciple: that disciple was known unto the high priest, and went in with Jesus in the palace of the high priest.** [16]**But Peter stood at the door without. Then went out that other disciple, which was known unto the high priest, and spake unto her that kept the door, and brought in Peter.**

Just as was stated back in chapter 1, every Bible student ought to take another look at the disciples before drawing any definitive conclusions about who they were in society. This disciple (commonly accepted to be John) was not only known of the high priest but had enough connections and influence to get Peter in and out of this palace. I'd say he had a little higher status in society than a *dumb fisherman* as the disciples are so often described.

[17]**Then saith the damsel that kept the door unto Peter, Art not thou also one of this man's disciples? He said, I am not.**

This is Peter's first denial of Christ.

[18]**And the <u>servants and officers</u> stood there, who had made a fire of coals; for it was cold: and they warmed themselves: and Peter <u>stood</u> <u>with them</u>, and warmed himself.**

Notice the comparison between Peter and Judas. Here Peter is standing with the servants and officers that came and arrested Jesus just as Judas was doing back in the garden (v.5). When you are not following Jesus, you will wind up standing in the way of sinners. **Blessed is the man that walketh not in the counsel of the ungodly, nor standeth in the way of sinners, nor sitteth in the seat of the scornful** (Psalm 1:1).

[19]The high priest then asked Jesus of his disciples, and of his doctrine. [20]Jesus answered him, I spake openly to the world; I ever taught in the synagogue, and in the temple, whither the Jews always resort; and in secret have I said nothing. [21]Why askest thou me? ask them which heard me, what I have said unto them: behold, they know what I said.

Jesus was asked about His disciples and His doctrine, but the only answer He gives is regarding doctrine. The reason is because doctrine is all that matters. It is fixed and will not change. It is all truth. It is what will save your soul.

A disciple can stand for truth one minute and change that stand the next. A disciple can lie, curse, flee, or any number of such things. Look at the context here as an example. All the disciples went their way (v.8) and not Jesus' way. Judas betrayed the Son of God. Peter is there denying Jesus and will soon curse and swear at someone for asking him if he follows Christ (Mark 14:67-71). Do not focus your attention on men because they may disappoint you. Instead, focus all your attention on Christ and His doctrine.

[22]And when he had thus spoken, one of the officers which stood by struck Jesus with the palm of his hand, saying, Answerest thou the high priest so? [23]Jesus answered him, If I have spoken evil, bear witness of the evil: but if well, why smitest thou me?

Jesus has done nor said anything wrong, and He still gets treated this way. He knows exactly who He's talking to, and He's not going to change His words just because He happens to be standing in front of the high priest. God truly is no respecter of persons (Galatians 2:6, Acts 10:34, Romans 2:11, and 2 Samuel 14:14 are just a few examples).

Men have a problem with respecting persons, even though we shouldn't (Deuteronomy 16:19, James 2:1-9). Even Paul when standing before Ananias, the high priest, in Acts 23 said, **God shall smite thee, thou whited wall: for sittest thou to judge me after the law, and commandest me to be smitten contrary to the law?** Then as soon as he is rebuked for speaking to the high priest in such a manner, he basically apologizes by saying

I wist not, brethren, that he was the high priest. Not Jesus though. He stands His ground and does not apologize for what He said.

²⁴Now Annas had sent him bound unto Caiaphas the high priest. ²⁵And Simon Peter stood and warmed himself. They said therefore unto him, Art not thou also one of his disciples? He denied it, and said, I am not.

Here is the second denial.

²⁶One of the servants of the high priest, being his kinsman whose ear Peter cut off, saith, Did not I see thee in the garden with him?

If anybody could recognize Peter in a lineup, I think it would be this man.

²⁷Peter then denied again: and immediately the cock crew.

Jesus told Peter this would come to pass in John 13. Even though Peter did not believe Him, Jesus' words still came to pass.

²⁸Then led they Jesus from Caiaphas unto the hall of judgment: and it was early; and they themselves went not into the judgment hall, lest they should be defiled; but that they might eat the passover.

This is the clearest representation of religion I have ever seen in the Bible. They refuse to go into this Gentile judgment hall building because doing so would make them unclean according to their religion. However, bringing false accusations and lies against an innocent man during an unsanctioned trial is ok (Matthew 27:59-63). Toying with a woman's life in order to trap a man into saying something contrary to God's law is ok (John 8). Plotting murder is ok (John 11:49-53, John 12:10). God forbid though that they should go into a Gentile building. Do you see the hypocrisy?

It is no different than a person living like hell except for when they come to church. They will lie, cheat, steal, fornicate, backbite, commit adultery, divorce their spouses, get drunk, along with God knows what else, but come Sunday morning their hair is done just right, their clothes are perfect, and their demeanor on the outside is representative of someone honorable. Yet on the inside they are a two-fold child of hell. These Pharisees are just like that.

²⁹Pilate then went out unto them, and said, <u>what</u> accusation bring ye against this man? ³⁰They answered and said unto him, If he were not <u>a</u> malefactor, we would not have delivered him up unto thee.

That is not an answer to the question. Pilate wanted to know *what* Jesus had done, and they can only respond with, *He's a malefactor.* Well, if He is guilty of a crime then why not answer the question by stating the crime? The reason no crimes are presented is because Jesus is not guilty of breaking any laws. He has done nothing wrong. They just want Him dead.

³¹Then said Pilate unto them, Take ye him, and judge him according to your law. The Jews therefore said unto him, It is not lawful for us to put any man to death: ³²That the saying of Jesus might be fulfilled, which he spake, signifying what death he should die.

The Jews are under the control of the Roman government, and they cannot lawfully put anyone to death without Rome granting them permission. That is why they brought Him to Pilate. If this were not the case, they would have simply put Him to death by stoning. However, stoning is not how Jesus said He would die.

If you recall back to John 3:14 and John 12:22-24, Jesus made it very clear that He would be lifted up from the earth just as Moses lifted up the serpent on a pole in the wilderness. This implicated a crucifixion death. The interesting truth about this is that Jesus had come to this earth with Rome in control for this prophecy to come true. They were the only ones to crucify.

If Jesus had come a few hundred years prior, He would either have been thrown in the lion's den or tossed into a fiery furnace (Daniel 3 and 6). Arriving anytime later, Rome would no longer be in power thus making the prophecy null and void. Oh, no. God knew what He was doing. Christ was sent into the world **when the fullness of the time was come** (Galatians 4:4).

³³Then Pilate entered into the judgment hall again, and called Jesus, and said unto him, Art thou the King of the Jews? ³⁴Jesus answered him, <u>Sayest thou this thing of thyself</u>, or did others tell it thee of me?

That is the question everyone must answer. Most people know who Jesus is and what He did for the world, but is it something they can say of themselves? In other words, do they believe in Him or are they just repeating what they have heard?

³⁵Pilate answered, Am I a Jew? Thine own nation and the chief priests have delivered thee unto me: what hast thou done?

Since the Jews never answered Pilate's question from verse 29, he does not know why Jesus is there, nor what criminal accusations are against Him.

36 Jesus answered, My kingdom is not of this world: if my kingdom were of this world, then would my servants fight, that I should not be delivered to the Jews: but now is my kingdom not from hence.

This is a very important statement in your Bible. Many denominations teach that when Jesus *failed* to establish His kingdom on earth, He decided to establish the church as a back-up plan. However, look at this statement closely and you will see that Jesus did not *fail* at anything.

Jesus said that right now, His kingdom is (present tense) not of this world. When He came to the earth the first time, being born of a virgin, it was not to set up an earthly kingdom. It was to die on that cross in order to redeem the entire world. There is coming a day however, according to Revelation, that He will rule from a throne at Jerusalem. He just did not come to do that the first time.

37 Pilate therefore said unto him, Art thou a king then? Jesus answered, Thou sayest that I am a king.

Pilate may not know the accusations against Jesus, but He knows the proclamations that have circulated throughout the Jewish community about Jesus being a king. He has even talked about it himself according to this verse, and Jesus knows.

How? Jesus is God. Surely, Pilate now has cause to be concerned about the judgment he is about to make.

Something else that must be considered is what happened roughly thirty years prior to this event. Matthew 2 tells us that when king Herod received word that the King of the Jews was born in Bethlehem of Judea, he had every baby boy and girl two years of age and younger executed. I do not believe it is possible that thirty years later people have forgotten those events.

Then, just a few days ago the Jews were shouting **Hosanna: Blessed is the King of Israel that cometh in the name of the Lord** (John 12:13) as Jesus entered Jerusalem. Now, standing before Pilate is a man that fits the age and description that scared Herod into his murdering spree. Surely, Pilate is thinking: *Maybe Jesus really is the King of the Jews.*

To this end was I born, and for this cause came I into the world, that I should bear witness unto the truth. Every one that is of the truth heareth my voice.

Recall John 14:6: **Jesus saith unto him** [Thomas]**, I am the way, the truth, and the life: no man cometh unto the Father, but by me.** Jesus did not come to set up an earthly kingdom. He came to bear witness of Himself, and to end His life on the cross thus paying the wages of sin for all the world.

38Pilate said unto him, What is truth? And when he had said this, he went out again unto the Jews, and saith unto them, I find in him no fault at all.

Great Pilate! You should find no fault in Him, but apparently you were not listening because you completely missed everything Jesus said. He came to bear witness of **the truth**, and those that are **of the truth <u>heareth</u>** Him. Pilate responds with **what is <u>truth</u>**, instead of asking what is THE truth. Pilate was looking for information regarding the accusations being brought against Him. He was not looking for the truth about Jesus Christ. He did not even hang around long enough to receive an answer to the question. He just turned around and walked out.

Pilate is a good picture of lost people today. Many lost people know truth about Jesus, but they do not know Him. They know He was born of a virgin. They know He died on a tree. They know He performed miracles, but there is a big difference between knowing truth and knowing THE TRUTH. Knowing THE TRUTH is when someone personally knows Jesus Christ. If all you have is truth about who Jesus is without knowing Him, you are still lost in your sin.

39But ye have a custom, that I should release unto you one at the passover: will ye therefore that I release unto you the King of the Jews?

This brings us right back to Jesus' triumphal entry into Jerusalem. Pilate is bringing to their remembrance what they were shouting just a few days ago when they called Jesus their King. I'm sure he does this to appeal to the crowd to skirt the responsibility of passing judgment on Jesus. He is hoping this might give him a way out of the situation.

40Then cried they all again, saying, Not this man, but Barabbas. Now Barabbas was a robber.

WOW! These people are choosing Barabbas over Jesus. They are choosing a robber over someone that has healed their sick, raised their dead, cleansed their diseased, and so much more. That barely even describes the awful choice they are making. Notice the wording of the Bible passages below.

Matthew 27:15-16: **Now at the feast the governor was wont to release unto the people a prisoner, whom they would. And they had then**

a notable prisoner, called Barabbas. Not only was Barabbas a robber, but he is famous. Everybody knew of him and what he had done.

Mark 15:7: **And there was one named Barabbas, which lay bound with them that had made insurrection with him, who had committed murder in the insurrection**. Murder is what made him so famous, and it appears he committed the murder during a robbery.

Luke 23:17: **(For of necessity he must release one unto them at the feast.)** Pilate releasing a prisoner was necessary, and these people had to make a choice.

In summary … Every living person, just like these people, must make a necessary choice between Barabbas and Jesus. You cannot choose both. For one to live the other must die. Therefore, trying to live and please the world while at the same time trying to please God is impossible. There is no such thing as a worldly Christian. You are either carnal, or you are seeking after God. You cannot be both.

Also, you need to understand that if you choose Barabbas, he brings death. If you choose Jesus, He brings life (John 14:6). **Know ye not, that to whom ye yield yourselves servants to obey, his servants ye are to whom ye obey; whether of sin unto death, or of obedience unto righteousness?** (Romans 6:16). It seems to be an easy choice, but so many struggle with choosing to follow Jesus. As a result, they have no joy, no peace, and even their love has diminished. Those things are fruits of the Spirit (Galatians 5:22-23), and the reason people do not experience such things is because they have chosen Barabbas over Jesus.

John 19

When Jesus therefore had received the vinegar, he said, It is finished
– John 19:30: only God can proclaim the redemptive work complete

¹Then Pilate therefore took Jesus, and scourged him.

With all the movies in existence about these events, I am confident most people know this is more than just a beating. They are literally ripping the flesh from His body.

²And the soldiers platted a crown of thorns, and put it on his head, and they put on him a purple robe, ³And said, Hail, King of the Jews! and they smote him with their hands.

The soldiers took time to make this crown and place the purple robe on Him as mockery. **And when they had platted a crown of thorns, they put it upon his head, and a reed in his right hand: and they bowed the knee before him, and mocked him, saying, Hail, King of the Jews!** (Matthew 27:29)

Through their actions they are saying, "Jesus is proclaimed to be the King of the Jews, and this is what we think about that." How horrible this scene must have been to witness.

⁴Pilate therefore went forth again, and saith unto them, Behold, I bring him forth to you, that ye may know that I find no fault in him.

This is the third time Pilate has made that declaration. If he really found no fault in Him, WHY HAVE HIM SCOURGED AND MOCKED!? Pilate is just like the world. They try to be complacent without choosing a side to stand on, but when people try to remain neutral in order to avoid making a decision on whether or not to follow Jesus, they are actually making a decision. There is no grey area. You are either following Him, or not. Choosing to remain neutral is simply saying no to Christ.

Pilate even tries to say he is not at fault for the treatment of Christ. **When Pilate saw that he could prevail nothing, but that rather a tumult was made, he took water, and washed his hands before the multitude, saying, I am innocent of the blood of this just person: see ye to it.** (Matthew 27:24). There is only one problem. He is at fault because it all happened under his watch and authority.

⁵Then came Jesus forth, wearing the crown of thorns, and the purple robe. And Pilate saith unto them, Behold the man! ⁶When the chief

priests therefore and officers saw him, they cried out, saying, Crucify him, crucify him. Pilate saith unto them, Take ye him, and crucify him: for I find no fault in him.

Come on Pilate. If you find no fault in Him the only logical choice is to set Him free. Not to turn Him over to someone else for execution.

[7]The Jews answered him, We have a law, and by our law he ought to die, because he made himself the Son of God.

This hypocritical crowd is just as bad as Pilate. They try to turn to the law as justification for their actions, but they have completely abused the law up to this point. They held an unlawful trial against Jesus, they brought in false witnesses to lie against Him, and even misused the law long before this day (revisit John 18:28 commentary). The only just person in this whole scene is Jesus Christ. **His glory is above the earth and heaven** (Psalm 148:13).

[8]When Pilate therefore heard that saying, he was the <u>more</u> afraid;

If he was the more afraid then he was already afraid, and for good reason. He is about to give these people the permission to crucify the Son of God even though he knows, in the back of his mind, that Jesus very well could be the King of the Jews.

[9]And went again into the judgment hall, and saith unto Jesus, Whence art thou? But Jesus gave him no answer.

Here is another example of what we have seen all the way through this Gospel: when people refuse light, Jesus will not give it. He tried to give Pilate THE TRUTH earlier, but Pilate just walked out the door without listening.

[10]Then saith Pilate unto him, Speakest thou not unto me? knowest thou not that I have power to crucify thee, and have power to release thee? [11]Jesus answered, Thou couldest have no power at all against me, except it were given thee from above: therefore he that delivered me unto thee hath the greater sin.

Jesus is the one controlling this entire line of questioning. Pilate tries to turn it around by attempting to scare Him with death, but what Pilate does not understand is that Jesus has every intention of dying. Death does not scare Him. No wonder Pilate is afraid. I am sure every person he has ever had to pronounce judgment on was scared out of their mind about death, but not Jesus. He is standing there with no thought or concern about being crucified.

The last statement **he that delivered me unto thee hath the greater sin** could be directed at one of two different people. Obviously, Jesus is talking about one man because He uses the singular pronoun, he. Therefore, this could be directed at Judas Iscariot or Caiaphas. Judas is the most logical one considering he betrayed the Lord, but if you remember back to John 11 it was Caiaphas who came up with the idea to have Jesus killed. Judas was simply a pawn in the overall scheme. Plus, Caiaphas is the one orchestrating all these events in direct violation of the law. He is supposed to be the one representing the law and making sure it is followed, but instead he is directly defying it. Because of those reasons I would argue Jesus' statement applies to Caiaphas rather than Judas.

[12]**And from thenceforth Pilate sought to release him: but the Jews cried out, saying, If thou let this man go, thou art not Caesar's friend: whosoever maketh himself a king speaketh against Caesar.** [13]**When Pilate therefore heard that saying, he brought Jesus forth, and sat down in the judgment seat in a place that is called the Pavement, but in the Hebrew, Gabbatha.**

Pilate is now being faced with the ultimate dilemma. He wants to let Jesus go, and he knows he should, but the Jews just said if he lets Him go it is a decision in direct defiance against Caesar. So, if Caesar were to hear about this, Pilate would be the next one to die. He has a real choice to make, and Jesus said every person would have to make this choice. **Whosoever will come after me, let him deny himself, and take up his cross, and follow me** (Mark 8:34).

Everybody has to choose to deny themselves in order to follow Jesus, but for some this literally means death as a result. Here, Pilate would literally lose his life, and this has proven true for many people in various places of the world throughout history. In other places the results may mean losing the lifestyle they once had. For example, in many religions if someone decides to stop following the family's religion to follow Jesus, that person is considered dead in the eyes of the family. Yes, some cases are more extreme than others, as illustrated by Pilate, but everybody must make this same choice: deny themselves, take up their cross, and follow Christ.

[14]**And it was the preparation of the passover, and about the sixth hour: and he saith unto the Jews, Behold your King!**

A review of the Levitical law and feasts days (Leviticus 23:4-6) shows that the Passover meal was eaten at evening (6 p.m.) when Nisan 15 began. The following morning hours (6 a.m. – 6 p.m.) were preparation hours for the 7-day feast of unleavened bread.

Please review the introductory commentary of chapter 5, and the appendix – Biblical Calendar.

[15]But they cried out, Away with him, away with him, crucify him. Pilate saith unto them, Shall I crucify <u>your</u> King? The chief priests answered, We have no king but Caesar.

Pilate tries one final plea with these people to receive the man they themselves were calling King just a few days ago. It does not work. Then, the Jews make the worst decision they could possibly make.

The chief priests answered, We have no king but Caesar.

They deny God as their King.

[16]Then delivered he him therefore unto them to be crucified. And they took Jesus, and led him away. [17]And <u>he bearing his cross</u> went forth into a place called the place of a skull, which is called in the Hebrew Golgotha: [18]Where they crucified him, and two other with him, on either side one, and Jesus in the midst.

We know from the other Gospels that Simon a Cyrenian also carried the cross. Today there seems to be a lot of debate over the details of these events. Why did Simon have to carry the cross? When did they get Simon to *help* Jesus? The debates would stop if people would read their Bible instead of consulting movies for their source of information.

Almost every movie shows Simon carrying the cross because Jesus was too weak to carry it Himself. However, you do not find support for that anywhere in the Bible. Nor do you find support that such speculation is justifiable.[41]

[19]And Pilate wrote a title, and put it on the cross. And the writing was JESUS OF NAZARETH THE KING OF THE JEWS. [20]This title then read many of the Jews: for the place where Jesus was crucified was nigh to the city: and it was written in Hebrew, and Greek, and Latin.

---

[41] Please see Appendix: *Simon a Cyrenian* for what the Bible says regarding this topic.

God made sure these three languages were provided so all who looked would be able to read it.

21Then said the <u>chief priests of the Jews</u> to Pilate, Write not, The King of the Jews; but that he said, I am King of the Jews. 22Pilate answered, What I have written I have written.

When reading through the Gospels, you will read the phrase *chief priests* quite often. However, this is the first time God called them the **chief priests <u>of the Jews</u>**. The Jews have just renounced God, so these priests are no longer *of God*, but *of the Jews*.

23Then the soldiers, when they had crucified Jesus, took his garments, and made four parts, to every soldier a part; and also his coat: now the coat was without seam, woven from the top throughout. 24They said therefore among themselves, Let us not rend it, but cast lots for it, whose it shall be: that the scripture might be fulfilled, which saith, They parted my raiment among them, and for my vesture they did cast lots. These things therefore the soldiers did.

The scripture that is being fulfilled is Psalm 22:18. The one piece of garment they did not tear was his coat because it was made without seams. That means the coat was made by weaving together one piece of thread starting from the top and ending at the bottom. It is a picture of the church.

The church is not made up of many individuals being sewn together. We are all one member knit together. **There is neither Jew nor Greek, there is neither bond nor free, there is neither male nor female: for ye are all one in Christ Jesus** (Galatians 3:28), **knit together in love** (Colossians 2:2). **So we, being many, are one body in Christ, and every one members one of another** (Romans 12:4). Not one member is above another no matter who you are, what you have done, or what office you hold. We are all one in Christ. Amen.

25Now there stood by the cross of Jesus his mother, and his mother's sister, Mary the wife of Cleophas, and Mary Magdalene.

The disciples might have gone *their* way after leaving the garden (John 18:8), but these women are right there until the end.

26When Jesus therefore saw his mother, and the disciple standing by, whom he loved, he saith unto his mother, Woman, behold thy son! 27Then

saith he to the disciple, Behold thy mother! And from that hour that disciple took her unto his own home.

Jesus could have turned Mary over to one of His other brothers (Mark 6:3), but He did not. This is most likely because spiritual relationships are stronger than physical ones. **My mother and my brethren are these which hear the word of God, and do it** (Luke 8:21).

Plus, John 7:5 told us that His brethren did not believe in Him at this point, and it is not until Acts 1:14 that we see the first evidence of their belief. Witnessing the infallible proofs of His resurrection (Acts 1:3) must have led them to their belief.

[28]**After this, Jesus knowing that all things were now accomplished, that the scripture might be fulfilled, saith, I thirst.** [29]**Now there was set a vessel full of vinegar: and they filled a spunge with vinegar, and put it upon hyssop, and put it to his mouth.** [30]**When Jesus therefore had received the vinegar, he said, <u>It is finished</u>: and he bowed his head, and gave up the ghost.**

Those are the last recorded words of Jesus before He dismissed His spirit and died (John 10:18). His first recorded words were as a twelve-year-old boy in Luke 2:49. And **he said unto them** [Mary and Joseph]**, How is it that ye sought me? wist ye not that <u>I must be about my Father's business</u>?** From His first recorded words to the last, He had one thing in mind: **to do the will of him that sent me, and <u>to finish his work</u>** (John 4:34).

[31]**The Jews therefore, because it was the preparation, that the bodies should not remain upon the cross on the sabbath day, (for that sabbath day was an high day,) besought Pilate that their legs might be broken, and that they might be taken away.**

Here are the Jews once again following their religious holy days. Never mind about having an innocent man killed, but they simply *must* comply with their holidays.

The reason for breaking their legs is so they would be unable to use them to support their body weight and thus die more quickly from suffocation.

[32]**Then came the soldiers, and brake the legs of the first, and of the other which was crucified with him.** [33]**But when they came to Jesus, and saw that he was dead already, they brake not his legs:**

Here is what the Bible states regarding the Passover lamb:

- Exodus 12:46: **In one house shall it be eaten; thou shalt not carry forth ought of the flesh abroad out of the house; neither shall <u>ye break a bone</u> thereof.**
- Numbers 9:12: **They shall leave none of it unto the morning, <u>nor break any bone of it</u>: according to all the ordinances of the Passover they shall keep it.**

Recall back to John 1:29 where John called Jesus the Lamb of God, and then reference 1 Corinthians 5:7 that describes Christ as being our Passover. His bones not being broken is vitally important according to scripture.

[34]**But one of the soldiers with a spear pierced his side, and forthwith came there out blood and water.** [35]**And he that saw it bare record, and his record is true: and he knoweth that he saith true, that ye might believe.** [36]**For these things were done, that the scripture should be fulfilled, A bone of him shall not be broken.** [37]**And again another scripture saith, They shall look on him whom they pierced.**

These two scriptures are yet to be fulfilled. Look carefully at the words: **that the scripture <u>should</u> be fulfilled**, compared to the words of scripture that were fulfilled in verses 24 and 28: **that the scripture <u>might</u> be fulfilled**. There is coming a day when all eyes shall look upon Jesus who was pierced yet not a bone of Him was broken (Zechariah 12:10, Revelation 1:7). For everyone to look upon Him that was pierced without any bones being broken, the events that we are reading about here in John had to take place. That is why the Bible says **these things were done, <u>that</u> the scripture <u>should</u> be fulfilled**.

I'll say it again: Jesus came to die, not to set up an earthly kingdom.

[38]**And after this Joseph of Arimathaea, being a disciple of Jesus, but secretly for fear of the Jews, besought Pilate that he might take away <u>the body of Jesus</u>: and Pilate gave him leave. He came therefore, and took <u>the body of Jesus</u>.**

I appreciate how God pays particular attention to detail in His word. When people show up to a funeral, they look in the casket and say something like, "Mr. So-and-so sure looks good." The truth is that lying in that casket is a body, not the person. Jesus' body needed to be taken away and placed in a tomb, but Jesus is long gone.

[39] **And there came also Nicodemus, which at the first came to Jesus by night, and brought a mixture of myrrh and aloes, about an hundred pound weight.** [40] **Then took they the body of Jesus, and <u>wound it in linen clothes</u> with the spices, as the manner of the Jews is to bury.**

We previously examined references showing that from the start to the finish of Jesus' life on earth, He set out to die on that cross. Even his body being wrapped in linen clothes is proof of that fact because the last time His body was wrapped like this was at His birth in Bethlehem. **And she** [Mary] **brought forth her firstborn son, and <u>wrapped him in swaddling clothes</u>, and laid him in a manger; because there was no room for them in the inn** (Luke 2:7).

[41] **Now in the place where he was crucified there was a garden; and in the garden a new sepulchre, wherein was never man yet laid.** [42] **There laid they Jesus therefore because of the Jews' preparation day; for the sepulchre was nigh at hand.**

The events we read about in John 18-19 began in the garden of Gethsemane and ended in this garden.

At this time, if you would like to read a detailed summary of the chronological events spanning the final week of Jesus' earthly life, please see the Appendix – *The last days of Jesus' ministry.*

John 20

And Thomas answered and said unto him, My Lord and my God –
John 20:28: Thomas claims Jesus to be God

¹**The first day of the week cometh Mary Magdalene early, when it was yet dark, unto the sepulchre, and seeth the stone taken away from the sepulchre.**

Mary Magdalene was one of the last people to leave the crucifixion, and one of the first to arrive at the tomb. See Matthew 27:55-61 with Matthew 28:1

²**Then she runneth, and cometh to Simon Peter, and to the other disciple, whom Jesus loved, and saith unto them, They have taken away the LORD out of the sepulchre, and we know not where they have laid him.**

Who are they? It is unclear who Mary might be referring to and there are only a few possibilities.

1. Nicodemus and Joseph of Arimathaea – According to Mark 15:47, Matthew 27:61 and Luke 23:55, Mary Magdalene witnessed them prepare Jesus' body for burial. Maybe she supposed them to have taken the body.
2. The Jews – This possibility is highly unlikely considering they took every precaution to avoid anyone taking actions to proclaim that a resurrection had occurred (Matthew 27:62-66).
3. The Romans – Just as unlikely. What would they have to gain or benefit by taking Jesus' body? Besides, if they had taken the body why unwrap it and fold the napkin (vs. 6-7)?

Nonetheless, it is very apparent that the disciples did not anticipate Jesus rising from the dead even though He told them He would on several occasions. See Matthew 12:40, 16:21, 17:23, 20:19, 27:63, Mark 8:31, 9:31, 10:34, Luke 9:22, 13:32, 18:33, 24:7, John 2:19-21.

³**Peter therefore went forth, and that other disciple, and came to the sepulchre. ⁴So they ran both together: and the other disciple did outrun Peter, and came first to the sepulchre. ⁵And he stooping down, and looking in, saw the linen clothes lying; yet went he not in. ⁶Then cometh Simon Peter following him, and went into the sepulchre, and seeth the linen clothes lie, ⁷And the napkin, that was about his head, not lying with**

the linen clothes, but wrapped together in a place by itself. **[8]Then went in also that other disciple, which came first to the sepulchre, and he saw, and believed.**

So, Peter and John did not believe Mary's report and had to see for themselves before they believed.

[9]For as yet they knew not the <u>scripture</u>, that he must rise again from the dead.

These disciples have spent several years with Jesus listening to Him expound the scripture, and teach others as well as themselves, but they were not entirely listening. Jesus told them He would die and rise again. They did not listen. He quoted scripture after scripture, but they were not listening. The disciples were just like the rest of Israel who only focused on the scriptures reporting Christ the Messiah ruling and reigning from His thrown at Jerusalem.

Luke 24:21 is a prime example. There Jesus appeared to two disciples on their way to Emmaus after He had resurrected and look at what they said. **We trusted that it had been he which <u>should have redeemed Israel</u>**. The scriptures that coincided with this thought are all they knew, and the scriptures regarding Messiah's death went in one ear and out the other.

For more proof, see John 2:22. **When therefore he was risen from the dead, his disciples <u>remembered</u> that he had said this unto them; <u>and they believed the scripture</u>, and the word which Jesus had said.**

[10]Then the disciples went away again unto their own home.

It is Sunday morning, and the women have just brought news that Jesus either rose from the dead based on the report of strange men in white apparel (Luke 24:1-12) or someone ("they" – v. 2) has taken away His body. Peter and John run to the tomb to find His body missing, and now what should they do? I guess the answer is to just go back home.

I wonder how many people go to church Sunday morning after Sunday morning to hear reports of Jesus rising from the dead only to leave in disbelief, bewilderment, and/or uncertainty only to return home as if nothing really had happened. I would be willing to bet it happens every single week.

[11]But Mary stood without at the sepulchre weeping: and as she wept, she stooped down, and looked into the sepulchre, [12]And seeth two angels in white sitting, the one at the head, and the other at the feet, where the body of Jesus had lain. [13]And they say unto her, Woman, why weepest thou?

She saith unto them, Because they have taken away my LORD, and I know not where they have laid him.

She still thinks someone took Jesus' body.

[14]**And when she had thus said, she turned herself back, and saw Jesus standing, and knew not that it was Jesus. [15]Jesus saith unto her, Woman, why weepest thou? whom seekest thou? She, supposing him to be the gardener, saith unto him, Sir, if thou have borne him hence, tell me where thou hast laid him, and I will take him away.**

This is truly a fitting thought by Mary to suppose Jesus to be the gardener. I understand they are in a garden and Mary supposing this man to be the gardener is a natural thought; however, notice what the Bible illustrates regarding a gardener.

The first man Adam had occupation as a gardener (Genesis 2:15). The Bible calls Jesus the last Adam (1 Corinthians 15:45), and how fitting it is for Mary to suppose the last Adam to be just like the first Adam!

Secondly, there are multiple reasons for her not recognizing Him. Maybe the sun is rising over the horizon and hard to see, or He is a rather long way off. Maybe she has so much racing through her mind that she would not recognize Him at first glance. On and on we could go, but there is only one reason that makes sense to me according to scripture: Jesus' body is still marred with not only the nail prints in His hands and feet, and a hole in His side, but with every wound He received from the scourging ordered by Pilate. That truly would leave Him unrecognizable. This is supported by biblical resurrection and glorification (1 Corinthians 15) where every individual's spirit and soul reenter the same body they had before death. Resurrection is the complete reversal of death. How you look at time of death is how you will look upon resurrecting, except with a very important change ... **For this corruptible** (your body) **must put on incorruption, and this mortal** (your body) **must put on immortality** (1 Corinthians 15:53).

Please examine each post resurrection appearance for support on this thought. See John 21:12, Matthew 28:17, Luke 24:16, and Mark 16:12. A curious phrase is found in the Mark passage. The Bible declares that Jesus **appeared in another <u>form</u>**. This is most interesting because of what Isaiah 50:6, Psalm 22:16-17, and Isaiah 52:14 declare concerning Christ's death.

- Isaiah 50:6: <u>**I game my back to the smiters,**</u> **and my cheeks to them that plucked off the hair: I hid not my face from shame and spitting**. We know from this passage and the Gospel accounts of the scourging that He experienced quite the beating.

207

- Psalm 22:16-17: **For dogs have compassed me: the assembly of the wicked have inclosed me: they pierced my hands and my feet. I may tell all my bones: they look and stare upon me**. This description sounds like the beating Christ received cut His body so deep that His bones were exposed.
- Isaiah 52:14: **As many were astonied at thee; his visage was so marred more than any man, and <u>his form more than the sons of men</u>**. Do you see my point? It appears the scourging left His form so marred that He was completely unrecognizable.

This thought is also supported by prophetical passages that describe His appearance. **They shall look upon me whom they have pierced** (Zechariah 12:10; see also Revelation 1:7), and **I beheld, and, lo, in the midst of the throne and of the four beasts, and in the midst of the elders, stood a <u>Lamb</u> <u>as it had been slain</u>** (Revelation 5:6). Again, the Bible seems to indicate that He still looks marred from all the events of the crucifixion.

I know this goes against what we have all seen produced by Hollywood where they represent Jesus as a perfectly formed man with holes in his hands, feet, and side based on John 20:27. But, why would He have those markings and not the marks from the scourging?

[16]**Jesus saith unto her, Mary. She turned herself, and saith unto him, Rabboni; which is to say, Master.**

The moment she heard Him say her name, she knew it was Jesus! Truly **the sheep hear his voice: and he calleth his own sheep <u>by name</u>, and leadeth them out. And when he putteth forth his own sheep, he goeth before them, and the sheep follow him: for they know his voice.** (John 10:2-3)

[17]**Jesus saith unto her, <u>Touch me not</u>; for I am not yet ascended to my Father:**

There are probably several reasons for why Jesus told Mary not to touch Him, and I have heard several from the pulpit throughout my life. Only one makes sense to me though.

Jesus' death on the cross was a fulfillment of the Old Testament offerings including the fulfillment of the Day of Atonement (see the book of Leviticus). Those sacrifices had to be presented to the LORD before they could be consumed by the priests. One additional requirement for the animal sacrifices was their flesh could not encounter any unclean thing. Leviticus 7:19 describes this condition under the law of the trespass offering. **And the**

flesh (flesh of the animal being sacrificed) **that toucheth any unclean thing shall not be eaten; it shall be burnt with fire**.   Therefore, Mary could not touch Jesus until He had presented Himself to the LORD.

but go to <u>my brethren</u>, and say unto them, I ascend unto my Father, and your Father; and to my God, and your God.

This small portion of scripture is absolutely loaded with truth pertaining to the theme of John.

Recall that Jesus is being presented as God manifest in the flesh. John 1:11-13 told us **He came unto his own, and his own received him not. But <u>as many as received him, to them gave he power to become the sons of God</u>, even to them that believe on his name: Which were born, not of blood, nor of the will of the flesh, nor of the will of man, but of God**. Now, for the first time in John, Jesus is referring to His disciples as His brethren. This relationship position is the result of a new birth, thus making the disciples and everyone else that believe on Jesus' name a son of God. This only happens after someone has believed in Jesus' death, burial, and resurrection. Thus, it is absolutely fitting for Jesus to wait until now to refer to the disciples as His brethren.

Also notice the two statements by Jesus that follow. Those two statements once again refer us back to the theme of John by showing Jesus as both God (deity) and man (humanity).

- **I ascend unto my Father and your Father**

Every time Jesus referred to God the Father as His Father the Jews wanted to kill Him for blasphemy (John 5:17-18, John 10:29-31) because such a statement meant that He was equal with God. Thus, Jesus is expressing to us His deity.

- **and to my God, and your God**

It is understandable for Jesus to say that He and the Father are one (John 10:30) considering He is indeed God; but for Jesus to state He is ascending "to my God" would have to mean that He is man. Only a man could, or would, make such a statement. Thus, Jesus is expressing to us His humanity.

Why are these two statements so important?

1. Because the unity of all believers that Jesus prayed for in the garden in John 17:20-21 has now been made possible. Hebrews 2:9-11 bears this out. **But we see Jesus, who was made a little lower than the angels for the suffering of death, crowned with glory and honour; that he by the grace of God should taste death for every man. For it**

became him, for whom are all things, and by whom are all things, in bringing many sons unto glory, to make the captain of their salvation perfect through sufferings. **For <u>both he that sanctifieth and they who are sanctified are all of one: for which cause he is not ashamed to call them brethren</u>**. The same unity that God the Father and God the son have exists between God the Son and all believers. What an incredible thing! God, who tasted death for every man and by whom are all things, is not ashamed to call us brethren. Praise His holy name!

2. Jesus (both God and man) is now currently in heaven seated beside God the Father making intercession and mediating to God the Father on our behalf (Hebrews 7:25, 1 Timothy 2:5). That is why the Bible states, **But now hath he obtained a more excellent ministry, by how much also he is the mediator of a better covenant, which was established upon <u>better promises</u>** (Hebrews 8:6). We can go to the true and living God in prayer regarding the trials, tribulations, struggles, heartaches, despairs, and every other thing pertaining to this life asking Him for the grace to overcome those situations, and Jesus will go to God the Father on our behalf professing how He knows exactly what we are going through. As a man, He **was in all points tempted like as we are, yet without sin** (Hebrews 4:15). He experienced hunger, sadness, despair, heartache, weariness of the flesh, etc., all as a man. God can truly relate to what we go through in this life for He experienced it all Himself. Truly, what better promises we have that did not exist before Calvary!

[18]Mary Magdalene came and told the disciples that she had seen the LORD, and that he had spoken these things unto her. [19]Then the same day at evening, being the first day of the week, when the doors were shut where the disciples were assembled for fear of the Jews, came Jesus and stood in the midst, and saith unto them, Peace be unto you.

First, I can understand their fear. The Jews just killed Jesus, and they must be thinking there is nothing preventing them from being killed next.

Secondly, just try to imagine Jesus suddenly appearing before you inside a sealed room. I do not think an actor exists anywhere in the world that could accurately portray such a reaction. Jesus telling them to be at peace must have been a necessity!

[20]And when he had so said, he shewed unto them his hands and his side. <u>Then</u> were the disciples glad, when they saw the LORD.

I'm going to reiterate what we previously discussed in verses 14-15. The disciples did not know this was Jesus standing in front of them until He showed unto them His hands and side. The only explanation for this is that His physical form has been altered. Whether this means His glorified state is a body different to the one He had before Calvary with holes in His hands, feet, and side, or that He is in the same brutally beaten, unrecognizable body is a conclusion you will have to draw for yourself.

What I do know, is that we Americans are bombarded with advertisements of "perfectly formed models" aided only by technology, that people desire such beauty for themselves (Romans 9:20). It is no wonder that when Christians talk of a glorified body, they immediately imagine perfect hair, perfect skin without scars or blemishes, perfectly functioning organs, and the energy of a teenager. No wonder this has become the acceptable norm surrounding this topic. However, if we read 1 Corinthians 15 carefully, it describes us having a CHANGED body. The change is that sin is completely eradicated, aging is no longer a factor, and the decaying of death is wiped away. We must get beyond our definitions of physical beauty when it comes to this topic because God considers every one of His creations beautiful despite our opinions (Psalm 139:14).

[21]Then said Jesus to them again, Peace be unto you: as my Father hath sent me, even so send I you.

This is one of the many verses involving *the great commission* – Jesus sending believers out into the world to preach the gospel.

Jesus originally sent the disciples out to the surrounding areas to preach the kingdom of heaven (the physical kingdom pertaining strictly to the Jews – Matthew 10:1, 5-6), and the kingdom of God (the spiritual kingdom pertaining to both Jew and Gentile – Luke 9:1-2, 6).[42] Now they are to continue what was started by beginning at Jerusalem and progressing unto the uttermost part of the earth (Acts 1:8) by preaching the things pertaining to the kingdom of God (Acts 1:3).

[22]And when he had said this, he breathed on them, and saith unto them, Receive ye the Holy Ghost:

Recall what we discussed in John 14:16-18, 26. Jesus promised He would not leave them comfortless when He departed out of this world and would send another comforter (the Holy Ghost) into them. The common

---

[42] See the author's work: Matthew for additional insight and commentary involving these two kingdoms.

teaching is that the disciples did not receive the Holy Ghost until Acts 2. If that were correct, Jesus was untruthful to them when He told them He would not leave them comfortless for there were several days that passed between His leaving the earth and the day of Pentecost.[43]

This is the only explanation I know to give. Those He promised would not be left comfortless in John 14 must have received the Holy Ghost at this point. Later in Acts 2, those of the 120 in the house who had not already received the Holy Ghost then became recipients.

[23]**Whose soever sins ye remit, they are remitted unto them; and whose soever sins ye retain, they are retained.**

Why is such authority given to these disciples? The answer is a dispensational truth.

When the disciples leave the upper room in Acts 2 to begin fulfilling the great commission, everything they will proclaim will be their word against the Old Testament scriptures. Yes, they are eyewitnesses to the accounts they are preaching (Acts 2:32). Yes, everything they are preaching regarding Jesus Christ is a fulfillment of the Old Testament scriptures, but to the devout Jew they will be witnessing to, their preaching will seemingly be going against scriptures hand delivered by God. You must admit this would be a hard truth to believe without some sort of proof. So, God does as He has always done when delivering men more truth. He enables the disciples/apostles to perform miracles, signs, and wonders simply because the Jews require those signs (1 Corinthians 1:22). Then, because of someone hearing the truth of the gospel, seeing the miracles wrought by the hands of these disciples, and believing on the Lord Jesus Christ they are saved by the grace of God.

How will they know their sins have been remitted? How will they know they have eternal life? They would get their assurance to such questions from these men. We get our assurance today from the word of God (Romans 10:9-13), but during this time, the word of God found in the New Testament is still yet to be recorded. Once the Holy Ghost brings all things to these disciple's remembrance (John 14:26) and guides them into all truth (John 16:13) to record God's word, the apostolic authority found here in these verses will shift from them to the word of God.

---

[43] Acts 1:3 declares that Jesus was seen of the disciples for forty days before ascending into heaven. Therefore, approximately 1 week transpired before the Holy Ghost descended in Acts 2 on the day of Pentecost.

24But Thomas, one of the twelve, called Didymus, was not with them when Jesus came. 25The other disciples therefore said unto him, We have seen the LORD. But he said unto them, Except I shall see in his hands the print of the nails, and put my finger into the print of the nails, and thrust my hand into his side, I will not believe.

Good ol' doubting Thomas. We Bible believers sure do like to give Thomas a hard time for not believing, but we are quick to forget that the rest of the disciples did not believe Mary's reports earlier. They doubted just as much as Thomas did.

Can Thomas be defended for his doubting, because maybe He has good reason? Cross reference Matthew 24:24-26 where Christ taught the disciples the things that would come to pass during the great tribulation. **Then if any man shall say unto you, Lo, here is Christ, or there; believe it not. For there shall arise false Christs, and false prophets, and shall shew great signs and wonders; insomuch that, if it were possible, they shall deceive the very elect. Behold, I have told you before. Wherefore if they shall say unto you, Behold, he is in the desert; go not forth: behold, he is in the secret chambers; believe it not**. The disciples told Thomas they saw Jesus while hiding in their locked secret chamber. Maybe Thomas immediately refers to what Christ had previously told them. I do not know for certain, but it is possible we should give Thomas the benefit of the doubt.

26And after eight days again his disciples were within, and Thomas with them: then came Jesus, the doors being shut, and stood in the midst, and said, Peace be unto you. 27Then saith he to Thomas, Reach hither thy finger, and behold my hands; and reach hither thy hand, and thrust it into my side: and be not faithless, but believing.

Jesus knew exactly what Thomas previously stated eight days prior and even offers him the opportunity to do exactly what he desired. Whether or not he did it, the scripture does not say. Nevertheless, the opportunity was provided.

28And Thomas answered and said unto him, My LORD and my God.

Thomas fully understands Jesus' deity. Why cannot other denominations and/or factions under the umbrella of Christianity understand this simple truth? Many teach Jesus to be a good man, and a great teacher recognized as a prophet. Jesus is indeed man, but He is more than just a man. Jesus was indeed a good teacher, and a great prophet, but He is so much more than that. He is God!

29Jesus saith unto him, Thomas, because thou hast seen me, thou hast believed: blessed are they that have not seen, and yet have believed.

If you are reading these words and believe, as I do, that Jesus Christ is God and died for our sins, these words apply to you and me! Truly we are blessed in this world of sorrow, pain, despair, turmoil, frustration, sin, and death but we have a hope that no unsaved person has. One day we will be absent from this body and present with the Lord (2 Corinthians 5:8) in a place with no more death, sorrow, crying, or pain for it will all be wiped away (Revelation 21:4). In this day we walk by faith but in that day, we will trade faith for sight for we shall see Him as He is (1 John 3:2-3). Hallelujah!

30And many other signs truly did Jesus in the presence of his disciples, which are not written in this book: 31But these are written, that ye might believe that Jesus is the Christ, the Son of God; and that believing ye might have life through his name.

The very theme of John. As a result of reading and studying this far into John … do you believe? Do you have life through His name?

John 21

Jesus saith unto him, If I will that he tarry till I come, what is that to thee? follow thou me – John 21:22: only God can command obedience

¹**After these things Jesus shewed himself again to the disciples at the sea of Tiberias; and on this wise shewed he himself.**

The sea of Tiberias is where Jesus fed the multitude and walked on water back in John 6.

²**There were together Simon Peter, and Thomas called Didymus, and Nathanael of Cana of Galilee, and the sons of Zebedee, and two other of his disciples.** ³**Simon Peter saith unto them, I go a fishing. They say unto him, We also go with thee. They went forth, and entered into a ship immediately; and that night they caught nothing.**

The most common preaching I have heard on these verses is that Peter backslides on the Lord. Instead of being a fisher of men that the Lord called him to be (Matthew 4:18-19), he reverted to his old life, and as a result he led the others astray. All that sounds good and can make for good preaching, but it is pure speculation. If we are going to speculate, we might as well consider all possibilities.

John 20:19 told us the disciples feared the Jews and that they were hiding out in closed quarters as a result. Given their fear, it is likely they will not want to be seen in public. Therefore, grocery shopping in the market would be a rather difficult thing to accomplish without being seen, so the simple solution would be to go fishing at night while the town is asleep.

Maybe, for them fishing is the easiest way to collect food and perhaps the fish are more active at night. There really is no absolute certainty for why they did what they did. We can speculate, just as we could have speculated Nicodemus' reasons for coming to see Jesus at night back in John 3. All we can say for sure is they went fishing, and Jesus appears to them the following morning.

⁴**But when the morning was now come, Jesus stood on the shore: but the disciples knew not that it was Jesus.** ⁵**Then Jesus saith unto them, Children, have ye any meat? They answered him, No.** ⁶**And he said unto them, Cast the net on the right side of the ship, and ye shall find. They cast therefore, and now they were not able to draw it for the multitude of**

fishes. ⁷**Therefore that disciple whom Jesus loved saith unto Peter, It is the Lord.**

We could say it is obvious how they knew it was the Lord because He knew exactly where the fish were. However, scripture gives us a better reason for how they knew Him to be Jesus. This happened before in Luke 5:1-11 and was the very reason they followed Jesus in the first place.

And it came to pass, that, as the people pressed upon him to hear the word of God, he stood by the lake of Gennesaret, And saw two ships standing by the lake: but the fishermen were gone out of them, and were washing their nets. And he entered into one of the ships, which was Simon's, and prayed him that he would thrust out a little from the land. And he sat down, and taught the people out of the ship. Now when he had left speaking, he said unto Simon, Launch out into the deep, and let down your nets for a draught. And Simon answering said unto him, Master, we have toiled all the night, and have taken nothing: nevertheless at thy word I will let down the net. And when they had this done, they inclosed a great multitude of fishes: and their net brake. And they beckoned unto their partners, which were in the other ship, that they should come and help them. And they came, and filled both the ships, so that they began to sink. When Simon Peter saw it, he fell down at Jesus' knees, saying, Depart from me; for I am a sinful man, O Lord. For he was astonished, and all that were with him, at the draught of the fishes which they had taken: And so was also James, and John, the sons of Zebedee, which were partners with Simon. And Jesus said unto Simon, Fear not; from henceforth thou shalt catch men. And when they had brought their ships to land, they forsook all, and followed him.

Now when Simon Peter heard that it was the Lord, he girt his fisher's coat unto him, (for he was naked,) and did cast himself into the sea.

Let's keep this as simple as we can. What does it mean that Peter was naked? Well, it means what it says. He was naked. Nakedness is when bare skin is exposed. That could mean someone is completely without clothing (Genesis 3:7, Ecclesiastes 5:15), or it could mean that a specific part of the body has been left bare of clothing exposing naked skin (Exodus 28:42). From the context, it seems Peter is out there on the boat with his shirt off because the only article of clothing mentioned is a coat. Nonetheless, nakedness is nakedness in the Bible whether you are talking about one specific area of exposed skin, or the entire body being exposed. It makes no difference.

Also, doesn't this seem a little odd to you? I'm talking about the fact that Peter gets dressed to go swimming. Today, people do the exact opposite by getting naked in as little clothing as possible to swim. Society should not dictate your dress code. The Bible should.

⁸And the other disciples came in a little ship; (for they were not far from land, but as it were two hundred cubits,) dragging the net with fishes.

If we use the common measurement of a cubit being equal to eighteen inches, this distance was equal to the length of a football field from goal line to goal line (100 yards).

⁹As soon then as they were come to land, they saw a fire of coals there, and fish laid thereon, and bread.

In John 6 Jesus fed the multitude in the wilderness close to this sea. Here He has prepared a table for His disciples. Both times Jesus provides and meets a need that man was not able to meet or provide on their own. He truly does supply our every need!

¹⁰Jesus saith unto them, Bring of the fish which ye have now caught. ¹¹Simon Peter went up, and drew the net to land full of great fishes, <u>an hundred and fifty and three</u>: and for all there were so many, yet was not the net broken.

God gives us in His word exactly what we need to know. Surrounding some topics, we are provided with plenty of information, and on others we are left desiring further details. With that being said, why did God give us the specific number of fish they caught? Is there something significant about the number 153? Perhaps God is simply allowing the penman's personality to be exposed within the writing. That is a truth that holds throughout all the New Testament epistles, and John is a fisherman after all. All fishermen I know consistently count their catch at the end of their fishing expeditions. At best the answer is unsure, but there are a few interesting things to consider.

1. The men fished all night without any success under their own labors. As soon as the Lord gets involved, they reap a benefit that could have, if not should have, broken their nets. **He that abideth in me** [Jesus], **and I in him, the same brigeth forth much fruit: for without me ye can do nothing** (John 15:5).

2. According to Luke 5, Christ initially called these men to be fishers of men. Once obedient to God's calling by preaching the gospel of Jesus Christ, sinners willingly repent and believe on Jesus Christ for the remission of sins, and God knows each person that is saved. None of them are lost. **My sheep hear my voice, and <u>I know them</u>, and they follow me: And I give unto them eternal life; and they shall <u>never perish</u>, neither shall any man pluck them out of my hand. My Father, which gave them me, is greater than all; and no man is able to pluck them out of my Father's hand** (John 10:27-29). **While I [Jesus] was with them in the world, I kept them in they name: those that thou gavest me <u>I have kept, and none of them is lost</u>, but the son of perdition; that the scripture might be fulfilled** (John 17:12). Perhaps this event portrays these truths, given the fact that God knew exactly how many fish were in the net, the net was not broken, and none of the fish were lost.

3. This last consideration is one I have run across several times in study. However, please take it as a grain of salt.

    If you look at each Gospel and count the number of people that are "personally blessed" by the Lord Jesus Christ, the total apparently comes to 153. "Personally blessed" is loosely exaggerated, however. See what I mean below.

    a. Matthew records 47 people (8:2, 15:22, 27:56, 27:57 just to name a few)
    b. Mark records 3 people (1:23, 7:32, 8:22)
    c. Luke records 94 people (the seventy sent out to preach – 10:1, ten lepers cleansed – 17:12, and Zaccheus – 19:2 to name the majority)
    d. John records 9 people

    The numbers mentioned above total 153. However, singling out those individuals means you would have to ignore the number in the multitudes that were fed, ignore the number of the disciples in the count, and quite possibly ignore a few more. That is why I said this count is loosely exaggerated.

[12]**Jesus saith unto them, Come and dine. And none of the disciples durst ask him, Who art thou? knowing that it was the Lord.**

Hopefully now you can see why I have put such emphasis on the fact that the disciples did not recognize Jesus physically. Again, it is uncertain what His physical features look like: still marred from the crucifixion, or a perfectly formed complexion? Nonetheless, the Bible yet again insinuates that Jesus looked differently. God wanted this to be evident to us for a reason.

¹³Jesus then cometh, and taketh bread, and giveth them, and fish likewise.

Look at what this verse tells us of Jesus on behalf of His servants.

- He supplies their temporal needs.
- He humbles himself to prepare a table for others. Having a sense of humility is something all Christians should portray.
- All laborers (including us) need rest and refreshment with the Lord.
- Christ is not dependent on our efforts to get things accomplished. He prepared a meal of fish that the disciples failed to catch.
- This pictures the marriage supper of the Lamb in Revelation 19.

¹⁴This is now the third time that Jesus shewed himself to his disciples, after that he was risen from the dead.

This is the third time as recorded by John (John 20:19, 26), but the seventh appearance chronologically.⁴⁴

¹⁵So when they had dined, Jesus saith to Simon Peter, Simon, son of Jonas, lovest thou me more than <u>these</u>? He saith unto him, Yea, Lord; thou knowest that I love thee.

Jesus asked Peter a very direct question, **"Lovest thou me more than these?"** I appreciate Peter's response, but my initial question is, who are these? Are they the disciples? Are they the fish? The answer is uncertain but notice Peter's response. He just simply states that He loves Jesus. He left out the phrase, "more than these." It is a humble answer and one that I very much appreciate.

Today you love Jesus more than your family, friends, acquaintances, things, possessions, and even your very life, but the day may come that we might deny the Lord just as Peter did. In that hour Peter put his love of life ahead of his love for Jesus. That is why I appreciate his humble reply. He knows his shortcomings and we should too. **<u>There hath no temptation taken you but such as is common to man</u>: but God is faithful, who will not suffer you to be tempted above that ye are able; but will with the temptation also make a way to escape, that ye may be able to bear it** (1 Corinthians 10:13).

---

⁴⁴ See the author's work: <u>Matthew</u> for additional commentary involving the chronological order of events following Jesus' resurrection.

219

He saith unto him, Feed my lambs.

Understanding that God's people are often portrayed as sheep in the Bible (1 Peter 2:25, Isaiah 53:6), we can safely conclude that God is telling Peter to feed the newborn young Christians.

[16]**He saith to him again the second time, Simon, son of Jonas, lovest thou me? He saith unto him, Yea, Lord; thou knowest that I love thee. He saith unto him, Feed my sheep.**

Applying the same thought process as above, these must be the more mature Christians that Peter is supposed to feed.

[17]**He saith unto him the <u>third time</u>, Simon, son of Jonas, lovest thou me? Peter was grieved because he said unto him the third time, Lovest thou me? And he said unto him, Lord, thou knowest all things; thou knowest that I love thee. Jesus saith unto him, Feed my sheep.**

I find it interesting how the number three seems to be so closely associated with Peter.

- He bragged or boasted three times in the upper room (Matthew 26:33-35, John 13:37)
- He slept three times in the garden (Mark 14:32-41)
- He denied the Lord three times.
- Here he has confessed his love for the Lord three times.
- Here he is told to feed God's people three times.
  - He indeed does do as Jesus asked:
    - In Acts 2 he feeds the Jews the gospel
    - In Acts 10 he feeds the Gentiles the gospel
    - In 1 and 2 Peter he feeds the church of God with doctrinal truths

[18]**Verily, verily, I say unto thee, When thou wast young, thou girdest thyself, and walkedst whither thou wouldest: but when thou shalt be old, thou shalt stretch forth thy hands, and another shall gird thee, and carry thee whither thou wouldest not.** [19]**This spake he, signifying by what death he should glorify God. And when he had spoken this, he saith unto him, Follow me.**

Jesus notifies Peter that he will die in such a way that would not be pleasant. We can conclude this based on the fact Peter was to be girded and carried to a place not of his choice. The Bible does not give us the specifics of his death, only that Peter continued to follow Christ even though he knew he was going to die. **Yea, I think it meet, as long as I am in this tabernacle, to stir you up by putting you in remembrance; Knowing that shortly I [Peter] must put off this my tabernacle, even as our Lord Jesus Christ hath shewed me** (2 Peter 1:13-14).

History, according to what I have read from the Smith's Bible Dictionary as recorded by early historians, tells us that Peter was crucified upside down in Rome under the emperor Nero around 67 or 68 A.D. It is understood and accepted that he requested this position because he did not want to be put to death in the same manner as Jesus.

[20]Then Peter, turning about, seeth the disciple whom Jesus loved following; which also leaned on his breast at supper, and said, Lord, which is he that betrayeth thee?

Considering they just finished breakfast, the Bible must be referring us to John leaning on Jesus' breast during the Passover meal (commonly called the last supper) in John 13:23.

[21]Peter seeing him saith to Jesus, Lord, and what shall this man do? [22]Jesus saith unto him, If I will that he tarry till I come, what is that to thee? Follow thou me.

Peter is a perfect representative of most Christians. He begins by asking about John to compare himself to him. What he needed to do, and what we all need to do, is to not worry ourselves with what everyone else is doing. We must make sure our spiritual relationship with Jesus Christ is where it ought to be. Often, we are so quick to base the measure of our spirituality by comparing ourselves to our immediate company of Christians, and this should not be. **For we dare not make ourselves of the number, or compare ourselves with some that comment themselves: but they measuring themselves by themselves, and comparing themselves among themselves, are not wise** (2 Corinthians 10:12).

[23]Then went this saying abroad among the brethren, that that disciple should not die: yet Jesus said not unto him, He shall not die; but, If I will that he tarry till I come, what is that to thee? [24]This is the disciple which testifieth of these things, and wrote these things: and we know that his testimony is true.

This is where commentators attribute John to the places where God had written, "disciple whom Jesus loved" (John 21:20, 21:7), and "that other disciple" (John 18:16, 20:3, 20:8). He must have been the penmen of this Gospel based on this information. Nevertheless, whoever the penman was is of little concern because ultimately the author is God.

[25]And there are also many other things which Jesus did, the which, if they should be written every one, I suppose that even the world itself could not contain the books that should be written. Amen.

      If people tried to record all that Jesus did while on earth, and what He has been doing for all believers in the past 2,000 years, there would not be enough room in all the world to contain the books. Truly, you can never fully describe God's love for us!

      It is my sincere hope that this book has been a help and a blessing to your soul, and that your understanding of John has increased. I pray that your continued walk with our Lord Jesus Christ would encourage you to tell others all that you have read and learned about Jesus being God manifest in the flesh.

      Also, just as v. 25 above illustrates, many more truths could have been stated within this book's pages. May you be the one to fill in the gaps with the additional commentary that could have been presented. Witness for Jesus to the lost. Be an encouragement to the saved and testify of the great and wonderful things Jesus has done for you. May God bless each of you!

APPENDIX

The Trinity

This article was originally written in 2013 as an internet publication for Landis Baptist Church in Landis, North Carolina, and has been placed in this book because of its relation to our discussion in John 1. This work has been updated to include additional information and truths that God has enabled me to learn since 2013.

This article comes in direct response to a comment one of my professors made while I attended Appalachian State University. I will not give her name, but the course was entitled: Women and the Study of Religion. During a class discussion she said "There is no biblical support for a trinity – at least there is not one verse saying a trinity exists. The idea came from the Council of Nicaea around 325 A.D. where the bishops decided a trinity existed after debating the matter."

At that time in my spiritual walk, I did not have a biblical rebuttal. In other words, I could not think of one single verse to counter her argument. Nonetheless, from that day on I began to uncover the truth for myself as to what the Bible has to say regarding three issues brought up among this council:

1) When should the resurrection be celebrated?
2) What is the relationship between the Father, Son, and Holy Ghost – are they all God?
3) Was Jesus Christ (the Son) created by God the Father?

Celebrating the resurrection

My wife sometimes gives me supportive criticism regarding some of my attributes of character. All of which I need, and fully appreciate. One of those attributes is how I will often answer a question with a question. I cannot honestly remember when or why I started doing that, although I think it might have had something to do with teaching high school for a few years. As a teacher I tried not to give answers, but to help students discover the answer for themselves.

I mention this so that when asked, "When should the resurrection be celebrated?" I can respond with, "Who said you SHOULD?"

All throughout the New Testament there are two specific observances (commonly called ordinances) that God commanded of us. One is to preach, teach, and baptize in the name of the Father, Son, and Holy Ghost. **Go ye therefore, and teach all nations, baptizing them in the name of the Father,** and of the Son, and of the Holy Ghost: **Teaching them to observe all things whatsoever I have commanded you: and, lo, I am with you alway, even unto the end of the world. Amen** (Matthew 28:19-20). The second is to remember the Lord's death through partaking of the Lord's Supper. **And when he had given thanks, he brake it, and said, Take, eat: this is my body, which is broken for you: this do in remembrance of me.** After the same manner also he took the cup, when he had supped, saying, This cup is the new testament in my blood: this do ye, as oft as ye drink it, in remembrance of me. For as often as ye eat this bread, and drink this cup, ye do shew the Lord's death till he come** (1 Corinthians 11:24-26).

So, the question I stated above is legitimate. Jesus made an explicit point for us to remember His death and not His resurrection because it is in His death where we have victory over sin and the grave. He shed His blood that we might have the remission of sins (Ephesians 1:7, Colossians 1:14, and Hebrews 9:22). He even stated, **it is finished** upon giving up the ghost on the cross. Therefore, His death takes precedence over the resurrection – so, again I ask: "Who said you should celebrate the resurrection?"

In all truthfulness, every time you magnify Jesus Christ, praise Him for what He has done, or call upon His name you are celebrating the resurrection. Jesus said in John 11:25, **I am the resurrection, and the life**, therefore honoring and exalting Him is indeed celebrating the resurrection.

Please do not misunderstand what I am saying. I did not say there was something wrong with setting aside one day each year to celebrate the resurrection of Jesus Christ. Nor did I say the resurrection was not important. It holds plenty of importance. His resurrection from the dead proved that He was exactly who He said He was – God manifest in the flesh. I am just simply wondering why the question was even brought up among this council considering there is not a single verse of scripture commanding us to do such a thing.

The Relationship between the Father, Son, and Holy Ghost

The simple answer to this question is 1 John 5:7 – [1]**For there are three that bear record in heaven, the Father, the Word, and the Holy Ghost: and these three are one.** Using this verse, and John 1:1-14 where Jesus Christ is described as being the Word, it is evident the members of the Godhead are all one. So, I cannot tell you the condition of my professor's heart, but here is a single verse supporting the trinity. This should be enough evidence to convince the gainsayer; however, the Bible has plenty of evidence to show their equality. Consider the few verses below that illustrate the truth of this matter.

First: God the Holy Ghost = God the Father

1. Notice what was said about Ananias and Sapphira in the early church out of the book of Acts – Acts 5:1-4. **But a certain man named Ananias, with Sapphira his wife, sold a possession, And kept back part of the price, his wife also being privy to it, and brought a certain part, and laid it at the apostles' feet. But Peter said, Ananias, why hath Satan filled thine heart to <u>lie to the Holy Ghost</u>, and to keep back part of the price of the land? Whiles it remained, was it not thine own? and after it was sold was it not in thine own power? why hast thou conceived this thing in thine heart? thou hast <u>not lied unto men, but unto God</u>.** It appears God and the Holy Ghost are one in the same.

2. Isaiah 6:8-9: **Also I heard <u>the voice of the Lord</u>, saying, Whom shall I send, and who will go for us? Then said I, Here am I; send me. And <u>he said</u>, Go, and tell this people, Hear ye indeed, but understand not; and see ye indeed, but perceive not.** Notice who was talking here compared to Acts 28:25-26 where this scripture is referenced. **And when they agreed not among themselves, they departed, after that Paul had spoken one word, <u>Well spake the Holy Ghost</u> by Esaias the prophet unto our fathers, Saying, Go unto this people, and say, Hearing ye shall hear, and shall not understand; and seeing ye shall see, and not perceive.** The Lord and the Holy Ghost must be equal.

3. Jeremiah 31:31-34: **Behold, the days come, <u>saith the LORD</u>, that I will make a new covenant with the house of Israel, and with the house of Judah: Not according to the covenant that I made with their fathers in the day that I took them by the hand to bring them out of the land of Egypt; which my covenant they brake, although I was an husband unto them, said the LORD: but this shall be the covenant that I will make with the house of Israel; After those days, <u>saith the LORD</u>, I will put my law in their inward parts, and write it in their hearts; and will be their God, and they shall be my people. And they shall teach no more every man his neighbor, and every man his brother, saying, Know the LORD: for they shall all know me, from the least of them unto the greatest of them, saith the LORD: for I will forgive their iniquity, and I will remember their sin no more.** Again, notice who spoke here compared to Hebrews 10:15-17 where this scripture is referenced. **Whereof <u>the Holy Ghost</u> also is a witness to us: for after**

226

that **he had said before,** This is the covenant that I will make with them after those days, **saith the Lord,** (more proof that the Holy Ghost = Lord) **I will put my laws into their hearts, and in their minds will I write them; And their sins and iniquities will I remember no more.**

Second: God the Father = Jesus Christ the Son

1. Look at the response Jesus gave the Jews about healing on the Sabbath, and then how the Pharisees reacted in John 5:16-18. **And therefore did the Jews persecute Jesus, and sought to slay him, because he had done these things on the sabbath day. But Jesus answered them, My Father worketh hitherto, and I work. Therefore the Jews sought the more to kill him, because he not only had broken the sabbath, but said that God was his Father, making himself equal with God.**

2. The same thing happened again in John 10:30-33. **I and my Father are one. Then the Jews took up stones again to stone him. Jesus answered them, Many good works have I shewed you from my Father; for which of those works do ye stone me? The Jews answered him, saying, For a good work we stone thee not; but for blasphemy; and because that thou, being a man, makest thyself God.**

3. Now, in response to the Jews' comment about Jesus "being a man" – He was a man, but he was also God. **There is no man that hath power over the spirit to retain the spirit; neither hath he power in the day of death: and there is no discharge in that war; neither shall wickedness deliver those that are given to it** – Ecclesiastes 8:8. So no mere man could simply dismiss his spirit if he wanted to die, but Jesus did on the cross in Luke 23:46. **And when Jesus had cried with a loud voice, he said, Father, into thy hands I comment my spirit: and having said thus, he gave up the ghost.**

4. Jesus performed many miracles while here on earth: healed the lame and the crippled, cured disease, raised the dead, caused the dumb to speak, and gave sight to the blind. Giving sight to the blind is particularly interesting. Mark 8:22-25: **And he cometh to Bethsaida; and they bring a blind man unto him, and besought him to touch him. And he took the blind man by the hand, and led him out of the town; and when he had spit on his eyes, and put his hands upon him, he asked him if he saw ought. And he looked up, and said, I see men as trees, walking. After that he put his hands again upon his eyes, and made him look up: and he was restored, and saw every man clearly.** Jesus

227

gave this man sight, and this is interesting because Psalm 146:8 states **The LORD openeth the eyes of the blind.** Jesus must be God.

Lastly: God the Holy Ghost = Jesus Christ the Son

Simple algebraic mathematics at this point would prove to you this last point. If God the Holy Ghost equals God the Father, and God the Father equals Jesus Christ the Son, then God the Holy Ghost equals Jesus Christ the Son. It is the transitive property of equality (if a=b, and b=c, then a=c). And people think the word of God does not belong in public school. Nonetheless, we will not allow mathematics to usurp any authority over the word of God, so here is what the Bible says.

1. Romans 5:8-9: **But God commendeth his love toward us, in that, while we were yet sinners, <u>Christ</u> dies for us. Much more then, being now justified by <u>his blood</u>, we shall be saved from wrath through him.**
2. 1 Peter 1:18: **Forasmuch as ye know that ye were not redeemed with corruptible things, as silver and gold, from your vain conversation received by tradition from your father; But with the precious <u>blood of Christ</u>, as of a lamb without blemish and without spot.**
3. Here we must look at a long passage because the sentence covers 8 verses: Colossians 1:9-14. **For this cause we also, since the day we heard it, do not cease to pray for you, and to desire that ye might be filled with the knowledge of his will in all wisdom and spiritual understanding; That ye might walk worthy of the Lord unto all pleasing, being fruitful in every good work, and increasing in the knowledge of God; Strengthened with all might, according to his glorious power, unto all patience and longsuffering with joyfulness; Give thanks unto the Father, which hath made us meet to be partakers of the inheritance of the saints in light: Who hath delivered us from the power of darkness, and hath translated us into the kingdom of his <u>dear Son: In whom we have redemption through his blood</u>, even the forgiveness of sins.**

These three sections of scripture plainly state we are redeemed and justified because of the shed blood of Christ. Now, look at Acts 20:28. **Take heed therefore unto yourselves, and to all the flock, over the which <u>the Holy Ghost</u> hath made you overseers, to feed the church of God, which <u>he hath purchased with his own blood</u>.** Isn't that interesting? The Holy Ghost is said to have purchased us with His shed blood. The only way these verses cannot be contradictory is if God the Holy Ghost equals God the Son.

Now, just in case someone thinks the pronoun, he, refers to God and not the Holy Ghost – please examine the commas. The phrase: "to feed the church of God" contained inside the commas is a parenthetical. It is extra information relating to the Holy Ghost, who is the subject (noun) of focus in the sentence. Therefore, the pronoun, he, must refer to the Holy Ghost.

Can I just reiterate that the Bible belongs in public education. You can reference it to teach any of the main subjects: Math, Science, History, and English.

Was Jesus Christ created by God the Father?

Simple Answer: No.

I imagine this question arose from the words that often describe the relationship between God the Father, and Jesus Christ: **only begotten Son** (found in John, Acts, Hebrews, and 1 John) and **the only begotten of the Father** (also found in John). We will discuss the use of this word as it relates to Jesus shortly.

First, we will take our study all the way back to creation to see what we can learn. Colossians 1:16-17 states the following words regarding Jesus Christ: **For by him were all things created, that are in heaven, and that are in earth, visible and invisible, whether they be thrones, or dominions, or principalities, or power: all things were created by him, and for him: and he is before all things, and by him all things consist**. You can see He was "before ALL things."

Next, consider Revelation 1:8: **I am Alpha and Omega, the beginning and the ending, saith the Lord, which is, and which was, and which is to come, the Almighty**. Just two verses show how Jesus was there before all things, and that He created all things. Therefore, God the Father could not have created God the Son.

Two more sections of scripture to finish the discussion. The first we have referenced previously - John 1:1-3: **In the beginning was the Word, and the Word was with God, and the Word was God. The same was in the beginning with God. All things were made by him; and without him was not any thing made that was made.** Here is yet more support that Jesus created all things, and when the beginning started Christ was there.

The second reference is found in Micah 5:2: **But thou, Bethlehem Ephratah, though thou be little among the thousands of Judah, yet out of thee shall he [Jesus] come forth unto me that is to be ruler in Israel; whose goings forth have been from of old, from everlasting**. Wow, what a statement! You cannot put a start date to Jesus' existence. If you were to investigate the past, eternally backwards, Jesus is and has always been.

What about the word begotten?

In the commentary of John 1, my desire was to not complicate the context of the chapter, so we briefly skimmed over the Bible's teaching of *begotten* throughout scripture. We learned how it refers to one's physical birth and spiritual birth, but now we need to see how this word relates directly to Jesus Christ. There are five places in scripture, apart from the book of John, which speak of Christ being begotten and every single time the verses illustrate Him in an *honored and exalted position given to Him by God the Father*. Those references are Psalm 2, Acts 13:33, Hebrews 1:5; 5:5, and 1 John 4:9. We will examine three of them.

Psalm 2

Why do the heathen rage, and the people imagine a vain thing? The kings of the earth set themselves, and the rulers take counsel together, against the LORD, and against his anointed saying, Let us break their bands asunder, and cast away their cords from us (vs. 1-3). The context is the heathen's desire to set themselves apart from God by taking counsel together to rise up against the LORD. They want the exalted position above God. How does God respond?

He that sitteth in the heavens shall laugh: the Lord shall have them in derision. Then shall he speak unto them in his wrath, and vex them in his sore displeasure (vs. 4-5). God laughs at them! Why anyone would think they can combat God and win is a mystery to me, and God chuckles at such a notion. Then, notice what He says.

Yet have I set my king [Jesus] **upon my holy hill of Zion. <u>I will declare the decree</u>: the LORD hath said unto me** [Jesus]**, Thou art my Son; <u>this day have I begotten thee</u>. Ask of me, and I shall give thee the heathen for thine inheritance, and the uttermost parts of the earth for thy possession. Thou** [Jesus] **shalt break them with a rod of iron; thou shalt dash them in pieces like a potter's vessel** (vs. 6-9). God makes known His decree for all the rulers and kings of the heathens to hear that there is one who is set upon the holy hill of Zion. A king who owns the heathen as an inheritance, receives the earth as His possession, and will rule all with a rod of iron (c.f. Revelation 2:27; 12:5; 19:15).

Also, do you see the exalted position God the Father has given His Son through His decree? **Thou art my Son; this day have I begotten thee** is a decree from all mighty God on behalf of Jesus Christ stating that Christ has the exalted position. Not those heathens who plotted and schemed to take it.

There is only one proper response man can give to God's decree. **Be wise now therefore, O ye kings: be instructed, ye judges of the earth. Serve the LORD with fear, and rejoice with trembling. Kiss the Son, lest he be angry, and ye perish from the way, when his wrath is kindled but a little. Blessed are all they that put their trust in him** (vs. 10-12). Simply put: Stop fighting against God. Instead, fear Him and trust Him. He has the exalted position over you.

Acts 13:26-33

Men and brethren, children of the stock of Abraham, and whosoever among you feareth God, to you is the word of this salvation sent. For they that dwell at Jerusalem, and their rulers, because they knew him [Jesus] **not, nor yet the voices of the prophets which are read every Sabbath day, they have fulfilled them** [the scriptures] **in condemning him. And though they found no cause of death in him, yet desired they Pilate that he should be slain. And when they had fulfilled <u>all that was written of him</u>, they took him down from the tree, and laid him in a sepulcher. But <u>God raised him from the dead</u>: And he was seen many days of them which came up with him from Galilee to Jerusalem, who are his witnesses unto the people. And we declare unto you glad tidings, how that the promise which was made unto the fathers, God hath fulfilled the same unto us their children, in that he hath raised up Jesus <u>again</u>, as it is also written in the second psalm, Thou art my Son, <u>this day have I begotten thee</u>**.

Look at the facts of the verses and notice Jesus' exalted position.

1. Jesus' condemnation and death was a fulfilment of Old Testament scripture. Very few people can boast of having prophetical scripture being written about them, and Jesus is one of them.
2. He was raised from the dead. There is an even shorter list of people who can make such a claim, and Jesus is on that list.
3. The promise that was made unto the fathers was fulfilled when Jesus was raised up <u>AGAIN</u>. That is very interesting indeed!

This second raising is not a reference to His bodily resurrection but is a reference to His exalted position over all creation. God the Father gave His Son a position of exaltation that no other person on earth can claim. Sure, some people had prophesies foretold and recorded about them like Jesus. Others were raised from the dead like Jesus. But no other person on earth has ever been given such an exalted position that Jesus Christ has received from God the Father. This is why God stated, **Thou art my Son, this day** (the day the Father made His decree from Psalm 2) **have I begotten thee**.

Our last stop will really show Jesus' exalted position given to Him by the Father.

Hebrews 1:1-9

God, who at sundry times and in divers manners spake in time past unto the fathers by the prophets, Hath in these last days spoken unto us by his Son, whom he hath appointed heir of all things, by whom also he made the worlds; Who being the brightness of his glory, and the express image of his person, and upholding all things by the word of his power, when he had by himself purged our sins, sat down on the right hand of the Majesty on high; Being made so much better than the angels, as he hath by inheritance obtained a more excellent name than they. For unto which of the angels said he at any time, Thou art my Son, this day have I begotten thee: And again, I will be to him a Father, and he shall be to me a Son? And again, when he bringeth in the first begotten into the world, he saith, And let all the angels of God worship him. And of the angels he saith, Who maketh his angels spirits, and his ministers a flame of fire. But unto the Son he saith, Thy throne, O God, is for ever and ever: a scepter of righteousness is the scepter of thy kingdom. Thou hast loved righteousness and hated iniquity; therefore God, even thy God, hath anointed thee with the oil of gladness above thy fellows.

WOW! Just take a step back and look at the exalted position Jesus has.

- In these last days God has spoken to us by his Son
- Jesus is heir of all things
- Jesus made all things
- He is the brightness of the Father's glory
- He is the express image of the Father's person
- He upholds all things by the word of His power
- He purged our sins by Himself

- He sat down on the right hand of the Father – the Majesty on high
- He is above all the angels, and all the angels should worship Him
- His throne is eternal, and His scepter is righteousness
- He hates iniquity
- He is anointed with the oil of gladness above thy fellows (Israel).

In a short summary: whenever you see the word begotten as it relates to Jesus Christ, it is referring to the exalted position the Father has given Him over all creation. Oh, what a savior we have in Jesus!

Why ye __must__ be born again

In the first three chapters of John, we have the following truths: Jesus Christ created all things, He gives light to every man that cometh into the world, He continues to give light to those that desire it, and apart from your physical birth, you must be born again.

What is wrong with your first birth? To answer this question, we need to go to the book of Genesis, chapter 5.

This is the book of the generations of Adam. In the day that God created man, in the likeness of God made he him; Male and female created he them; and blessed them, and called their name Adam, in the day when they were created. Man was created in God's likeness, and in God's image (Genesis 1:26), but keep reading. **And Adam lived an hundred and thirty years, and begat a son in his own likeness, after his image; and called his name Seth**. This may not seem like much at first glance, but we have a dramatic turn of events.

When Adam was created no sin was in the world. Adam later transgressed against the commandment of God by eating of the forbidden fruit from the tree of knowledge of good and evil, and thus sin entered the world. It was after this that Adam and his wife Eve conceived and bore a son in his likeness, after his image. Oh yes, this likeness and image is very much like the likeness and image that Adam was created in, but with one major difference – sin.

We all are in this generation of Adam. We all are sinners. **God that made the world, and all things therein, seeing that he is Lord of heaven and earth, dwelleth not in temples made with hands; Neither is worshipped with men's hands, as though he needed any thing, seeing he giveth to all life, and breath, and all things; And hath made of one blood all nations of men for to dwell on all the face of the earth** (Acts 17:24-26a). So, it does not matter what ethnic background you come from, what language you speak, or what color your skin is because the same blood that was in Adam is in us.

What can we expect because of being born physically? **Wherefore, as by one man sin entered into the world, and death by sin; and so death passed upon all men, for that all have sinned** (Romans 5:12). The answer is you will die.

If you were to continue reading of the generations of Adam in Genesis 5 you would see death in almost every fourth verse. Why? **For the wages of sin is death** (Romans 6:23). As a direct result of Adam's transgression, every person born in this world is born a sinner, a debt must be paid, and the only wage payable to satisfy this debt is death. You are going to die.

People say, "I don't like to talk about death." "I don't like to think about death." What people need is to face facts. You are going to die. This may seem like a dreary subject with no hope in sight, but Jesus Christ has provided the only means of hope. **For as in Adam all die, even so in Christ shall all be made alive** (1 Corinthians 15:22).

Christ paid our sin debt by dying on the cross. If you do not trust in Him and die without being born AGAIN, you will die in your sins and spend eternity in hell. **Ye shall die in your sins: for if ye believe not that I** [Jesus] **am he, ye shall die in your sins** (John 8:24). You MUST be **born again, not of corruptible seed** (Adam's seed)**, but of incorruptible, by the word of God, which liveth and abideth for ever** (1 Peter 1:23). According to all that we have read in the word of God – upon believing on the Son of God, based on what is written in God's word, you experience a new birth[45] and have everlasting life. You will still die a physical death, but now you will be absent from the body and present with the Lord (2 Corinthians 5:8) in a place with no tears, pain, sorrow, or crying (Revelation 18:7). Oh, how gracious and glorious God is!

---

[45] Some churches support a belief that you can lose this new birth. Two things to consider: 1) Why would God call the life you have after being born again "eternal/everlasting" if you can lose it? 2) How do you lose "a birth" when a birth is an event that cannot be altered or changed.

Jesus walked on water

According to the Gospel accounts, immediately after Jesus fed roughly five thousand men with five loaves and two fishes, He walked on the sea as the disciples made their way toward Capernaum unto Bethsaida (Matthew 14:22-32, Mark 6:45-52, and John 6:15-21). I can't help but wonder as to why He would do such a thing when everything He did served a specific purpose. He did not waste actions, words, or moments of opportunity and a few examples should be sufficient to illustrate these three points.

First, He came to this earth in the form of a man (Philippians 2:6-7) to accomplish death. The Bible states during the transfiguration account in Luke 9:31 that Moses and Elias **spake of his decease which he should accomplish at Jerusalem**. Everything He did went to fulfil that purpose. He even often avoided answering people's questions when the inquirers posed questions to be argumentative rather than true heart felt inquisitions for truth. Also, it was stated in John 4:4 how **he must needs go through Samaria**. The point is, He always had a purpose for anything He did. So, why walk on water? What was Jesus trying to show or tell us? We will examine the context of Matthew 14:22-27 before discussing 2 possible explanations.

And straightway Jesus constrained his disciples to get into a ship, and to go before him unto the other side, while he sent the multitudes away. And when he had sent the multitudes away, he went up into a mountain apart to pray: and when the evening was come, he was there alone. But the ship was now in the midst of the sea, tossed with waves: for the wind was contrary. And in the fourth watch of the night Jesus went unto them, walking on the sea. And when the disciples saw him walking on the sea, they were troubled, saying, It is a spirit; and they cried out for fear. But straightway Jesus spake unto them, saying, Be of good cheer; it is I; be not afraid.

From the context of the passage, I'm sure Jesus had to constrain His disciples to go to the other side of the sea without Him because: 1. they arrived with Him, so surely, they wanted to depart with Him, and 2. While recently on the sea, they thought they were going to be killed by a storm. Had it not been for Jesus calming the sea, I'm sure they reckoned they would have perished (see Mark 4:35-39 along with the walking on water passage in Mark 6:45-52).

Also, it needs to be noted that the disciples did not abandon Jesus. One might think that the disciples deserted Jesus leaving him stranded on the other side of this sea, and this is simply not the case. Notice how the multitudes of people arrived at this desert place where Jesus fed them in Matthew 14:13: **He** [Jesus] **departed thence by ship into a desert place apart: and when the people had heard thereof, they followed him on foot out of the cities**. Jesus could have simply walked around the water like these people did. So again, why did Jesus walk on water? Well, the shortest distance between two points is a straight line, so walking on the water was the fastest route. This idea will prove important shortly.

Please keep in mind as you read through the following possible explanations that they are simply points of interest derived from truths within the Bible. We do not have a single verse stating, "Jesus walked on water because" ... therefore, these points are in fact speculations based on biblical truths.

1. Picture of what Jesus does for individuals within the nations

According to Revelation 17 verses 1 and 15, water is a picture of nations. **And there came one of the seven angels which had the seven vials, and talked with me, saying unto me, Come hither; I will shew unto thee the judgment of the great whore that sitteth upon many waters...The waters which thou sawest, where the whore sitteth, are peoples, and multitudes, and nations, and tongues**. Verse 2 explains **the inhabitants of the earth have been made drunk with the wine of her** [great whore] **fornication**. As a result of this great whore's influence and control over the inhabitants of the earth, they have become completely filled with the sin of fornication. Sin is everywhere, and all around them, as is the same for us today: **Behold, I was shapen in iniquity; and in sin did my mother conceive me** (Psalm 51:5). Just as these disciples found themselves tossed with waves amid this sea, all peoples find themselves struggling with sin. See below how this truth is illustrated in the life of Paul - Romans 7:15-25.

For that which I do I allow not: for what I would, that do I not; but what I hate, that do I. If then I do that which I would not, I consent unto the law that it is good. Now then it is no more I that do it, but sin that dwelleth in me. For I know that in me (that is, in my flesh,) dwelleth no good thing: for to will is present with me; but how to perform that which is good I find not. For the good that I would I do not: but the evil which I would not, that I do. Now if I do that I would not, it is no more I that do it, but sin that dwelleth in me. I find then a law, that, when I would do good, evil is present with me. For I delight in the law of God after the inward man: But I see another law in my members, warring against the law of my mind, and bringing me into captivity to the law of sin which is

in my members. **O WRETCHED MAN THAT I AM! WHO SHALL DELIVER ME FROM THE BODY OF THIS DEATH?** Can you see the struggle with sin Paul describes? You and I are no different, but thankfully God provides us with an answer to this question. **I THANK GOD THROUGH JESUS CHRIST OUR LORD. So then with the mind I myself serve the law of God; but with the flesh the law of sin**. Jesus Christ dealt with sin once and for all on our behalf, and He'll continue to help us with this struggle, just as He came to the disciple's aid during the fourth watch of the night. It doesn't matter who you are, what tongue you speak, or what nationality you are part of. Christ paid for your sins. You can have remission of your sins if you will repent and believe on the Lord Jesus Christ (Acts 10:43, 17:30, Luke 24:30, and Romans 10:9).

2. How Jesus walked out of hell and into Paradise

A lot of Bible truth must be presented before illustrating this point. Note the verses below where our journey begins with Jesus on the cross.

- While Jesus was hanging on the cross, the Bible tells us in Mark 15:33-37: **And when the sixth hour was come, there was darkness over the whole land until <u>the ninth hour</u>. And <u>at the ninth hour</u> Jesus cried with a loud voice, saying, Eloi, Eloi, lama sabachthani? which is, being interpreted, My God, my God, why hast thou forsaken me? And some of them that stood by, when they heard it, said, Behold, he calleth Elias. And one ran and filled a spunge full of vinegar, and put it on a reed, and gave him to drink, saying, Let alone; let us see whether Elias will come to take him down. And Jesus cried with a loud voice, and gave up the ghost**.
- According to the Bible there are twelve hours of sun light in each day. To keep arguments regarding geographical locations out of this topic, the following statement by Jesus is true for where He was at the time. John 11:9: **Jesus answered, Are there not <u>twelve hours</u> in <u>the day</u>? If any man walk in <u>the day</u>, he stumbleth not, because he seeth <u>the light of this world</u>**.
- The Jewish day begins in the evening, not in the morning as we reckon it. Take the first day of creation as an example and notice the evening is mentioned as the beginning of a 24-hour period. Genesis 1:5: **And God called the light Day, and the darkness he called Night. And <u>the evening and the morning</u> were the first day.**
- While on the cross, Jesus spoke with the repentant thief. Luke 23:39-43: **And one of the malefactors which were hanged railed on him,**

saying, If thou be Christ, save thyself and us. But the other answering rebuked him, saying, Dost not thou fear God, seeing thou art in the same condemnation? And we indeed justly; for we receive the due reward of our deeds: but this man hath done nothing amiss. And he said unto Jesus, Lord, remember me when thou comest into thy kingdom. And Jesus said unto him, Verily I say unto thee, To day shalt thou be with me in paradise.

Taking all the verses above into consideration, along with Acts 2, Psalm 16, and Revelation 1 we have the following facts:

1. Acts 2, Psalm 16, and Revelation 1 tell us that Christ went to hell before going to Paradise. He did not go there to suffer, but simply to get the keys to death and hell (Revelation 1:18), to dump all our iniquities there that were placed on Him (Isaiah 53:6, this event was pictured through the "scapegoat" released into the wilderness in the Old Testament - Leviticus 16), and to preach unto the spirits there in prison (1 Peter 3:19).
2. A new day began at evening for the Jews (approximately 6 p.m.)
3. Jesus died around the 9th hour of a 12-hour time frame, therefore there were only 3 hours remaining before the next day began
4. Before dying, Jesus told the thief He would be with him today in Paradise, therefore He's limited to 3 hours to get from hell to Paradise.

Next, our journey takes us to Luke 16:19-26 where we get a clear description of hell and Paradise.

There was a certain rich man, which was clothed in purple and fine linen, and fared sumptuously every day: And there was a certain beggar named Lazarus, which was laid at his gate, full of sores, And desiring to be fed with the crumbs which fell from the rich man's table: moreover the dogs came and licked his sores. And it came to pass, that the beggar died, and was carried by the angels into Abraham's bosom: the rich man also died, and was buried; And in hell he lift up his eyes, being in torments, and seeth Abraham afar off, and Lazarus in his bosom. And he cried and said, Father Abraham, have mercy on me, and send Lazarus, that he may dip the tip of his finger in water, and cool my tongue; for I am tormented in this flame. But Abraham said, Son, remember that thou in thy lifetime receivedst thy good things, and likewise Lazarus evil things: but now he is comforted, and thou art tormented. And beside all this, between us and you there is a great gulf fixed: so that they which would pass from hence to you cannot; neither

can they pass to us, that would come from thence. Apparently, hell and Paradise were close enough to be seen by the inhabitants of each. We also know from Matthew 12:40 that this is in the heart of the earth - **For as Jonas was three days and three nights in the whale's belly; so shall the Son of man be three days and three nights in <u>the heart of the earth</u>**.

Did you notice what was separating hell and Paradise? A great gulf. This is the only place in the Bible where the word gulf appears, so we must determine its meaning. It could be a deep abyss, or a body of water based on the definitions of the word. If this is indeed a body of water, we then have proof from the life of Christ that crossing it would be no problem for Him - He could walk on it. And, given the time frame Jesus is dealing with, the quickest route is to walk on the water and not around it. This seems to go hand in hand with the details of Matthew 14.

How long was Jesus' ministry?

I do not want to make this into a big deal, but it seems people derive their durations for Jesus' ministry based predominantly on logic instead of the Bible.

Some commentators claim His ministry could not have lasted longer than a year and they support their argument by stating the Bible was translated incorrectly. Considering God Himself said His word was forever settled in heaven (Psalm 119:89), it liveth and abideth forever (1 Peter 1:23, 25), and that it would not pass away (Matthew 24:35, Mark 13:31, Luke 21:33), we can thus disregard their claims.

Other commentators derive a 3½ year ministry based on the Gospel of John (more on this shortly) and add to the Bible their logic that Christ would have needed an extra 6 months to complete everything recorded in the Gospels.

I personally want to throw logic out the window whenever possible. According to the Gospels, it appears Jesus' ministry could not have lasted any longer than three years. To determine how much time has passed while examining the Gospels, you have to look for key indicators like dates or events that always happen at the same time each year. The feast of Passover is a good indicator.

Only three Passover feasts are mentioned throughout the Gospel of John. They are in John 2:13, 6:4, and 11:55.[46] Since this feast occurs every year at the same time, we can accurately determine when a calendar year has passed. If we then examine the whole book, we have the timetable represented below.

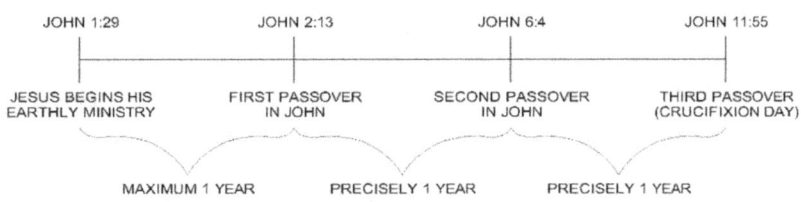

Therefore, Jesus' ministry on this earth must have been a maximum of 3 years if we go strictly by the Bible.

---

[46] This last Passover is the only one common to the other Gospels. It is the day Jesus died (see the Appendix – *The last days of Jesus' ministry* for more details). Therefore, we have to focus our attention to John to answer this question.

To narrow down this time frame even further, notice what Jesus says in Luke 13:6-9. **He spake also this parable; A certain man had a fig tree planted in his vineyard; and he came and sought fruit thereon, and found none. Then said he unto the dresser of his vineyard, Behold, <u>these three years</u> I come seeking fruit on this fig tree, and find none: cut it down; why cumbereth it the ground? And he answering said unto him, Lord, let it alone this year also, til I shall dig about it, and dung it: And if it bear fruit, well: and if not, then after that thou shalt cut it down**. This directly relates to the time frame illustrated above where Israel refused to receive Jesus Christ despite hearing Him preach for three years. If we cross reference Mark 11:12-14 and Matthew 21: 19-21 we will see that Jesus cursed the fig tree on the 10th day of Nisan[47] just before He went to be crucified on the 14th, so Jesus did not grant the dresser's request of an additional year for the fig tree to bear fruit. With that information, I would conclude His ministry did not exceed three years in length.

Now, as I mentioned before, I am not going to make this into a big deal. I do not get upset when I hear someone say His ministry was 3½ years simply because if Jesus had not died on that cross, paying the wages of our sin (Romans 6:23) to reconcile us to Himself, that He might present us holy and unblameable and unreproveable in His sight (Colossians 1:21-22), it would make no difference if He ministered on earth for twenty minutes or two thousand years; we would still be lost in our sin. I am just glad that God had a ministry and died for us despite the specific length of time it took.

---

[47] See Appendix – *The last days of Jesus' ministry*

The last days of Jesus' ministry

I have often wondered why controversy exists among various denominational churches over a "Wednesday" crucifixion vs. a "Good Friday" crucifixion. They all seem to agree the women discovered Jesus' missing body on Sunday around sunrise (approximately 6 a.m.) for the average church member knows the Bible states **In the end of the sabbath, as it began to dawn toward <u>the first day of the week</u>, came Mary Magdalene and the other Mary to see the sepulchre** (Matthew 28:1). However, when trying to get answers regarding the specifics of when Jesus was crucified, the answer is usually traditional in nature instead of consulting the Bible.

"That's the way we've always celebrated it" is so often the response.

I desire to know what the Bible proclaims, and scripture has plenty of information to give. We will examine dozens of passages to receive the full story, but first notice the calendar below.

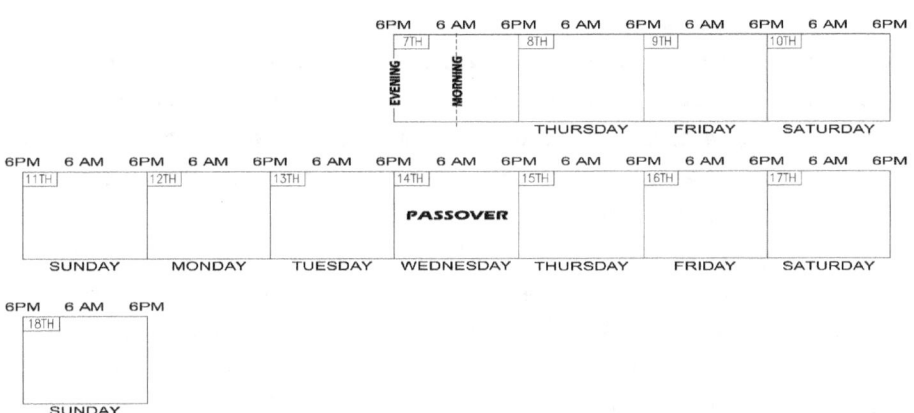

The first few things you need to be aware of are…

1) The Jewish day begins at "evening," approximately 6 p.m. instead of midnight like we are accustomed to. This will prove to be vital once we discuss the day of the crucifixion, but as a bonus, hopefully Genesis 1:5b will not seem backwards the next time you read it. **And the <u>evening and the morning</u> were the first day**.

2) Passover is the 14th day of the Jewish month Nisan – the first month of the Jewish calendar. **In the first month, that is, the month Nisan, in the fourteenth day of the first month <u>at even</u> is the LORD's Passover** (Esther 3:7 with Leviticus 23:5). The Passover feast would begin around 6 p.m. in the evening when Nisan 14 officially started.

The reason I have dedicated this day to a Wednesday will be fully presented as we progress forward.

3) God separated each day into two twelve-hour periods called day and night. **And God called the light Day, and the darkness he called Night. And the evening and the morning were the first <u>day</u>** (Genesis 1:5a). We know they are both 12-hour periods because **Jesus answered, Are there not <u>twelve hours in the day</u>**? (John 11:9)

As we cover each day shown on the calendar, an updated calendar will be presented. Our search detailing the crucifixion and resurrection account begins on the 8th day of the month Nisan.

<u>Nisan 8 – Jesus goes to Bethany</u>
John 12:1-8: **Then Jesus <u>six days before the passover</u> came to Bethany, where Lazarus was, which had been dead, whom he raised from the dead. There they made him a supper; and Martha served: but Lazarus was one of them that sat at the table with him. Then took Mary a pound of ointment of spikenard, very costly, and anointed the feet of Jesus, and wiped his feet with her hair: and the house was filled with the odour of the ointment. Then saith one of his disciples, Judas Iscariot, Simon's son, which should betray him, Why was not this ointment sold for three hundred pence, and given to the poor? This he said, not that he cared for the poor; but because he was a thief, and had the bag, and bare what was put therein. Then said Jesus, Let her alone: against the day of my burying hath she kept this. For the poor always ye have with you; but me ye have not always.**

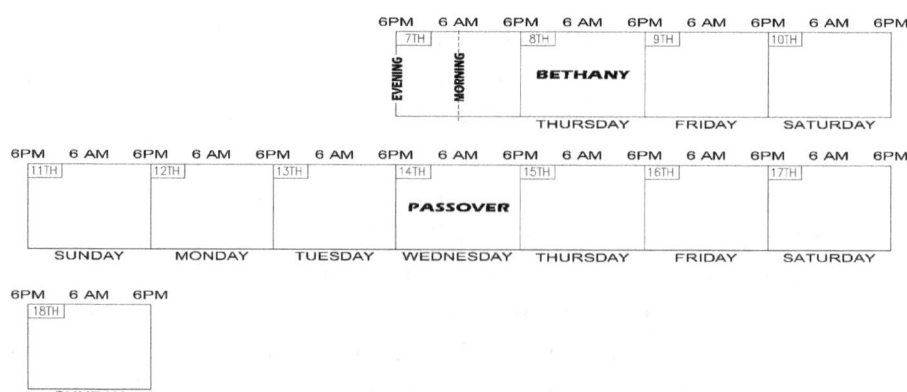

244

<u>Nisan 9 – Triumphal entry into Jerusalem</u>

Remaining in the twelfth chapter of John, begin at verse 12: **On the next day much people that were come to the feast, when they heard that Jesus was coming to Jerusalem, Took branches of palm trees, and went forth to meet him, and cried, Hosanna: Blessed is the King of Israel that cometh in the name of the Lord. And Jesus, when he had found a young ass, sat thereon; as it is written, Fear not, daughter of Sion: behold, thy King cometh, sitting on an ass's colt** (John 12:12-15). This is the day commonly referred to as "Palm Sunday." But, as you can see, and soon to be fully presented, this could *NOT* have happened on a Sunday.

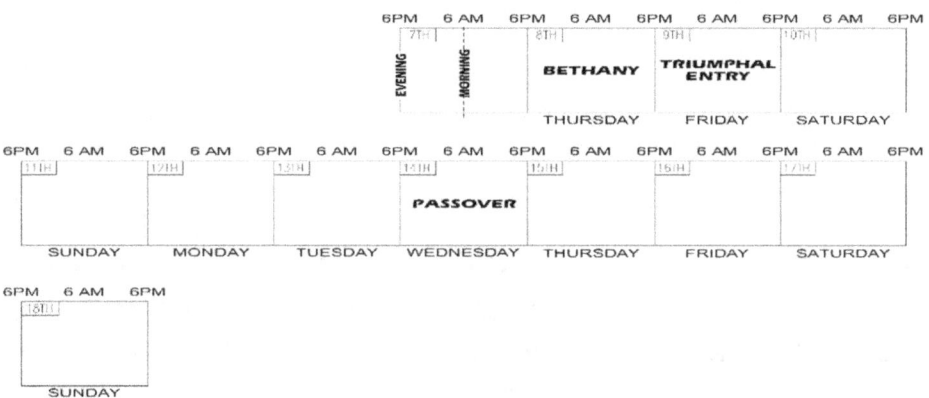

<u>Nisan 10 – Fig tree cursed and Temple cleansed</u>

Now we will go to Mark 11 where verses 1-10 connect us with what we read from John regarding the triumphal entry, but we want the information that follows beginning in verse 11. **And Jesus entered into Jerusalem, and into the temple: and when he had looked round about upon all things, and now <u>the eventide was come</u>, he went out unto Bethany with the twelve. <u>And on the morrow</u>, when they were come from Bethany, he was hungry: And seeing a fig tree afar off having leaves, he came, if haply he might find any thing thereon: and when he came to it, he found nothing but leaves; for the time of the figs was not yet. And Jesus answered and said unto it, No man eat fruit of thee hereafter for ever. And his disciples heard it. And they come to Jerusalem: and Jesus went into the temple, and began to cast out them that sold and bought in the temple, and overthrew the tables of the moneychangers, and the seats of them that sold doves; And would not suffer that any man should carry any vessel through the temple.** (Mark 11:11-16).

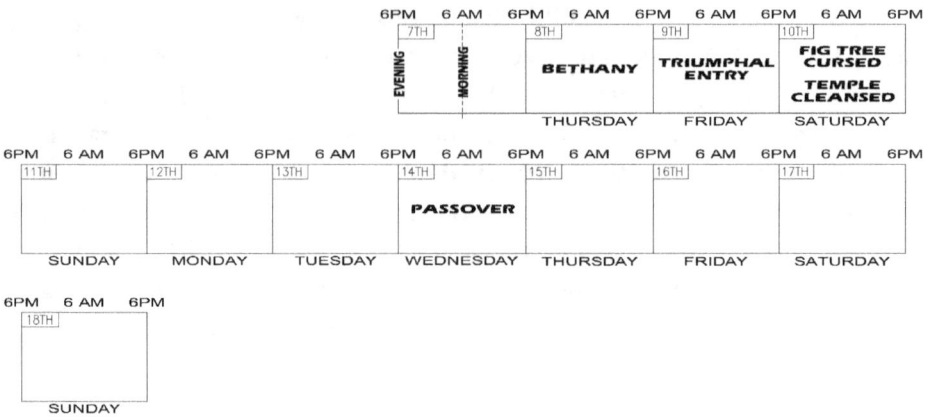

I would argue, based on scripture, that Jesus cleansing the temple was the final straw for the Jewish leaders who sought to kill Him. The basis of my argument is simply based on Exodus 12:1-6. **And the LORD spake unto Moses and Aaron in the land of Egypt, saying, This month shall be unto you the beginning of months: it shall be the first month of the year to you. Speak ye unto all the congregation of Israel, saying, <u>In the tenth day of this month they shall take to them every man a lamb</u>, according to the house of their fathers, a lamb for an house: And if the household be too little for the lamb, let him and his neighbor next unto his house take it according to the number of the souls; every man according to his eating shall make your count for the lamb. Your lamb shall be without blemish, a male of the first year: ye shall take it out from the sheep, or from the goats: And <u>ye shall keep it up until the fourteenth day</u> of the same month: and <u>the whole assembly of the congregation of Israel shall kill it in the evening</u>.**

This describes perfectly what happened to Jesus. On the fourteenth day He was taken into custody. The whole assembly of Israel that gathered at the hall of judgement shouted and cried for Him to be crucified, and He was nailed to a cross that very afternoon. To me, it only makes sense that on the tenth day of Nisan the Jewish leaders must have officially set their plans into motion to have Jesus killed.

Nisan 11 – Olivet Discourse

Mark 11:18-20: **And the scribes and chief priests heard it, and sought how they might destroy him: for they feared him, because all the people was astonished at his doctrine. And <u>when even was come,</u> he went** out of the city. **And in the morning, as they passed by, they saw the fig tree dried up from the roots. And Peter calling to remembrance saith unto him, Master, behold, the fig tree which thou cursedest is withered away.** According to this scripture we have moved into the 11th day of Nisan. This chapter of Mark matches Matthew 21 where Jesus begins a series of teachings referred to as the Olivet Discourse because he gave it near the Mt. of Olives. This discourse does not end until the beginning of Matthew 26, where we read: **And it came to pass, when Jesus had finished all these sayings, he said unto his disciples, Ye know that after two days is the feast of the passover, and the Son of man is betrayed to be crucified** (Matthew 26:1-2). The phrase "after two days" means three days later, or on the third day. Therefore, Passover occurs three days later.

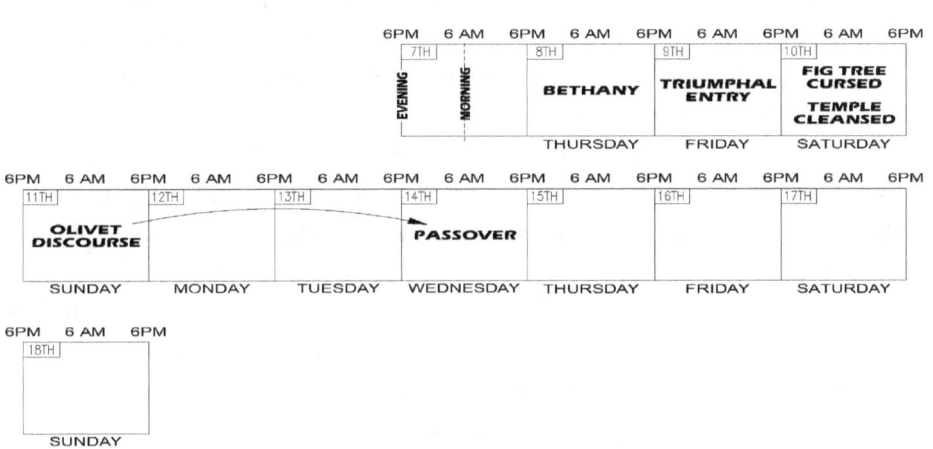

Nisan 14 through 18 – Crucifixion to the Resurrection

The first Passover feast happened in Egypt the night before the Israelites made their exodus out from under Egyptian bondage. If you recall note 2 at the beginning of this discussion, this feast began shortly after the start of Nisan 14 at evening. This brings us to the following events that occurred on the 14th:

1. Jesus and His disciples eat the Passover meal in the upper room.
2. They leave the upper room to go to the garden of Gethsemane.
3. Jesus is betrayed by Judas Iscariot and arrested in the garden.
4. He is taken before the high priest and the Sanhedrin for trial where false witnesses bear testimony against Him.
5. He is presented to Pilot and Herod to be condemned to death.

6. He is scourged, mocked, beaten, crowned with thorns, and smitten even though Pilate found no fault with Him.

7. Barabbas is released from his condemnation and Jesus takes his place to be crucified at the place of the skull called Golgotha.

   - See Matthew 26-27, Mark 14-15, Luke 22-23, John 13 and 18-19 for reference.

We will jump ahead to Jesus being on the cross. Please recall John 11:9, from note 3 at the beginning of this discussion, that there are 12 daytime hours according to scripture. With that in mind, read Mark 15:33-34, and 37. **And when the <u>sixth hour</u> was come, there was darkness over the whole land until the <u>ninth hour</u>. And at the ninth hour Jesus cried with a loud voice, saying, Eloi, Eloi, lama sabachthani? which is, being interpreted, My God, my God, why hast thou forsaken me? And Jesus cried with a loud voice, and gave up the ghost**. Given Jesus died at the ninth hour of a twelve-hour window, there are three hours remaining until the start of Nisan 15. I'll explain why this is important shortly.

Jesus also stated numerous times that He would be in the grave for 3 days and 3 nights. **For as Jonas was three days and three nights in the whale's belly; so shall the Son of man be three days and three nights in the heart of the earth** (Matthew 12:40). Connecting this with the women arriving at the tomb on the first day of the week, Jesus had to die on Wednesday to be in the heart of the earth from Thursday through Saturday for the women to discover His absent body on Sunday.

God's word is perfect. Hallelujah!

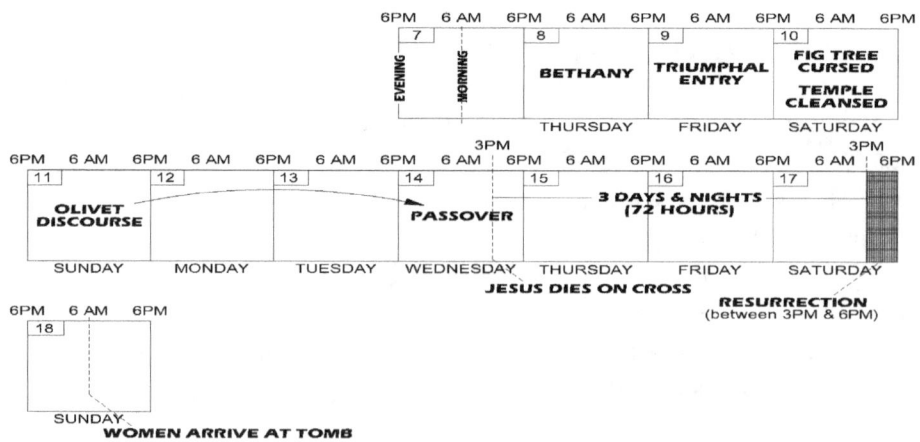

The reason I placed the resurrection between 3 and 6 pm on Saturday is because of what the Bible proclaims. Eight times in the Gospels, the scripture states Jesus would resurrect *on* the third day (Matthew 16:21, 17:23, 20:19; Mark 9:31, 10:34; Luke 9:22, 13:32, 18:33, 24:7). One occurrence states Jesus would resurrect *in* three days (John 2:19-21). And twice the scripture states that Jesus would resurrect *after* three days (Matthew 27:63, Mark 8:31). Is this a contradiction? God forbid! The explanation is simple: Christ died Wednesday at 3 pm and resurrected Saturday between 3 and 6 pm allowing Him to rise *on* the third day *after* being *in* the grave for 72 hours. Indeed, God's word is perfect!

Now comes what most *Good Friday* believers would call a flaw in what has been presented thus far. The Jews observe one particular day each week called the Sabbath (Saturday) where no servile work is done. Knowing this fact, many people read Mark or Luke, and based on what is written in the Bible, a Friday death seems to be the only logical answer. **And Jesus cried with a loud voice, and gave up the ghost. And now when the even was come, because it was the preparation, that is, the day before the sabbath, Joseph of Arimathaea, an honourable counsellor, which also waited for the kingdom of God, came, and went in boldly unto Pilate, and craved the body of Jesus** (Mark 15: 37, 42-43). So, it does seem that Christ died on a Friday, BUT you must run all the scriptural references.

Just think for a few moments. If Jesus died on Friday, He would not have been in the heart of the earth for three full days and nights, as he promised (Matthew 12:40). Friday afternoon to Sunday morning in no way equals 72 hours. Nonetheless, investigate the Gospel of John because there is where we get the extra information we need to tie this entire puzzle together.

When Jesus therefore had received the vinegar, he said, It is finished: and he bowed his head, and gave up the ghost. The Jews therefore, because it was the preparation, that the bodies should not remain upon the cross on the sabbath day, (for that sabbath day was an high day,) – John 19:30-31a. This day following Passover was not the weekly Saturday Sabbath. Many people just assume this Sabbath to be Saturday, but God's word tells us this Sabbath was a high day.

Please understand that there are many Sabbaths in scripture. You have the weekly Sabbath (Saturday), many annual Sabbaths regarding feasts of the Lord (Leviticus 23), a 7-year Sabbath, and even a 50th year Sabbath in scripture. So, which Sabbath is God referring to regarding the day after Jesus died? Leviticus 23 holds the answer.

In the fourteenth day of the first month (this is the day Jesus was crucified) **at even is the LORD's passover. And on the fifteenth day of the same month is the feast of unleavened bread unto the LORD: seven days ye must eat unleavened bread. In the first day ye shall have an holy convocation: ye shall do no servile work therein** (Leviticus 23:5-7). The 15th started a 7-day feast unto the LORD, and this day was considered a Sabbath. Therefore, Jesus died on the 14th, the day before an annual Sabbath, and resurrected at the close of the weekly Saturday Sabbath.

Hallelujah!! Isn't the Bible a glorious book? It has all the answers you need, without any contradictions. We must be diligent enough to search the scriptures.

Lastly, I'll try to explain why Jesus dying three hours before the Passover day ended was so important. While Jesus hung on the cross, there were 2 malefactors crucified with him. Notice what the Bible tells us in Luke 23:39-43. **And one of the malefactors which were hanged railed on him, saying, If thou be Christ, save thyself and us. But the other answering rebuked him, saying, Dost not thou fear God, seeing thou art in the same condemnation? And we indeed justly; for we receive the due reward of our deeds: but this man hath done nothing amiss. And he said unto Jesus, Lord, remember me when thou comest into thy kingdom. And Jesus said unto him, Verily I say unto thee, To day shalt thou be with me in paradise.** This is important because Jesus did not just die and go to Paradise. The Bible teaches that He went into hell (Psalm 16, Acts 2:25-31), and probably took all mankind's sin and iniquities to dump there that were placed on and in His body (Isaiah 53:5-6, 1 Peter 2:24) as was pictured by the scapegoat in the Old Testament (Leviticus 16:21-22). He preached to the spirits there in prison (1 Peter 3:18-20), and then left hell (He can leave because He now holds the keys – Revelation 1:18), crossed the gulf separating hell and Paradise (Luke 16), and kept his appointment with the repentant malefactor. All this had to be done in 3 hours.

Don't you just love the Bible!?

Simon a Cyrenian

Have you ever wondered about the man who was compelled to carry Jesus' cross? Why was he chosen for such a task? What happened to him after the event? This is an effort to shed some light on these questions, and to look at part of the crucifixion story. To do this, we will have to examine all the Gospels simultaneously. We will begin in Mark, chapter 15.

Why was Simon chosen?

Mark 15:16-22:

Pilate has just conformed to the people's demands to crucify Jesus and set Barabbas free. **And the soldiers <u>led him away into the hall</u>, called Praetorium; and they call together the whole band. And they clothed him with purple, and platted a crown of thorns, and put it about his head, And began to salute him, Hail, King of the Jews! And they smote him on the head with a reed, and did spit upon him, and bowing their knees worshipped him. And when they had mocked him, they took off the purple from him, and put his own clothes on him, and <u>led him out</u> to crucify him. And they compel one Simon a Cyrenian, who passed by, coming out of the country, the father of Alexander and Rufus, to bear his cross. And they bring him <u>unto</u> the place Golgotha, which is, being interpreted, The place of a skull.** From the information here in Mark you need to understand a few things:

1. Jesus was in the judgment hall being mocked by the soldiers.
2. Jesus was then led out of the judgment hall where they found Simon to bear His cross.
3. Simon carried the cross <u>unto</u> Golgotha (this is important).

Matthew 27:27-32

Then the soldiers of the governor <u>took Jesus into the common hall</u>, and gathered unto him the whole band of soldiers. And they stripped him, and put on him a scarlet robe. And when they had platted a crown of thorns, they put it upon his head, and a reed in his right hand: and they bowed the knee before him, and mocked him, saying, Hail, King of the Jews! And they spit upon him, and took the reed, and smote him on the head. And after that they had mocked him, they took the robe off from him, and put his own raiment on him, and led him away to crucify

him. And as they came out, they found a man of Cyrene, Simon by name: him they compelled to bear his cross. So, Matthew supports exactly what we saw in Mark.

Luke 23:26

And as they led him away, they laid hold upon one Simon, a Cyrenian, coming out of the country, and on him they laid the cross, that he might bear it after Jesus. Again, the same information we gathered from Mark and Matthew is stated, but with one extra piece of information: Simon followed Jesus while carrying the cross.

John 19:16-18

Then delivered he him therefore unto them to be crucified. And they took Jesus, and led him away. And he [Jesus] bearing his cross went forth into a place called the place of a skull, which is called in the Hebrew Golgotha: Where they crucified him, and two other with him, on either side one, and Jesus in the midst. Now, we see yet again some extra information. Here it is reported that Jesus carried the cross into, not unto, like we saw in Mark. This is NOT a Bible contradiction. When you put all the information together, the events are as followed:

- Jesus was taken into the judgment hall to be mocked by the soldiers.
- As they came out of the hall, they found Simon to carry Jesus' cross.
- Simon carries the cross behind Jesus unto Golgotha.
- The soldiers take the cross off Simon and place it on Jesus at Golgotha, and Jesus carries the cross into Golgotha.

Most movies you watch about Jesus and the crucifixion show that Simon was chosen because Jesus was too weak from the beatings to carry His own cross. Yet, no support of that is found in the Bible. Jesus never began to carry His cross until they reached the place of the crucifixion. They chose Simon to carry the cross to continue their mockery. The robe, crown of thorns, and everything else was mocking the fact that Jesus was said to have been a "King." Therefore, as they come out of the judgment hall, they get the "King's subject" to carry the cross while following the King to His death. It was all intended for mockery.

This entire event was pictured in the Old Testament by Abraham and Isaac – Genesis 22:3-8(a). **And Abraham rose up early in the morning, and saddled his ass, and took two of his young men with him, and Isaac** his son, and clave the wood for a burnt offering, and rose up, and went **unto** the place of which God had told him. **Then on the third day Abraham lifted up his eyes, and saw the place afar off. And Abraham said unto his young men, Abide ye here with the ass; and I and the lad will go yonder and worship, and come again to you. And Abraham took the wood and the burnt offering, and laid it upon Isaac his son; and he took the fire in his hand, and a knife; and they went both of them together. And Isaac spake unto Abraham his father, and said, My father: and he said, Here am I, my son. And he said, Behold the fire and the wood: but where is the lamb for a burnt offering? And Abraham said, My son, God will provide himself a lamb for a burnt offering.** The same events about Jesus happened with Isaac and Abraham

- The donkey carried the wood unto the place of the sacrifice.
- Isaac then carries the wood into the place of the sacrifice.

This pictures the death of Jesus Christ because of the very interesting and important prophesy mentioned in verse 8. Isaac was never sacrificed. God stopped Abraham from doing it. Isaac was a sinner just like you and me, and the sacrifice of his blood would amount to very little in the eyes of a holy and righteous God. But Jesus was a spotless, undefiled, completely sinless, perfect sacrifice for you and me (1 Peter 1:18-19, 2 Corinthians 5:21), and He did exactly what Genesis said He would do: **GOD WILL PROVIDE HIMSELF A LAMB**. Jesus went to that cross on purpose to die for you and me, to accomplish death (Luke 9:31), and to finish the work of God the Father (John 4:34, John 19:30).

Hallelujah!!

What happened to Simon after the event?

If you return to Mark 15, you will notice the following words: **And they compel one Simon a Cyrenian, who passed by, coming out of the country, the father of Alexander and Rufus, to bear his cross.** Why is this information included in the Bible? I don't believe God places words just to take up space.

If you try to cross reference the name Alexander, you will find four other verses containing this name. I cannot tell for certain if one of them matches the name of Simon's son in Mark 15; however, only one other verse in the Bible includes the name Rufus. Romans 16:13: **Salute Rufus chosen in the Lord, and his mother and mine**. It appears to be quite possible that

Simon returned home to talk with his family about what he was compelled to do for Jesus. As a result, Rufus believes on the name of the Lord Jesus Christ and is saved by the grace of God. He then begins to live a life as holy and acceptable as possible unto his savior Jesus Christ (Romans 12:1). Again, I cannot be dogmatic, but with the information we have, this seems to be exactly what happened.

Biblical Calendar

The calendar below is provided to give you a visual for the feast days mentioned in our introductory discussion of chapter 5. The year represents the calendar year when Christ died on the cross. This truth is further discussed in the appendix - The last days of Jesus' ministry.

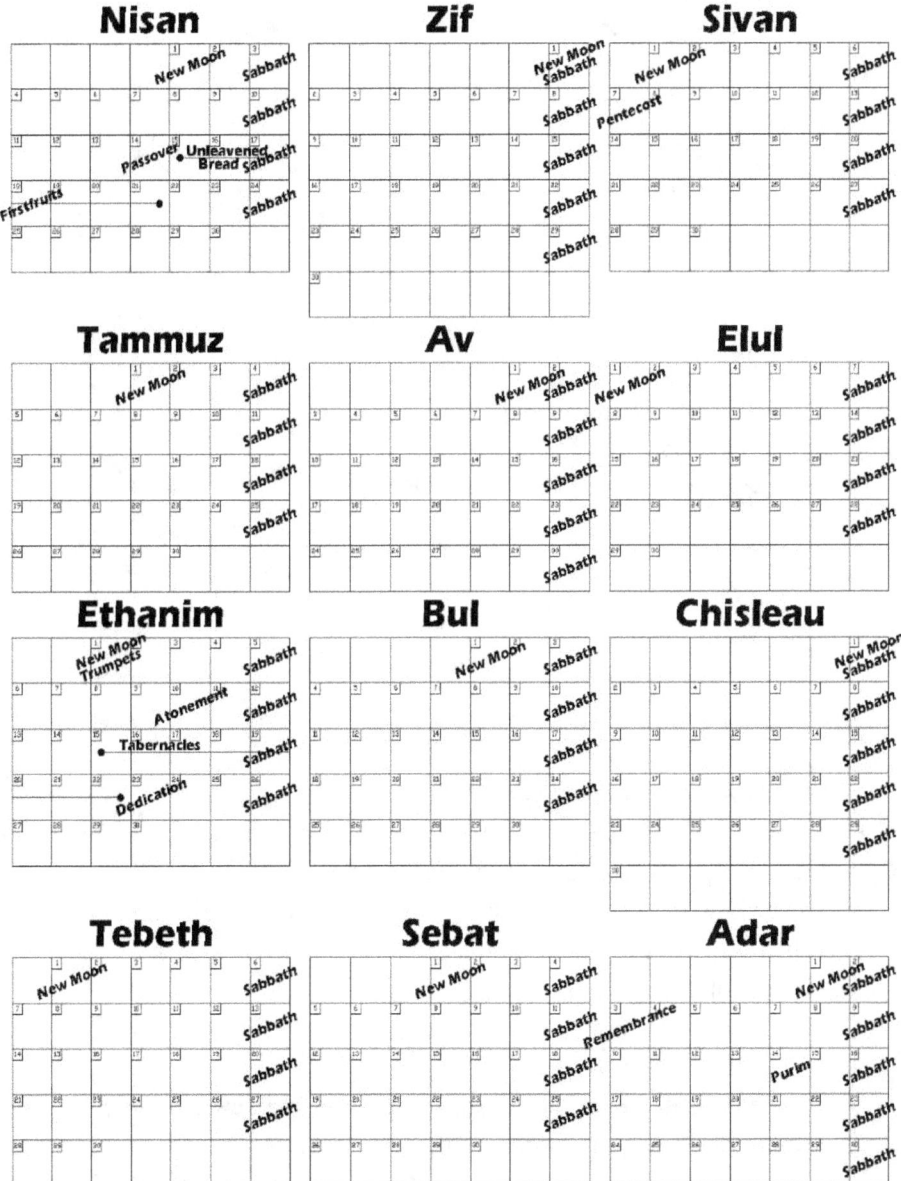

Below you will find a chart correlating the biblical calendar with the Roman/Civil calendar that is widely used throughout the world today. Also, we will examine parts of the Bible that give support for the length of a biblical year.

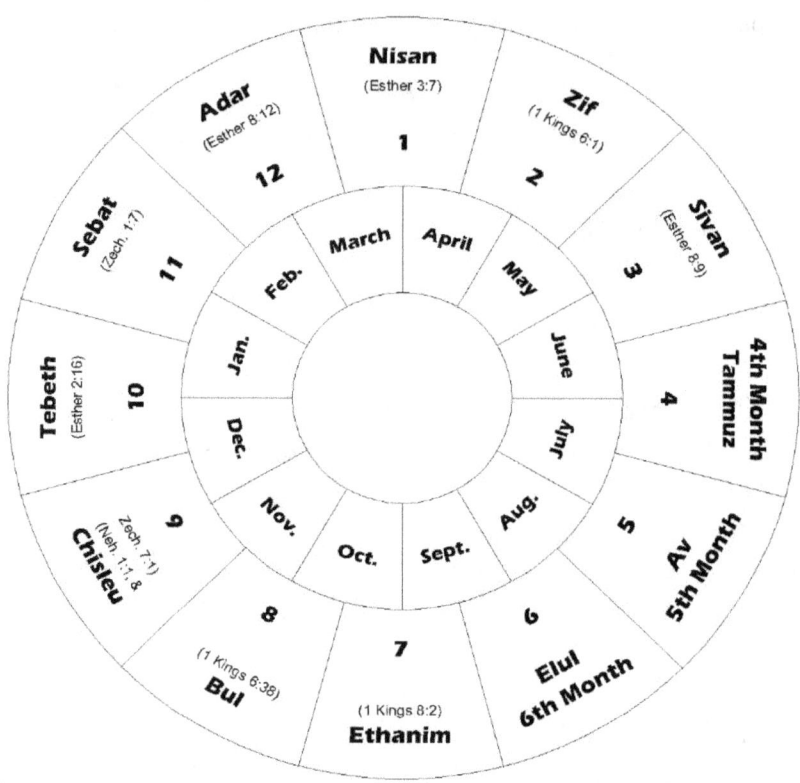

*The first month of a biblical year is the month Nisan.
*The fourth, fifth, and sixth months are identified by number in the Bible, but the names of these months are not given in scripture.

- According to today's Jewish calendar those months are named as followed...

     Tammuz: 4th month

     Av: 5th month

     Elul: 6th month

- Please note however, according to history, the Jewish names of each month on the Jewish calendar changed to adopt Babylonian titles after returning from Babylonian exile during the time of Ezra. Thus, the names of months 4, 5, and 6 above might very well have been different originally.

- The names of each month after Babylonian exile, which are still being used today (as far as I am aware), are as followed…

1 – Nissan	7 – Tishri
2 – Iyar	8 – Cheshvan
3 – Sivan	9 – Kislev
4 – Tammuz	10 – Tevet
5 – Av	11 – Shevat
6 – Elul	12 – Adar

The Roman/Gregorian calendar consists of 365 days with an extra day being observed at the end of February every four years (called a leap year). According to scripture however, there are only 360 days in a biblical year. Considering there are 12 months, each month must have 30 days each. See the references below for details.

REVELATION 11:1-3

These verses will give us support to each month having exactly 30 days.

And there was given me a reed like unto a rod: and the angel stood, saying, Rise, and measure the temple of God, and the altar and them that worship therein. But the court which is without the temple leave out, and measure it not; for it is given unto the Gentiles: and the holy city shall they tread under foot <u>forty and two months</u>. And I will give power unto my two witnesses, and they shall prophesy <u>a thousand two hundred and threescore days</u>, clothes in sackcloth.

- If we divide a thousand two hundred and threescore days (1,260) by forty and two months (42), we get exactly 30 days per month.

GENESIS 7 – 8: Noah and the flood

In these two chapters of the Bible, God gives us precise dates while telling us of Noah and the flood. I do not believe those dates were included in God's word just for entertainment purposes, but were put there to help us determine, not only the duration of time they were on the ark, but to also give us evidence for the number of days in a biblical year.

Please reference the calendar above, as needed, while reading through the following passages.

Gen. 7:11: **In the six hundredth year of Noah's life, in the second month, the seventeenth day of the month, the same day were all the fountains of the great deep broken up, and the windows of heaven were opened**.

- This is the starting date of the flood waters: Zif 17

Gen. 7:24 and 8:3b-4: **and the waters prevailed upon the earth an hundred and fifty days. And the waters returned from off the earth continually: and after the end of the hundred and fifty days the waters were abated. And the ark rested in the seventh month, on the seventeenth day of the month, upon the mountains of Ararat**.

- If we start on Zif 17, and add 150 days (exactly 5 months considering each month has 30 days each) we are now on Ethanim 17.

Gen. 8:5: **And the waters decreased continually until the tenth month: in the tenth month, on the first day of the month, were the tops of the mountains seen**.

- This adds 74 days to our count to bring us to Tebeth 1.

Gen. 8:13: **And it came to pass in the six hundredth and first year, in the first month, the first day of the month, the waters were dried up from off the earth: and Noah removed the covering of the ark, and looked, and, behold, the face of the ground was dry**.

- This adds 90 days to our count to bring us to Nisan 1.

Gen. 8:14: **And in the second month, on the seven and twentieth day of the month, was the earth dried. And God spake unto Noah, saying, Go forth of the ark, thou, and thy wife, and thy sons, and they sons' wives with thee**.

- This adds 56 days to our count to bring us to Zif 27
- This means Noah and his family were on the ark for one year and 10 days (started Zif 17 and ended Zif 27 the following year). The total number of days, based on everything we covered, was exactly 370 (150 + 74 + 90 + 56).
- 370 days = 1 year and 10 days, therefore 1 year is 360 days.

7's in John

- 7 occasions John refers to himself, but not by name – 13:23, 18:15-16, 19:26, 20:2-8, 20:5, 21:7, 21:20
    - called "disciple whom Jesus loved" and "that other disciple"
- 7 statements by John the Baptist – Chapter 1 (1:15-36)
- 7 Days – chapters 1 & 2 (1:29, 1:35, 1:43, and 2:1)
- 7 mentions of "hour" of death (2:4, 7:30, 8:20, 12:23, 12:27, 13:1, 17:1)
- 7 individuals testify to Jesus' deity
    - John the Baptist (1:34)
    - Nathanael (1:49)
    - Peter (6:69)
    - Martha (11:27)
    - Thomas (20:23)
    - John (20:31)
    - Jesus Himself (10:36)
- 7 times Jesus speaks to woman at the well – chapter 4 (4:7-26)
- 7 miracles before crucifixion
    - Water into wine (2:1-11)
    - Nobleman's son healed (4:46-54)
    - Impotent man healed (5:1-9)
    - Multitude fed (6:1-14)
    - Calming of the storm (6:15-21)
    - Blind man healed (9:1-7)
    - Lazarus raised from the dead (11:38-45)
- 7 similarities between first and second miracle
    - Both in Cana of Galilee
    - Both on third day (2:1, 4:43)
    - Jesus rebuked someone prior to each miracle
        - Mary (2:4)
        - Nobleman (4:48)
    - Both showed obedience to Jesus' word
    - Both illustrated God's word through spoken word
    - Both mentioned servants
    - Both followed with witnesses believing
- 7 mentions of "come/cometh down from heaven" – chapter 6
- 7 times Jesus claims to be the bread of life – chapter 6

- 7 times Jesus mentions words came from the Father (7:16, 8:28, 8:46, 12:49, 14:10, 14:24, 17:8)
- 7 "I am" statements by Jesus – this shows Jesus to be the **I am that I am** of Exodus 3:14
    - Bread of life (6:35)
    - Light of the world (8:12, 9:5)
    - Door of the sheep (10:7)
    - Good shepherd (10:11)
    - Resurrection and the life (11:25)
    - The way, truth, and life (14:6)
    - The true vine (15:1)
- 16 times the word "cannot" is used in John, but under 7 specific contexts
    - Natural man cannot enter the kingdom of God (3:3-5)
    - Lost cannot go where Christ is (7:34, 8:21-23)
    - Unsaved cannot hear the word (8:43)
    - Scripture cannot be broken (10:35)
    - World cannot receive Holy Ghost (14:17)
    - Believer cannot bear fruit of himself (15:4)
    - The Lord cannot teach us more rapidly than we can learn (16:12)
- 7 things the Shepherd does for His sheep – chapter 7
- 7 descriptions of the sheep are given – chapter 7
- 7 times Jesus instructs to pray in His name (14:13-14, 15:16, 16:23-24, 16:26)
- 7 specific witnesses of Jesus' deity are given
    - The Father (5:37, 8:18)
    - The Son (8:14, 18:37)
    - Holy Spirit (15:26, 16:13-14)
    - The word (1:45, 5:39 & 46)
    - Jesus' works (5:17 & 36, 10:25, 14:11, 15:24)
    - The forerunner (1:7, 5:33-35)
    - The disciples (15:27, 19:35, 21:24)
- 7 times "a little while" is used in 16:16-19
- Chapter 17 commentary – four different sevens are provided
    - Jesus requests glorification for 7 reasons
    - Jesus asks 3 things for His people based on 7 reasons
    - 7 things mentioned about the relation of believers to the world
    - 7 things Jesus prayed to have in common with all believers

- 7 times Pilate goes in or out of the judgment hall (18:29, 18:33, 18:38, 19:1, 19:4, 19:9, 19:12)
- Chapter 21 – 7 men go fishing (21:2-3)
- 19 times the word "behold" is used in John, but 7 specifically relate to Jesus
    - Lamb of God (1:29 & 36)
    - His love (11:3 & 36)
    - Thy King (12:15 & 19:14)
    - The world is gone after Him (12:19)
    - His glory (17:24)
    - The man (19:4-5)
    - His hands (20:27)

www.ingramcontent.com/pod-product-compliance
Lightning Source LLC
Chambersburg PA
CBHW060800120626
46557CB00001B/45